Spirituality and Social Embodiment

Spirituality and Social Embodiment

Edited by L. Gregory Jones and James J. Buckley

Blackwell Publishers Ltd

British Library Cataloguing in Publication Data

A CIP catalogue record for this book is available from
the British Library

Library of Congress Cataloguing-in-Publication Data

Data applied for

ISBN 0-631 20482-2

Printed in Great Britain by
The Alden Press, Oxford.

CONTENTS

SPIRITUALITY AND SOCIAL EMBODIMENT: EDITORS' INTRODUCTION

"Spirituality" often takes us out of the socially embodied world into a more inward (mystical) space, while "social embodiment" calls us beyond our selves to more material realities. Little doubt that many forms of modern theology have succumbed to these temptations, mimicking Alasdair MacIntyre's therapists and managers while protesting against one side or the other. The essays of this volume search for a way beyond such forms of spirituality and embodiment.

We hope the essays will be read both individually and together. We also hope that, when they are read together, theologians and students of theology will read them in different orders in different settings—including a different order than the one we have chosen. We begin with L. Gregory Jones' essay because he directly confronts Bernard of Clairveaux's socially embodied spirituality with the more popular spirituality of Thomas Moore's *Care of the Soul*, displaying the marked contrasts between disciplined practices of Christian spirituality and the simulacra of consumer spirituality. Rowan Williams' essay moves from modern preoccupation with the true self's interior space to the New Testament's insistence of the inseparability of ethics and spirituality—a non-competitive justifying grace calls us to an "epiphanic depth". Anna Williams continues the journey into the tradition by raising up Aquinas' *Summa Theologiae* as a model of mystical theology, both an exhortation to contemplation and an act of contemplation. Frederick Bauerschmidt argues against conceptions of Julian of Norwich as a disembodied mystic and in favor of her theology as embedded in Christ's mystical body politic. David Yeago proposes that Martin Luther's mature theology defines the church as a tangible "Christian, holy people" within history, constituted by distinctive public practices, in contrast to more individualistic consequences of the Reformation.

Nicholas Lash brings us clearly back to our century arguing that the state (here, the British state) is in a crisis it cannot recognize, and the Church is called to embody its vocation to and for humankind in Newman's social refraction of Christ's three offices in priestly devotion, a polity that resists religious nationalisms, and prophetic thought in the face of a culture that has given up on the common quest for truth. Finally, Willie Jennings argues that "essentialist" definitions of African-American spirituality arise from a protest against the colonialist's theologically derogatory vision of the African; but they also re-establish the colonialist vision of the African as always presenting an inauthentic Christian.

There is hardly a single thesis here. But all seek ways to place our spiritualities, socially embodied, before the God who desires to redeem us, body and soul.

A THIRST FOR GOD OR CONSUMER SPIRITUALITY? CULTIVATING DISCIPLINED PRACTICES OF BEING ENGAGED BY GOD

L. GREGORY JONES

There is a phenomenal interest in "spirituality" these days. This is true among academics, where there has been a resurgence of interest in significant figures from diverse religious traditions, including such Christian writers as Hildegard of Bingen and Julian of Norwich. It is even more the case among popular audiences, where books on spirituality have become a booming market over the last decade. Among other groups, there is a sense that spirituality offers resources for the contemporary world that have been unfairly neglected.

What should Christians make of the interest in spirituality? There are, to be sure, clear *alternatives* to Christian practice and belief available among both academic and popular books on "spirituality".[1] Even so, it is more difficult and important to ask whether popular books ambiguously connected to Christianity—for example, books authored by such writers as Thomas Moore and M. Scott Peck—are helpful or harmful to *Christian* spirituality. Do these interests in spirituality augur a genuine rediscovery of "the sacred", as several recent titles have suggested?[2] Are they signs of a renewed commitment to Christian practice, an indication of a resurgent set of interests in Christian life following the experiments with secularization? Or are they a peculiarly Western, or perhaps even parochially American, phenomenon? Are they simply the latest move in an increasingly commodified world, signs of people desperately searching to find a new commodity yet one which can

Prof. L. Gregory Jones
Department of Theology, Loyola College in Maryland, Baltimore, MD21210-2699, USA

also satisfy the desires other commodities have failed to quench? Can Christians embrace these burgeoning interests in spirituality, yet initiate people into specific spiritual practices so they foster communion with God and one another? Or are we left with a stark either/or, turning from false gods to God?

Obviously, there is no one answer that can adequately respond to the range of these questions or that can comprehensively address the wide variety of materials available, much less the range of intellectual options and arguments being advanced. Admittedly, there are risks in placing much stock in the trends and tendencies of popular consumption of religious literature. After all, popular devotional materials have long been available. Even so, the recent literature has reached far into the popular consciousness of many people, and is in need of careful examination.

Hence, it is important to examine the sorts of questions identified above in order to assess theologically the effects of "contemporary spirituality" both on the cultural landscape and, more specifically, on the understandings of God and the shape of Christian life which are increasingly regnant in churches and seminaries. Such an assessment is essential because, after reading a significant sample of the popular literature, I am convinced that much contemporary spirituality is shaped by consumer impulses and captive to a therapeutic culture. It systematically avoids the disciplined practices necessary for engagement with God.[3] Further, this literature separates spirituality both from theological convictions and practices on the one hand, and social and political realities and commitments on the other. The literature makes it more rather than less difficult to retrieve and embody authentically Christian spiritual practices, practices which provide the context for disciplined engagements with the God of Jesus Christ.

To be sure, the interest (as revealed in the massive sales!) reflects important yearnings among contemporary people that are both a sign of potential openness to central Christian themes *and* a judgment on the failures of Christian communities to respond appropriately to them. Yet, while Christians need to acknowledge those yearnings as authentic signs of restless hearts, the literature itself does not encourage the reader to find one's rest in God. Rather, like a good tourist, the reader is encouraged to go on brief forays, sampling exotic "lands" of ideas, but ultimately always returning to the home of his or her individual experience. The reader is offered a journey without a *telos* except the ceaseless motion of self-discovery or, more likely, self-invention. As such, the literature is dangerous because its invocation of "spirituality" suggests that it will help readers nurture and discover authentic relationships with God when what it offers is a synthetic substitute of vague, self-referential religiosity.

Hence, Christians ought to be wary of "spirituality" even while nurturing, through spiritual practices, people's often inchoate desires and yearnings.[4] But that can only be done if we recognize the dramatic differences between

Christian spiritual practices and appeals to a generic "spirituality". In order to show how and why this is the case, my analysis begins with a brief explication of a figure widely accepted as a major interpreter of Christian "spirituality": the medieval monk Bernard of Clairvaux. I explore Bernard's writing to show how a Christian appropriation of what has recently been identified as "spirituality" involves the transformation of our desires so we learn to engage God through participation in particular, ongoing, and disciplined practices. I then turn in the second section to an examination of one of the most popular and substantive books in contemporary spirituality, Thomas Moore's *Care of the Soul*. There I display the ways in which Moore's perspective sharply diverges from Bernard's. In the third section, I explore reasons why contemporary spiritualities such as Moore's have become so popular and why they represent (at best) an impoverishment or (at worst) a corruption of Christian practices of learning to know and love God. Finally, in the concluding section I respond to some potential objections to my use of Bernard as a contrast to the literature of contemporary spirituality.

I

One problem with much contemporary discussion about "spirituality" is that many of the people do not know much about the traditions of Christian spirituality—or they read those figures through the lens of modern assumptions about spirituality as a topic separate from, and essentially unrelated to, either theology or politics. Hence I begin by describing Bernard's thought, specifically his series of sermons on The Song of Songs.[5]

Bernard aims to show people how to seek the One by whom they are themselves sought. As he describes it in *De diligendo Deo*, echoing Augustine's *Confessions*,

> No one has the strength to seek you unless he has first already found you. For it is a fact that you will to be found in order that you may be sought and you will to be sought in order that you may be found. It is possible, therefore, to seek you and to find you, but it is not possible to anticipate you.[6]

This seeking and being sought is shaped by Bernard's understanding of the natural human desire for God. We have such a natural desire because human beings are created in the divine image. Any movement toward God, then, is already shaped by God's gracious gift in creation. Human desire describes that longing, that thirst, for God which God's grace has already instilled in human hearts—and which remains unfulfilled except through friendship with God. That is, while people need to exhibit "care of the soul", for Bernard, that is inseparable from desiring to know God. There can be no knowledge of ourselves apart from knowledge of God.

Unfortunately, sin and evil have distorted human desires, leading to failures in knowledge—particularly failures in self-knowledge. Fundamentally, we are tempted to mistake our present condition in the world with the purpose for which we were created. For Bernard, authentic self-knowledge begins with a sober acknowledgement of how "unlike" God we have become as a result of sin and evil.

> There must be no dissimulation, no attempt at self-deception, but a facing up to one's real self without flinching and turning aside. When a [person] thus takes stock of himself in the clear light of truth, he will discover that he lives in a region where likeness to God has been forfeited, and groaning from the depths of a misery to which he can no longer remain blind, will he not cry out to the Lord as the Prophet did: 'In your truth you have humbled me'?[7]

Our desire for God is awakened and renewed by acknowledging the ways in which our desires have been distorted, our quests for knowledge corrupted by self-deception, and our lives damaged by the sin and evil we have done and had done to us. If our acknowledgement of our life in this "region of unlikeness" leads to prayers for forgiveness and renewal, then the love of God will be deepened. Further, we will grow toward friendship with God— ultimately, for Bernard, toward "spiritual marriage."[8]

Bernard suggests that the waters of our desire for God are drawn from the well of charity—that charity which is none other than God's self-gift in Jesus Christ and the Spirit. For Bernard, Jesus is the source of all virtues and knowledge (see Sermon 13), of wisdom, justice, holiness and redemption (Sermon 22), of life and fruitfulness (Sermon 48).[9] God's charity transforms our desire from selfish acquisitiveness into self-giving love reflected in the indwelling love of Father, Son, and Spirit. Hence, Christian living involves a journey of learning to know oneself precisely as one who is known by God. This journey of self-knowledge requires awareness both of our absence from God, our "unlikeness", and also of our presence with God, our being renewed in the divine image by God's Spirit learned through such practices as prayer and almsgiving. Our self-knowledge of our "unlikeness" from God becomes a step towards the knowledge of God; as Bernard continues, God "will become visible to you according as his image is being renewed within you. And you, gazing confidently on the glory of the Lord with unveiled face, will be transformed into that same image with ever increasing brightness, by the work of the Spirit of the Lord" (36.6).

Christian spiritual living thus is shaped by both the absence and presence of God. Self-knowledge, understood as awareness of our estrangement from God and, by God's grace, our knowledge that delights in God, is the context in which we engage in practices that move us forward in the journey toward spiritual marriage with God. Our awareness of estrangement from God, and of our sense of God's absence, moves us to repentance through compunction over sin, recognizing in response to God's gracious love the ways in which sin inhibits our friendship with Christ. He describes our self-knowledge of being unlike God as a "sowing in tears". Indeed, Bernard elsewhere characterizes those tears which accompany our compunction over sin and estrangement from God as a "kind of baptism."[10]

Our tears, our good desires, and our good works are the seeds which enable us to "sow righteousness" through particular practices of Christian living:

> You therefore have sown righteousness for yourself if by means of true self-knowledge you have learned to fear God, to humble yourself, to shed tears, to distribute alms and participate in other works of charity; if you have disciplined your body with fastings and prayers, if you have wearied your heart with acts of penance and heaven with your petitions. This is what it means to sow righteousness. (37.2)

These practices contribute to our knowledge of God, enabling what we sow in tears of self-knowledge to be reaped in joy in our knowledge of God. We reap the joy associated with awareness of the gift of God's grace, God's charity. In this sense, we are drawn ever closer to God through the delight of loving friendship, a closeness nourished through careful attention to, and embodiment of, the practices of Christian living.

At the same time, however, another sense of our tears is attributable not to human sin so much as to the predicament of living in this time between the times. We mourn as we long for God's Kingdom, for the consummation of the lover's desire to be with the beloved, for the time when there will be no more suffering, no more tears, no more injustice. As Bernard puts it, "Why should the absence of Christ not move me to frequent tears and daily groaning? 'O Lord, all that I long for is known to you, my sighing is no secret from you'" (59.4; the internal citation is to Ps. 37:10).

Thus, Christian living, set in the context of the desire to know God, sees the ongoing need for practices of righteousness, sees the relations between God's forgiveness and our holiness, sees our tears—both of compunction and of mourning—as means to witness to God more faithfully. As Michael Casey describes Bernard's view, the one who seeks God and possesses a "sober mind" will

> be circumspect with regard to himself, regretfully recognising his failures; he will strive always to be pleasing to God; and finally, with regard to his neighbours, he will aim to serve and to prove himself useful [see Sermon 57.11]. In other words, vigilance for the coming of the bridegroom is not a passive matter of looking down the road with longing, but it is expressed through attention to the details of evangelical living.[11]

As Christian spiritual living involves seeking the One who has already sought us, so also our journey of encountering both the absence and the presence of God requires active receptivity. We must become aware both of that absence, that lack, by which our desire is awakened and we yearn for a better life, and of God's presence through which we find a response to our yearning. To have only the former would tempt us to despair; but to have only the latter, at least in this world, would give a false sense of self-sufficiency.

As such, Christian spiritual practices teach us to become detached from those features of our world which separate us from God and to cling to the One who alone can satisfy our desire for communion. We then learn how to love the world in the light of God's love. Unlearning the patterns of disordered desire and learning to order our affections involves ongoing attention throughout the journey of Christian living; though there is growth in this life, our unlearning and learning await eschatological fulfillment. This is also true of our desire, which in this life knows both surplus and lack. In God's Kingdom, according to Bernard, our desire to know and love God will know no lack, will find fulfillment in our endless delight in God. The practices of Christian spiritual disciplines constitute the school for this divine pedagogy, teaching us how to find the fulfillment which human beings naturally—but all-too-often desperately and misguidedly—desire.

Bernard is, however, acutely aware of the slowness by which human beings typically learn this divine pedagogy. He sketches a three-fold movement as human beings grow through participation in Christian spiritual disciplines. In the first, human beings respond to grace by acting through will-power and self-restraint, compelling themselves to do what is right. Through practice, they develop good habits and so learn that external constraints and coercion are less necessary. They learn to act virtuously. Finally, in a third movement, they find that good behavior is increasingly easy to practice and delightful in itself.[12] These movements require ongoing practice, and Bernard notes that acting perfectly from delight is possible only in the next life.[13]

Bernard believes that virtuous living is linked to a desire to know God: as he puts it, "God is sought by good works" (75.4). This should not be confused with the infamous "works-righteousness", for Bernard clearly holds that even our natural desire for God is a gift of grace.[14] Virtuous living is found in active receptivity through which our desires are transformed by the knowledge and love of God.

Of course, Bernard thought the practices of monastic living provide the best classroom for the divine pedagogy. Or, more specifically, the practices embedded in the Benedictine *Rule* provide the classroom. Bernard's sermons, addressed to his fellow monks, presuppose as their context the friendships, daily rituals, and institutional configurations of the community. This includes the liturgical life of the community, particularly prayer; an emphasis on internalizing Scripture through meditation and song; and the very fabric of support and accountability which the monks learned to expect from one another, particularly through the authority of masters in the community. These disciplined practices and friendships provide the context wherein knowledge of self and knowledge of God might be discovered and, over time, deepened.

Bernard's preaching is itself a practice by which the desire to know and love God could be cultivated as the monks were engaged by the Word. Talal Asad's assessment of medieval monasticism is instructive: "The sermons that give authoritative exegesis of biblical texts provide a new vocabulary by which the monks themselves can redescribe, and therefore in effect construct, their memories in relation to the demands of a new way of life. This redescription of memories depends on a long and complex process. In it, (1) the authoritative preacher and the monk addressed, (2) the monk interacting with fellow monks, (3) the confessor and the monk in confession, and (4) the remembering religious self and the secular self remembered, all contribute in the production of a moral description by which the monk's desires and feelings are reconstructed."[15]

It should be clear that, for Bernard, the journey of Christian life is neither simple nor easy. It requires disciplined practices of being engaged by God through both the darkness of God's absence and the light of God's presence. Complacency must be avoided, and growth in the knowledge of both God and the self will require repentance and the practice of virtue—including, especially, such virtues as patience, gentleness, a "zeal for justice", gratitude, and charity. Further, we are not necessarily the best interpreters of our own lives; we need friends on the journey, particularly as we turn to others who provide guidance, correction, and support as we unlearn sin and learn to become friends of God. At the same time, Bernard is aware that disciplined practices are necessary also to combat the dangers, temptations, and enemies encountered on the journey. The practices of Christian spiritual living require us to be both humble and vigilant, drawn forward by the love of God and the forces of memory and hope.[16]

Bernard's conception of Christian "spirituality" cannot be divorced either from theological convictions or from social and political realities. The cultivation of desire for God entails holy living and an ever-present suspicion of the temptation for self-interested power. Christian living requires a zeal for justice, an awareness of the forces that seek to divide and destroy both oneself and others, and a commitment to having one's own desires and relationships shaped by the self-gift of God in Jesus Christ and the Spirit. I will return in the final section to worries one might register about Bernard's specific politics or the applicability of his vision for non-monastic contexts; for now, the important point is to recognize that his conception and practice of Christian spirituality works against the modern temptation to read spirituality (or Bernard's writings) as a topic unrelated to theology or politics.

Yet that is precisely what contemporary spiritualities all-too-frequently invite their readers to do. In order to show how and why this is the case, I turn to an exploration of Thomas Moore's *Care of the Soul*.[17]

II

One way to read a book such as Moore's is as a collection of folk wisdom to help nourish people along their journey of learning to love and know the triune God. This is, after all, one way that Christians have often read the Book of Proverbs: wisdom that is not sufficient on its own but receives its determinative significance from the larger story of God with God's people.[18] This is also part of the attraction of The Song of Songs in Christian spirituality; as Bernard's sermons indicate, the Song of Songs provides intimations of natural desire which nourish people which nonetheless, when set within the larger story of God with God's people, also transform that desire into the communion with God which alone can satisfy it.

Yet Moore's book ultimately offers an *alternative* to Christian engagements with God rather than a useful collection of wisdom to supplement more specifically Christian practices and beliefs. *The Care of the Soul* is instructive because it is neither as superficial as some of the worst examples of popular spirituality nor as captive to secular models of "therapy".[19] Indeed, Moore recognizes that there are no quick techniques to make a spiritual person; rather, spirituality must be cultivated over time and can be described as a craft. Further, unlike many "self-help" guides to spirituality, Moore notes in his last two chapters that the "care of the soul" requires moving beyond oneself to care for the world—though he unsurprisingly emphasizes aesthetic and ecological concerns while virtually ignoring the significance of other social and political interactions and commitments.

In terms of his "method", Moore explicitly criticizes "therapeutic manipulations" as reductive in their attempts to conform people to certain standards (see pp. 19–20; 206–208). He also recognizes the importance of finding ways to move beyond modern bifurcations of the mind and the body, of reason and the emotions. He does this by invoking the significance of the imagination in learning to see the world differently.

So far, so good. Yet Moore's dominant perspective in the book turns out to replicate some of the worst features of a consumer spirituality. Although there are numerous problems with Moore's assumptions and descriptions, I will explore three themes where Moore's perspective, typical of many writers and readers of contemporary spirituality, diverges sharply from the traditions of Christian spirituality as exemplified by Bernard of Clairvaux: God, the self, and practices. In each case, Moore's perspective distorts and undermines Christian practices of being engaged by God.

First, for Moore, the primary reality which spirituality explores is "The Sacred", clearly to be distinguished from "God" (much less the Christian identification of the Triune God). Moore indicates that while his notion of "care of the soul" uses Christian terminology, "what I am proposing is not specifically Christian, nor is it tied to any particular religious tradition. It does, however, imply a religious sensibility and a recognition of our absolute need for a spiritual life" (p. xv).

One way to read this suggestion is that Moore is mining Christian practices and convictions for wisdom that might introduce religious seekers to sensibilities that need to be more fully developed as the seekers learn to desire to know God. Yet Moore systematically avoids any discussion of God. He commends polytheism as a "psychological model" (at least formally distinguishing it from "religious belief"), noting that human beings live better with multiplicity rather than striving for a "unity of personality". Later in the book, he moves toward a polytheistic sensibility for religious belief as well: "Polytheistic religions, which see gods and goddesses everywhere, offer useful guidance toward finding spiritual values in the world. You don't have to *be* a polytheist in order to expand your spirituality in this way. In Renaissance Italy, leading thinkers who were pious and monotheistic in their Christian devotion still turned to Greek polytheism for a wider range of spirituality" (p. 241).[20]

Moore's criteria for the sacred are determined by what the individual person finds useful, and he clearly thinks one needs to move beyond specific "Christian devotion" in order to discover the full range of "spiritual values" in the world. But Moore's criteria are unclear for distinguishing good "gods" from bad ones, other than usefulness to one's self. In Moore's world, any myth—particularly ones from Greece, to which he continually appeals in his discussions—will do so long as it is useful in helping cultivate a sense of "soul". Surprisingly, Moore never considers whether the Christian doctrine of the Trinity might provide a different, and perhaps superior, way to deal with issues of unity and multiplicity; nor does he provide any discussion of how we distinguish multiplicity from fragmented chaos. Further, he seems blissfully unaware that the Christian doctrine of the Trinity might enable catechized believers to understand how they can learn from other traditions while remaining faithful to God.

Moore's polytheistic "sacredness" does not so much oppose the Christian doctrine of God as coopt it. He leaves room for the Christian God in his pantheon, tempting readers to be inclusive of all gods and to feel that in doing so they are continuing to be Christians. Yet this is actually more rather than less dangerous to authentic Christian engagement with the God of Jesus Christ (a God who rather clearly opposes *any* idolatry). Indeed, Moore's seeming generosity in including the Christian God in his polytheistic pantheon of spirituality produces a "non-critique" of Christianity that undermines Christian practice and thought more than does the most strident atheism.

Second, Moore's conception of the self (including our "soul") focuses almost exclusively on the self-sufficiency of one's interior life. There is little sense in Moore that self-knowledge is difficult, or that knowledge of our-selves might be primarily of the importance of ongoing formation and transformation of desires in relation to God. Moore leaves judgments about how to "care for the soul" to the individual reader, wholly independent of any need for catechesis or being inducted into a particular tradition. As a result, the individual self, as autonomous chooser, is the primary referent for cultivating a sense of "soul" and for determining which gods are most useful in that cultivation.

Moreover, there is little sense of sin in Moore's analysis. Cultivating a sense of the sacred mainly requires more attentiveness to beauty. Moore lacks Bernard's acute awareness of the ways in which we are afflicted by self-deception and by conditions which require conversion from patterns whereby we and others are diminished and destroyed. Admittedly, language about sin can become debilitating if separated from the larger story of God's dealings with God's people: the goodness of Creation, the saving grace of Jesus's life, death and resurrection, and the promised consummation of God's Kingdom through the Holy Spirit. Yet Moore's analysis does not offer a vision of the self which fits into those horizons, correcting the potential distortions and corruptions about sin; rather, he avoids the language alto-gether. Moore fails to see any need for repentance or confession. There is virtually no sense in which God is an Other who interrupts our lives, offering us a judgment of grace which enables holy living; nor is there much need for the practices and friendships of Christian community in which we unlearn sin and learn to desire the knowledge of God and of ourselves. For Moore, the self is to be cultivated in its own individuality in everyday life—but little else is needed or required.

Here again, Moore's language of "soul" sounds similar enough to Chris-tianity that his non-critique of Christian understandings of the purpose and destiny of human life becomes more dangerous than explicit critiques. Who could possibly be against "caring for the soul"? But what if, from a Christian perspective such as Bernard's, the way in which Moore's "care" is to be developed actually reinforces and intensifies our distance from God, our tendencies to self-deception, our failures to attend to the pain and suffering of others? In other words, the "care of the soul" all too easily becomes the feeding of what Iris Murdoch calls our "fat, relentless ego."

The problems with Moore's conceptions of the sacred and of the self become even clearer when we turn to a third theme: Moore either ignores or privatizes Christian practices and, in so doing, undermines their signific-ance for Christian living. Moore thinks that "formal religious practice" can be useful for cultivating spirituality, and notes that a loss of such practice "deprives the soul of valuable symbolic and reflective experience." Yet formal religious practice is of only instrumental significance, and must be tailored to fit one's own needs and perceptions. Moore observes that every tradition is subjected to "fresh imagination" in a series of "reformations" that transform what otherwise might be a "dead tradition" into "the base of a continually renewing spiritual sensibility." He then notes that "an individual's life may reflect this cultural dynamic in religion, going through various phases, experiencing conflicting allegiances and convictions and surviving radical reforms and reinterpretations" (p. 212).

Moore uses his own life as an example, charting the movement from his very specific involvement in a Catholic seminary over several years to his decision to leave the seminary and to cultivate a sense of sacredness apart from formal religious structures.[21] Indeed, his journey is from active participation in institutional Christianity *to* an alternative religious tradition he terms "care of the soul".

> Now I find myself a practicing therapist writing about transforming psychotherapy by recovering a religious tradition called care of the soul— which originally was the work of a curate or priest. Even though my current work has nothing explicitly to do with the established church, it is deeply rooted in that tradition. Catholicism is being shaped and lived, for better or worse, in this so-called lapsed—I might say radically reformed—Catholic. The teachings I grew up with and studied intensely have now been refined, tuned and adjusted in a personal reformation that I by no means planned, but that apparently is being accomplished. Those teachings are the ultimate source of my own spirituality. (p. 214)

Moore appreciates his prior participation in Catholicism for the ways in which it has helped provide the roots and ultimate source for his own spirituality. But that spirituality is now separated from the practices of the "established church", and the criterion for what Moore thinks it means to be Catholic is his own "personal reformation". As a "practicing psychotherapist", his "practice" has migrated from the Church to salvation by therapy alone!

Moore makes this contrast even more sharply when he distinguishes "two ways of thinking about church and religion."

> One is that we go to church in order to be in the presence of the holy, to learn and to have our lives influenced by that presence. The other is that church teaches us directly and symbolically to see the sacred dimension of everyday life. In this latter sense, religion is an 'art of memory,' a way of sustaining mindfulness about the religion that is inherent in everything we do. (p. 214)

It evidently does not occur to Moore that perhaps by going to church to worship the triune God, and having our life shaped by that worship, Christians might simultaneously learn what it means to see everyday life in relation to God and to see how our everyday lives need to be formed and transformed by God. Moore is rightly worried about people who can worship God on Sunday but live remarkably secular lives the rest of the week.

Yet in addressing that problem he adds a new one, namely undermining the conviction that being engaged by God through practices of worship and discipleship might actually transform or, more radically, challenge in at least some respects our culturally-influenced senses of what is "sacred" in life.

Moore is acutely aware of the potential dangers of "formal religion", noting that it "always lies on a cusp between the divine and the demonic." In particular, he thinks it "justifies and inflames the emotions of a holy war, and it fosters profound guilt about love and sex" (p. 216). Yet though Moore notes that "spirituality is powerful, and therefore has the potential for evil, as well as for good" (p. 229), he offers no criteria to evaluate those practices which are conducive to "care of the soul" from those which divide and destroy. Contrary to Moore's assumption, the issue is not a choice between "formal religion" or "generic spirituality"; rather, it is whether there are adequate criteria for distinguishing good practices from bad ones, authentic politics from their corrupt simulacra. He suggests that "our culture is in need of theological reflection that does not advocate a particular tradition, but tends the soul's need for spiritual direction" (p. 229). He does not recognize that this claim advocates a particular tradition—namely, one which denies any tradition beyond my own preferences. Hence Moore, in his continual reliance on the self's own intuitions, constructions, and reformations, neither provides criteria for distinguishing a tradition's good practices from evil ones nor, more problematically, *can* he—except in the form of recommendations which I, in my own reflection, am free to reject if *I* judge them inadequate to the care of *my* soul. More pointedly, Moore cannot provide such criteria because he has no sense of a *telos* of what human beings are called to be and become.

Even so, Moore is strongly in favor of ritual: "Ritual maintains the world's holiness. Knowing that everything we do, no matter how simple, has a halo of imagination around it and can serve the soul enriches life and makes the things around us more precious, more worthy of our protection and care" (p. 226). To his credit, Moore recognizes that it is possible to have rituals "that have no soul." He also notes that rituals that are "made up" are not always just right. Hence he recommends that "formal religion and tradition" can help guide us in giving ritual a more important place in life. Yet it is not clear what criteria should be used to distinguish "good" rituals from "bad" ones. Nor is it clear that there are *any* specific rituals or practices necessary for, or constitutive of, caring for the soul. Even more, what rituals one does participate in are ultimately in the service of one's own preferences and needs; so, for example, Moore learned from the church that "candles should be made of beeswax and that the choice of bread and wine at a dinner is particularly important" (p. 227).

Throughout, Moore's readers are invited to become tourists in a vast religious marketplace: gleaning insights from here and there, cultivating a sense of "soul" amidst the varieties of cultural and religious differences.

There is no sense of formation, no need for re-formation or trans-formation, except as it seems suitable to that individual "I" waiting to emerge. In effect, Moore substitutes the random rituals of a religious tourist for Bernard's disciplined quest for self-knowledge through journeys toward God.

What emerges is something substantially different from the practices of Christian spiritual traditions, practices by which people participate in the formation and transformation of desires to know and love God. For Moore, by contrast, the primary specification for rituals or practices of a "spirituality of the soul" is that they provide "insight"—presumably, insight into how "I" can experience my individual life more fully. Moore indicates that "Truth is not really a soul word; soul is after insight more than truth" (p. 246). In this, Moore has imbibed more ancient theory and practice than he perhaps suspects, but unfortunately it is an updated version of one form of Gnosticism, the ancient Christian heresy.[22]

To be sure, Moore is not Gnostic in his appreciation for the "soul" of the material world and in his attention to such themes as embodiment. In this respect, Moore's account is vastly superior to those patterns of generic spirituality which are explicitly in flight from material realities. Yet Moore's proposals result in a version of "spirituality", and of "practice", which cannot be understood as proverbial wisdom offering milk for a journey toward more substantive Christian food. Whereas Christian practices involve disciplined engagement of doing things together, Moore's rituals and practices are arbitrary activities without a *telos*—even when they may be appropriated from Christian traditions. Moore prescribes a consumer spirituality and impoverished practices that undermine, rather than serve, our capacity to invoke and respond to God. The *telos* of Christian practices of spirituality is knowing the unknowable God; but for Moore, there is no *telos* other than a richer sense of my own experience and my connectedness to the "soul".

By this point, it ought to be clear just how stark the contrasts are between the consumer spirituality of Thomas Moore and the patterns of Christian spiritual practices described by Bernard of Clairvaux. For Moore, the self is the source and referent of religious searching, whereas for Bernard the self is only known through being addressed and known by God. Further, whereas for Moore the self is a stable source of self-expression, for Bernard the self is continually put into question as it seeks to unlearn habits of sin and evil and to learn—by the grace of God—to become a friend of God. For Moore, there is no need for specific practices of spiritual living, except as the self decides that they might be useful; by contrast, for Bernard it is precisely through being initiated into Christian spiritual practices that we learn how to live less untruthfully in relation to God.

Even so, Moore's perspective would be less troubling if he were more up-front about his co-optation of some aspects of Christianity, and his rejection of others. Post-Christian or anti-Christian spiritualities that explicitly reject central Christian claims and practices offer alternative and competing practices and convictions about the character of transcendent reality, the world, and the purpose and predicament of human beings. They explicitly seek to draw together theological convictions, spiritual practices, and political realities in ways of life that diverge from (and perhaps intend to counter) Christian practices. Insofar as this occurs, the alternatives can be clearly delineated and disagreements can be intelligibly debated.

Yet proposals such as Moore's remain blissfully removed from these debates. Moore refuses to explain the shape of his theological convictions (or lack thereof) in any detail, or to show how one's "care of the soul" or even "care of the world" might attend to massive suffering and horrifying evils on the one hand, and the need for political arrangements that can sustain and nourish fragile institutional commitments of families, communities, and other organizations on the other. Indeed, one suspects that readers who want to take "care of the soul" will find themselves less rather than more likely to become involved in the urgent task of cultivating and nourishing communities and institutions that combat evils great and small while fostering moral and political goodness.

It is not so much that Moore's book is removed from, or "above", the debates about the interrelations of theology, spirituality, and politics. Rather, his book replicates a conception of spirituality that fails to acknowledge its own implicit anti-theological commitments and individualistic conception of politics. For Moore, the "sacred" is to be cultivated in personal, indeed private, experiences that may or may not have any connection either to the social and political world around the self or to more specific beliefs about "God"—much less the God Christians believe is the Creator of all that is, became enfleshed in Jesus Christ, and promises to bring Creation to its consummation in "a new heaven and a new earth." Unfortunately, Moore is not unique; as I will suggest in the next section, he is simply one of the more popular figures in a long line of people who have sundered Christian spiritual practices from theological convictions and social and political engagements. Hence, we have one final contrast between Moore and Bernard: whereas for Moore spirituality is its own activity, essentially unrelated to either theology or moral and political realities, for Bernard they are inextricably interrelated.

Thus far, I have displayed how much of what passes for "contemporary spirituality" neither emerges from within Christian practices of being engaged by God nor can be construed as compatible with those practices. But I have not yet adequately explained why accounts such as Moore's have seemed to resonate with so many people.

III

Books on contemporary spirituality are both astonishingly popular and often immune to specific criticisms. Even so, a number of diverse yet overlapping explanations converge to provide a clearer understanding of the popularity and the dangers of consumer spirituality. Obviously, a full explanatory account cannot be offered here; however, I identify and briefly explore the significance of five different explanations.

First, contemporary spirituality plays into an increasingly prevalent consumer mentality. People in capitalist societies who are trained to think of things as commodities subject to individual, consumer preference are easily tempted to think of religious commitments in similar terms.[23] This contributes to the temptation to see everything—at its most extreme, even God—in instrumental terms, as things to be used rather than enjoyed. In Martin Buber's terms, this involves the transposition of "thous" into "its". Rather than understanding *desire* as an indication of a human lack only satisfied by the knowledge and love of God through transformed living, desires signify the need for new levels of consumption by the self.

This consumer mentality also suggests a levelling of diverse religious traditions: they become brand names selling essentially the same product with slightly different packaging. Hence, rather than seeking to understand—through often painstaking conversation—the similarities and divergences between, say, one's own practices of Christian spiritual disciplines and a Buddhist's, the temptation is to see them as offering different packaging of the same reality: a basically undifferentiated sense of the sacred.

We should not underestimate the force that book publishing and marketing bears on "spirituality". The existence of books designed to be read by individuals encourages a sense that the primary authority, if not also the ultimate referent, for spiritual life is my own experience. Even though Moore's book at one place encourages people to participate in "formal religious practice," the very shape of the book's argument militates against it—as does his characterization of his own relationship to Catholicism. Just as good business practice suggests that "the consumer is always right," so in contemporary spirituality is the individual reader.

This bears on a second explanation for the popularity of contemporary spirituality, namely that it celebrates individuality over-against other authority. Phyllis Tickle's *Re-Discovering the Sacred* celebrates this resistance to external authority, and credits a post-World War II mood in the U.S. (and, in some sense, the 1960s) as its primary source. There is no doubt some truth in such an observation, though its roots go much deeper and wider. If it were only the effects of so-called "baby boomer" sensibilities, then a pendulum-swing might occur in subsequent generations.[24] In addition to the forces of consumer capitalism undermining any authorities beyond the individual, we need to take into account several other factors, including what Philip Rieff has characterized as "the triumph of the therapeutic." Rieff's book, published in 1966, contains the following prescient observations about how a "therapeutic" mentality would encourage an increase in "spirituality" and a refusal of any doctrines beyond those an individual cultivates for oneself:

> In the emergent culture, a wider range of people will have 'spiritual' concerns and engage in 'spiritual' pursuits. There will be more singing and more listening. People will continue to genuflect and read the Bible, which has long achieved the status of great literature; but no prophet will denounce the rich attire or stop the dancing. There will be more theater, not less, and no Puritan will denounce the stage and draw its curtains. On the contrary, I expect that modern society will mount psychodramas far more frequently than its ancestors mounted miracle plays, with patient-analysts acting out their inner lives, after which they could extemporize the final act as interpretation.

But according to Rieff the effect of this psychodramatic interest in spirituality is not a return to classical practices and doctrines of Judaism or Christianity; rather, it consists of a consumer's desire to pick and choose one's own spirituality through broad experimentation. In Rieff's words, "The wisdom of the next social order, as I imagine it, would not reside in right doctrine, administered by the right [people], who must be found, but rather in doctrines amounting to permission for each [person] to live an experimental life."[25]

What Rieff finds horrifying, Moore celebrates; but they agree that individuals are becoming the ultimate authorities for cultivating and evaluating experiments with spirituality. In such a world, there is no need for—indeed no real place for—clergy or even spiritual directors, much less the sorts of institutions necessary to sustain ongoing practices over time. Counselors or therapists might be helpful in offering new ideas, or clarifying the individual's preferences, but no specific directions or disciplines are necessary.

A third explanation broadens these judgments, suggesting that there is actually a set of religious convictions entailed not only in the literature of contemporary spirituality but also among the North Americans who consume it—namely, one or another version of Gnosticism. As I suggested above, Moore's perspective does not fit all of the features which are typically attributed to ancient Gnosticism; further, it is a mistake to assume that Gnosticism was a unified notion in the ancient world.[26] Even so, Moore's book—like much of contemporary spirituality—bears enough similarity to warrant attribution of the term. The clearest similarity is the exaltation of the self's experience and the desire to discover salvation within one's own personal experiences. In so doing, a syncretistic approach to religious faith is adopted. As Hans Jonas observes about ancient Gnosticism,

> The gnostic systems compounded everything—oriental mythologies, astrological doctrines, Iranian theology, elements of Jewish tradition, whether biblical, rabbinical, or occult, Christian salvation-eschatology,

Platonic terms and concepts. Syncretism attained in this period its greatest efficacy.[27]

Philip J. Lee has recognized these gnostic tendencies in modern cultures—particularly (though not exclusively) modern Protestant North American cultures. He notes, "Gnostics, whether of the second century or the twentieth century, will not be constrained in the use of material. They will employ whatever is available, in whatever way they choose, to answer the needs of gnostic faith, which is to say, the spiritual needs of the self."[28] Though he writes of general cultural tendencies, Lee's point could easily be taken as a direct commentary on Moore's *Care of the Soul*.

Lee's critique aims at helping reform and recover the practices of classical Protestant Christianity. However, Harold Bloom finds Lee's diagnosis more powerful than his prognosis. Bloom explicitly agrees with Lee's assessment of the prevalence of Gnosticism in American religious culture, but he thinks it is more pervasive and more delightful. Bloom goes so far as to characterize Gnosticism as "The American Religion," observing that "the American Christ is more an American than he is Christ."[29]

Bloom thinks that American Gnosticism has been developing for the better part of two centuries.

> Unlike most countries, we have no overt national religion, but a partly concealed one has been developing among us for some two centuries now. It is almost purely experiential, and despite its insistences, it is scarcely Christian in any traditional way. A religion of the self burgeons, under many names, and seeks to know its own inwardness, in isolation. What the American self has found, since about 1800, is its own freedom—from the world, from time, from other selves. But this freedom is a very expensive torso, because of what it is obliged to leave out: society, temporality, and other. What remains, for it, is solitude and the abyss.

A few pages later Bloom links this experiential interest in the self to its own gnostic form of salvation: "Experiential faith, largely divorced from doctrine, would have left an emptiness in America but for something more vibrant that replaced doctrine, in timeless *knowing* that in itself saves."[30]

To be sure, Bloom's approving analysis of a gnostic American religion is impressionistic and often overstated. Yet Lee's more careful analysis, along with Bloom's provocative insights, point together to a dominant cultural reality that helps to explain the popularity of books like Moore's. That reality represents a divergence from , and a challenge to, Christian practices and convictions.

How did these sensibilities take hold with such considerable force, particularly in North America? This is a complex question, and one which—at least in my judgment—eludes a comprehensive causal historical explanation. However, these sensibilities seem also to be linked to broad intellectual and political commitments that have been developing over an extended historical period, and have become prominent in modern cultures.

Hence, a fourth explanation for the popularity of contemporary spirituality points to the constellation of these intellectual and political commitments in modernity.[31] For example, spirituality in modernity—and specifically that experience identified as "mysticism"—tends to be consigned, by both its advocates and its detractors, to the realm of "private", personal experience completely separated from the "public" realm of rationality, institutions, and politics. Spirituality's advocates see it as a potential means to unite people around the world beyond political or institutional divisions. This unity can be achieved both diachronically through time and synchronically across diverse cultures and religions. Note, for example, the following comments offered in a British review of two works on mysticism in the March 20, 1913 edition of the *Times Literary Supplement*:

> Mysticism in its essence is absolutely autonomous. It needs no institutions, no dogmas, no historical traditions. Those it finds among its surroundings, and for the most part gratefully or dutifully accepts; but it can stand without them. For this reason it is in all essentials the same at all times and in all places. The masterpieces of mystical literature, such as the Fourth Gospel, the Theologica Germanica, and the Revelations of Julian of Norwich, require no trained historical or literary faculty to understand them, and they leap over the denominational barriers which divide Christendom into hostile camps. They are for all time and for every nation; kindred spirits understand them and love them at once.[32]

It does not take much imagination to see how this description, which supposedly unites Christendom, could in the late twentieth century be extended to show the unity of all humankind's quest for the sacred beyond *any* cultural or religious divisions.

Indeed, this separation of "spirituality" from politics, institutions, doctrines, and (most broadly) the material world has become entrenched in many of our habits of thinking. Take, for example, three pivotal intellectual grids by which we now tend to evaluate issues of spirituality and mysticism: William James's *Varieties of Religious Experience*, Ernst Troeltsch's typology of Church-Sect-Mysticism in *The Social Teaching of the Christian Churches*, and Max Weber's sharp distinction between privatized mysticism and rationalized politics (developed in a variety of his writings). In each case, mysticism and spirituality are confined to the realm of private, apolitical experiences of the self that are essentially unrelated—if not actually inimical—to the worlds of social and political dynamics.

This bifurcation of spirituality and politics is one of the reasons that contemporary spirituality can be consumed as a luxury consumer good, primarily designed for middle- and upper-class folks. One will not be confronted with the massive suffering around the world, or even around the corner from where one lives. Nor will the reader be confronted with Amos's stinging prophetic indictments and Jesus's call to costly discipleship. Rather, the reader is invited to an increasingly inward journey that leaves the world largely as it already is.

The presumption created by such intellectual grids and habits of thought and "practice" is that the sacred has little if anything to do with morality, social institutions, or political power.[33] What really matters are the inner experiences of isolated individuals, cultivated and evaluated largely by those same individuals. This both distorts our readings of the patterns and practices of many spiritual figures and communities within the history of Christianity and masks the social values and commitments entailed in much of contemporary spirituality.[34]

However, Christians cannot rest in the comfortable position of blaming only these economic, cultural, and intellectual developments for the popularity of consumer spirituality. A fifth set of explanations points to the ways in which Christians themselves have contributed to these developments. Though Christians have traditionally claimed that we have been created for communion with God, and (in Augustine's terms) that our hearts will be restless until they rest in God, contemporary churches on the whole have done an abysmal job in sustaining the sorts of practices and disciplines necessary for that communion, for that rest. This is, at least in part, the result of our failure to notice the gap between what we mean by "spirituality" and what, for example, St. Paul means by invoking the importance of "life in the Spirit" (despite many modern interpretations which have too easily equated them). For St. Paul, life in the Spirit is not an opposition to the material world but a pattern of life enabled by the Holy Spirit through particular practices and disciplines which conform humanity to Jesus Christ. To be sure, there has been no one pattern of Christian spirituality in the diverse histories of Christian communities down through the centuries; however, there have been practices, presumptions, and beliefs which provide, together, a more coherent conception of Christian spirituality than is found in much contemporary spirituality.

The failure of churches to recognize the gaps between Christian practices and consumer spirituality is also, at least in part, due to a lack of ongoing practices of catechesis. Too many churches have failed to help shape a specifically Christian understanding of God, and in particular to recognize that learning to know God involves the transformation of our desires as well as struggles to unlearn patterns of sin and self-deception.[35]

The churches in general—and theologians in particular—need to re-read the histories of our own spiritual traditions to examine where and when we have contributed to sowing the seeds which have now come to fruition in contemporary spirituality. Various markers could be identified, including the introduction of discussions of "spirit" over-against "matter", and the ways in which that transmutes our sense of what the Pauline "Life in the

Spirit" entails; or the beginning of the separation of "love" and "knowledge" in the late medieval era, and the ways in which that separation affected and affects constructions of relations between the "self" and "community"; or the patterns and presumptions which eventually disjoined the discipline of theology from spirituality, resulting in the increasing modern disjunction between theology and sanctity.[36] There is, in this context, plenty of historical housecleaning that needs to be undertaken.

At the same time, however, there have been significant gains in Christian practices of spiritual disciplines over the years—and also new complexities and understandings that have had to be, and continue to have to be, negotiated. This includes, most notably, feminist contributions both through new insights and retrievals of significant traditions of women's spiritual practices.[37] Even though I have been charting some of the ways in which Christian practices have become corrupted in the contemporary phenomenon of consumer spirituality, it would be mistaken to read the history of Christian spiritual practices as a contemporary decline from some prior golden age in the patristic era, or the middle ages, or even the early days of the Reformation. There is no era that we either can or should try to replicate, whether it be twelfth-century Clairvaux or another time. There is much we can learn from such twentieth century figures as Edith Stein or Dorothy Day, just as we also can learn from John Wesley or Martin Luther, Hildegard of Bingen or Thomas Aquinas, Gregory of Nyssa or his sister Macrina.[38]

But in order appropriately to learn the lessons they have to teach, we need to recognize the different patterns of practices and beliefs by which diverse people and traditions have sought to be engaged by God. Though there are undoubtedly significant differences among the figures identified above, much less many others who could have been named, they shared in common certain presumptions, practices, and beliefs that provide important contrasts to the presuppositions that guide consumer spirituality—contrasts I have exemplified through the work of Bernard of Clairvaux.

IV

Even though the contrasts that I have suggested between Moore and Bernard ought to be clear, as ought also (though left implicit) the ways in which Bernard's thought challenges the presumptions of modernity's conceptions of spirituality, there are still important objections one might make to my account. By way of conclusion, I identify three potential sets of objections, and respond briefly to each.

First, it might be suggested that I have missed the point by comparing a twelfth-century monastic with a twentieth-century person who left the monastery in order to reach ordinary people with advice about spirituality in "everyday" life. Admittedly, there are some relevant disanalogies, and it is somewhat unfair to contrast a saint whose spiritual writings have long been considered a classic with a contemporary figure whose books, while best-sellers, are not likely to be mistaken for enduring classics.

Even so, several relevant features also need to be emphasized. For example, the important contrasts between the two are not that one is a monk and the other writing for every-day people, nor that one wrote in the Middle Ages, while the other is writing for contemporary people. Bernard's claims are not idiosyncratic; similar visions and patterns of practices have been developed and commended by remarkably diverse figures throughout the Christian tradition. Rather, the important contrasts lie in their conceptions of God and of the nature and destiny of human life, the practices they do or do not commend, and the attentiveness of their "spirituality" to issues of social and political import.

Put more bluntly, Bernard's conception of "spiritual" living is no less practicable for ordinary believers than is Moore's. To be sure, there will be some divergences when and if the practices are removed from the monastery and adapted for people living in the world. Among those divergences will likely be a critique of an excessive focus on spiritual "humiliation" that, while often overstated by critics of Christian spiritual traditions, nonetheless has significant force. In its place will be a deepened appreciation for the joy and beauty of God's good Creation.

There are numerous examples of people who have taken the rich and complex practices of monastic Christianity and adapted them for serious Christian spiritual living in the world. For visible examples, one could point to the Wesleyan class-meetings in eighteenth-century England, to twentieth-century Catholic Worker houses, or to contemporary Latin American base communities. What is required is a willingness to participate in disciplined practices of being engaged by the God of Jesus Christ. This may not be *easily* adapted into everyday life; but the relative ease is more typically a limitation of our willingness to have our everyday lives shaped by the grace of God than it is a problem with the practices commended.

Second: it might be objected that my invocation of Bernard presents a false contrast with Moore. Whereas Moore's book is designed to nurture people who for one reason or another are unconvinced by either the convictions or the practices of "institutional" or "traditional" Christianity, the appeals to Bernard present Christian spiritual practice as a take-it-or-leave-it proposition. To be sure, my analysis and comparisons have been, for the sake of space, overly schematized; greater specification and attention to the dynamics of contemporary belief and practice is needed. However, what is needed are not more examples of consumer spirituality, in which the traditions of Christian spiritual practices are either caricatured or ignored (and which, unwittingly, all too often replicate modernity's problematic construals of "spirituality"); rather, Christians ought to learn from figures such as Bernard or Julian of Norwich, adapting and re-forming *our* practices as needed and as are appropriate. In this way, Christian spirituality would also more effectively address those whose yearnings and inchoate desires have led them towards the consumption of spirituality.

At the same time, it is important to remember that the practices of Christian spirituality are *communal* and part of traditions; so the discernments ought to be conducted in those contexts, rather than by isolated individuals. Further, insofar as popular literature needs *good* examples of Christian spiritual living, we ought to be working from within the best of the Christian tradition's understandings of how spirituality, theology, and politics are interrelated. Bernard is one impressive example whose views, like those of Hildegard of Bingen or Catherine of Siena, ought to resonate with many Christians and interested seekers from a variety of traditions and viewpoints.

In addition, Bernard's thought provides important criteria for distinguishing good practices from bad ones, healthy ways of reforming traditions from simply engaging in "personal reformations". Those criteria are grounded in what conduces to authentic desire and knowledge of the Triune God, understood in rich and complex ways reflective of both psychological and social realities. Bernard's thought suggests that we ought to be wary of those religious practices which are *self*-interested, for they all-too-easily foster self-deception and the sustenance of "my" power at the expense of others. For Bernard, it is only if Christians become perfectly holy (an eschatological hope) that we will be able to learn to trust our self-interest, and then only because our self-interest has become transparent to God.

A third potential objection: it might be suggested that my invocation of Bernard is mistaken, for he was a male clerical figure in a position of power; both his life and his writings reflect power which replicate the problems of Christianity's connection to patriarchy and politics. Though this objection also is significant in relation to Moore, Peck, and several other writers of contemporary "spirituality"—namely that their spiritualities are designed mainly for middle-class people who seem unaware of the horrifying suffering and powerlessness that many people are forced to endure—it should be acknowledged that there is much in Bernard's life that lends credence to this critique. Bernard was too comfortable in engaging the worldly power-politics of his day. This was most notably the case in relation to the Crusades and in his conflict with Peter Abelard, which occurred (through Bernard's maneuvering) in political rather than in theological arenas. Even so, this can to a significant degree be attributed to the gaps that most people struggle with—including the saints—between the insights and convictions we hold on the one hand, and the fragile and often mistaken discernments we make in our lives on the other.

Yet there is also force to the critiques that suggest that Christian spiritual practices need to be less concerned with cleansing our interior lives and more concerned about a "spirituality" of justice. There is considerable significance in the suggestion that *both* Moore and Bernard are too focused on the self—Moore through an all-too-easy contentment with caring for one's own soul, and Bernard through a more complex account of the project of self-knowledge in relation to the knowledge of God. Bernard's conception of spiritual practices suggests a need for greater dispossession of the self, for humility and an abandonment of pride. But, the objector might respond, what about those who are already dispossessed and suffer ongoing humiliations not from God but at the hands of other human beings—particularly men? Is Bernard's theology not counsel for further dispossession and humiliation?

Such an objection is important, and needs to be included in a full understanding of the interrelations of spirituality, theology, and politics. Even so, I would suggest that Bernard's account of Christian spiritual practices provides a rich framework in which these concerns about political realities can be ably developed and his own problematic formulations criticized. To be sure, Bernard's sermons were directed, at least in the first instance, to his fellow monks. But it would not be difficult to show how the themes of desire, knowledge, and the importance of unmasking our illusions can be developed in significant ways for the powerful and the powerless alike.[39] Since Bernard's thought is so richly centered on the desire to know the God of Jesus Christ, learning to be engaged by this God can and should enable transformations of our thinking and living so *any* illusory constructions of the world or of persons can be challenged and unmasked.

It is not surprising to find so many people drawn to themes of "spirituality"; after all, if Bernard and others in the Christian tradition are right, we were created for communion with God and we will be restless and unsatisfied until we discover that communion. However, I have argued in this essay that much contemporary literature in spirituality—exemplified by Thomas Moore—makes it more rather than less difficult to discover that communion. We need less consumer spirituality and more of those practices of Christian living that enable us to be engaged by God, both in our sense of God's absence and in our delight in God's presence. In this sense, we need less "spirituality" and more "life in the Spirit." For it is on that journey of seeking to become God's friends, in response to God's gracious love, that our hearts will be nourished and finally enabled to find their active, delighted rest.[40]

NOTES

1   For an instructive discussion, see Linda Woodhead, "Post-Christian Spiritualities," *Religion* 23 (1993) pp. 167–181. I regret that I only came across Professor Woodhead's essay after mine was substantially finished; she and I have overlapping interests and criticisms. Professor Woodhead focuses particularly on academic authors and the contents of their arguments, and on figures who are more explicitly "post-Christian"; by contrast, I focus on the cultural significance of popular spirituality and its avoidance of Christian *practice*, and on figures who are more ambiguously connected to institutional Christianity.

2   Recent books by Robert Wuthnow and by Phyllis A. Tickle, considerably different in aim and content, nonetheless both share the title *Rediscovering the Sacred*.

3   My description of practices in this essay follows, at least in broad outlines, that offered by Alasdair MacIntyre in *After Virtue* (2nd ed.): "By a 'practice' I am going to mean any

coherent and complex form of socially established cooperative human activity through which goods internal to that form of activity are realized in the course of trying to achieve those standards of excellence which are appropriate to, and partially definitive of, that form of activity, with the result that human powers to achieve excellence, and human conceptions of the ends and goods involved, are systematically extended" (Notre Dame, IN: University of Notre Dame Press, 1984) p. 187. MacIntyre's account requires that practices be situated within an account of the narrative unity of human life and of traditions. A full theological account of practices needs to describe them in relation to God's active presence for the life of the world. For further theological reflection on practices, see my *Transformed Judgment* (Notre Dame, IN: University of Notre Dame Press, 1990).

4   I put the term "spirituality" in scare quotes because of the problems surrounding the use of that term. That is, the noun "spirituality" has a complex history; there is no such notion in ancient languages until the 5th century, and there the terms refer primarily to people who "live in the Holy Spirit". The notion of "spirituality", and particularly one which is differentiated from the material world, emerges only in the later middle ages—and there it is still related to Christian practices. In the early modern era, the term was often used pejoratively to refer to enthusiastic or quietistic movements. In the twentieth century, it has come to refer to a wide variety of experiences and patterns, many of which surround not so much attempts to express personal and ecclesial responses to God as attempts to cultivate or respond to a sense of the "sacred". Hence at least one of the problems in attempting to compare and evaluate diverse patterns of "spirituality" is that it is not always clear what conceptual boundaries the term is meant to mark. See the discussion in Philip Sheldrake, *Spirituality and History: Questions of Interpretation and Method* (New York: Crossroad, 1992), esp. pp. 32–56.

5   For an instructive analysis of Bernard's thought, to which I am indebted, see Michael Casey, *A Thirst for God: Spiritual Desire in Bernard of Clairvaux's Sermons on the Song of Songs* (Kalamazoo, MI: Cistercian Publications, 1988). I am also indebted to Rowan Williams' discussion of Bernard in his "Know Thyself: What Kind of Injunction?" in Michael McGhee (ed.) *Philosophy, Religion and the Spiritual Life* (Cambridge: Cambridge University Press, 1992) pp. 211–228.

6   Bernard, *De diligendo Deo* 22, cited in Casey, *A Thirst for God*, p. 85.

7   Bernard, Sermon 36.5, in *On the Song of Songs II*, tr. Killian Walsh (Kalamazoo, MI: Cistercian, 1976). Further citations to sermons will be to this edition and translation, and will be cited parenthetically in the text.

8   For Bernard, "spiritual marriage" occurs when the soul gives itself wholeheartedly and unreservedly to responding to its experience of the love of God. See the discussion in Casey, *A Thirst for God*, esp. pp. 191–200.

9   See also the discussion in Casey, *A Thirst for God*, pp. 54ff., 94.

10   Bernard, *Sermo in octava Paschae* 1.7, cited in Casey, *A Thirst for God*, p. 126.

11   Casey, *A Thirst for God*, p. 268.

12   See Bernard's comment at the close of Sermon 57 (57.11): "We find a contemplative Mary in those who, co-operating with God's grace over a long period of time, have attained to a better and happier state. By now confident of forgiveness they no longer brood anxiously on the sad memory of their sins, but day and night they meditate on the ways of God with insatiable delight, even at times gazing with unveiled face, in unspeakable joy, on the splendor of the Bridegroom, being transformed into his likeness from splendor to splendor by the Spirit of the Lord."

13   See Bernard, Sermon 23, and the treatise *On Grace and Free Choice*. See also the discussion in Casey, *A Thirst for God*, pp. 245–251.

14   Two points are worth noting, at least in passing. First, Luther himself loved Bernard's writings, suggesting that perhaps many protestant interpreters of Luther have misread his worries about "works righteousness" by failing to read Luther as an interpreter of people such as Bernard. Second, Bernard's account obviously precedes modern discussions of the relationship between "nature" and "grace", and—so I would argue—offers important insights and alternatives to those often fruitless debates.

15   Talal Asad, *Genealogies of Religion* (Baltimore, MD: Johns Hopkins University Press, 1993), p. 144.

16   See the discussion in Casey, *A Thirst for God*, pp. 54–59, with specific citations to various sermons in which Bernard deals with these themes.

17   Thomas Moore, *Care of the Soul* (New York: HarperCollins, 1992). The book made it to #1 on the *New York Times* Best-Seller list, and spent over 46 weeks on the list. Further citations to this book will be given parenthetically within the text. See also my "Spirituality Life," *The Christian Century* (Nov. 6, 1996), in which I critically analyze Moore's most recent book, *The Re-Enchantment of Everyday Life*.

18   The Book of Proverbs was frequently used, particularly in the early church, in the context of catechesis. Gregory of Nyssa reports that Macrina frequently turned to the Wisdom of Solomon for the moral education of children. See "The Life of St. Macrina", in *Saint Gregory of Nyssa: Ascetical Works*, tr. Virginia Woods Callahan (Washington, D.C.: Catholic University of America Press, 1967), p. 165.

19   I provide a more extended critique of these issues in my "The Psychological Captivity of the Church in the U.S.," in Carl E. Braaten and Robert W. Jenson (eds,) *Either/Or* (Grand Rapids, MI: Eerdmans, 1995), pp. 97–112. See also my critiques as these issues bear on forgiveness in *Embodying Forgiveness: A Theological Analysis* (Grand Rapids, MI: Eerdmans, 1995), especially chapter 2.

20   Moore seems unaware of, or at least does not acknowledge, the fact that some "polytheistic religions" have practised rituals such as child-sacrifice. Surely even on his own terms not all polytheistic religions offer "useful guidance toward finding spiritual values in the world".

21   Moore is identified on the back cover of the book as having been "a monk", though he never took formal vows.

22   On the other hand, Moore may be well aware of his gnostic proclivities and affirm them. After all, the epigraph to the major section "Spiritual Practice and Psychological Depth" is from the Gospel of Thomas: "Recognize what is before your eyes, and what is hidden will be revealed to you."

23   For an analysis of how these sorts of assumptions have affected Christian thinking about congregations and issues of "church growth", see Philip D. Kenneson, "Selling [Out] the Church in the Marketplace of Desire," *Modern Theology* 9/4 (October 1993) pp. 319–348.

24   To some extent, this may be happening with the resurgent interest in fundamentalist groups and, within the African-American community, the Nation of Islam.

25   Philip Rieff, *The Triumph of the Therapeutic: Uses of Faith After Freud* (Chicago, IL: University of Chicago Press, 1966), p. 26. See also Alasdair MacIntyre's critique of therapeutic culture in *After Virtue*.

26   Indeed, some versions of "Gnosticism" were part of the early Christian movements; only over time did the Church discover and articulate the ways in which Christian practice and doctrine diverged from various versions of Gnosticism. However, the contemporary appellation of the term "Gnosticism" typically refers to those versions that were more explicitly non- or even anti-Christian. For an excellent compilation of texts with historical introductions, and which emphasizes Gnosticism's proximity to Christianity, see Bentley Layton, *The Gnostic Scriptures* (New York: Doubleday, 1987).

  Even so, I would argue that it is a mistake for *Christians* to return (often unwittingly) to one or another version of ancient Gnosticism without attending to the developments of the Christian tradition—including, for example, the ways in which Bernard of Clairvaux and many others refine and challenge those conceptions and practices. Yet this is what is often done, particularly in contemporary spirituality.

27   Hans Jonas, *The Gnostic Religion* (Boston: Beacon Press, 1963), p. 25.

28   Philip J. Lee, *Against the Protestant Gnostics* (New York: Oxford University Press, 1987), p. 12.

29   Harold Bloom, *The American Religion: The Emergence of the Post-Christian Nation* (New York: Touchstone, 1992), p. 25.

30   Bloom, *The American Religion*, pp. 37, 49.

31   My analysis in what follows is indebted in several ways to F.C. Bauerschmidt's excellent, extended discussion in his currently unpublished "Politics and Mysticism".

32   *Times Literary Supplement*, No. 584, March 20, 1913, cited in F.C. Bauerschmidt's Ph.D. dissertation, *Julian of Norwich and the Mystical Body Politic of Christ* (Duke University, 1996), p. 26.

33   See also David S. Yeago's important argument that protestant (and particularly Lutheran) construals of the "law-gospel" dialectic have left many people unable to resist the twin

temptations of gnostic theology and antinomian morality. "Gnosticism, Antinomianism, and Reformation Theology: Reflections on the Costs of a Construal" *Pro Ecclesia* II/1 (Winter 1993) pp. 37–49.

34   For confirmation of this judgment in relation to specific historical figures, see Bauerschmidt on Julian of Norwich; Denys Turner on Augustine and Bonaventure in *The Darkness of God* (New York: Cambridge University Press, 1995); and Rowan Williams on *Teresa of Avila* (Wilton, CT: Morehouse, 1991).

35   There are, admittedly, many important questions underspecified in the above description of a "specifically Christian understanding of God". I have deliberately left them under-specified in the interest of casting as broad a net as possible; I would argue that many figures who would otherwise have disagreements about (for example) what constitutes sin, or how holiness is best lived, or how best to characterize God's triune character, would nonetheless share a commitment to the broad description I offer here. And it is the divergences from that broad description that are most worrisome about consumer spirituality. For further discussion of the importance of transformation and struggling to unlearn patterns of sin, see my *Transformed Judgment*.

36   On these markers, see in order: Sheldrake, *Spirituality and History*, esp. pp. 32–56; Sarah Coakley, "Visions of the Self in Late Medieval Christianity," in McGhee (ed.), *Philosophy, Religion and the Spiritual Life*, pp. 89–104; and Hans Urs von Balthasar, "Theology and Sanctity," in *Explorations in Theology Vol. I: The Word Made Flesh* (San Francisco, CA: Ignatius Press, 1989), pp. 181–210.

37   See, for example, Sarah Coakley's collection of essays, *Powers and Submissions: Essays on Spirituality, Feminism and Philosophy* (forthcoming, Blackwells); the work of Caroline Walker Bynum, especially *Jesus as Mother: Studies in the Spirituality of the High Middle Ages* (Berkeley, CA: University of California Press, 1982); and Margaret R. Miles, *Practicing Christianity: Critical Perspectives for an Embodied Spirituality* (New York: Crossroad, 1988).

38   Though I cannot explore the issues in this context, there are also important lessons to be learned from specific engagements with the practices of diverse religious traditions. That is, after all, one of the lessons we need to learn from Aquinas, whose own work was influenced by his engagements with Jewish and Muslim thinkers. See the discussion in David B. Burrell, *Knowing the Unknowable God* (Notre Dame, IN: University of Notre Dame Press, 1986).

39   For one example, see Williams' discussion in "Know Thyself: What Kind of Injunction", pp. 223–226.

40   I am grateful to F.C. Bauerschmidt, James J. Buckley, Michael Cartwright, Angela Russell Christman, Rodney Clapp, Stephen Fowl, Stanley Hauerwas, and Susan Jones for their criticisms of earlier versions of this essay.

INTERIORITY AND EPIPHANY: A READING IN NEW TESTAMENT ETHICS

ROWAN D. WILLIAMS

1

Common to a good deal of contemporary philosophical reflection on human identity is the conviction that we are systematically misled, even corrupted, by a picture of the human agent as divided into an outside and an inside— a 'true self', hidden, buried, to be excavated by one or another kind of therapy, ranging from the intellectual therapy of the post-Cartesian tradition (the modern 'philosophy of mind', the epistemological struggle) to the psychological therapy of another 'analytic' tradition, the tradition inaugurated by Freud and still flourishing in various serious and more popular forms. Modern ethics and theology alike have been haunted by a presence usually called the *authentic* self: an agent whose motivation is transparent, devoid of self-deception and of socially conditioned role playing. As a therapeutic fiction, this is a construct of great power and usefulness. I suspect, though, that it is also a fiction that is intellectually shaky and, in the last analysis, morally problematic. It plays with the idea that my deepest, most significant or serious 'interest' is something given and something unique; it brackets the difficult issue of how we are to think through our human situation as embodying a common task, in which the sacredness of the authentic self's account of its own interest is not the beginning and the end of moral discourse.

'No depth exists in subject until it is created. No *a priori* identity awaits us … Inwardness is a process of becoming, a work, the labour of the negative. The self is not a substance one unearths by peeling away layers until one gets to the core, but an integrity one struggles to bring into existence.'[1] This sharp

The Rt. Revd. Rowan D. Williams
Bishop of Monmouth, Bishopstow, Newport, Gwent NP9 4EA, UK

formulation by a contemporary American philosopher who attempts to bring Hegel, Heidegger, Marx and Freud into fruitful conversation concentrates our thinking very effectively. For if there is no pre-existent 'inwardness', where is the 'real' self to be found or made but in the world of exchange—language and interaction. More particularly, this statement of the question makes it clear that the self as self-conscious is the product of *time*. We tend to conceive interiority in terms of space—outer and inner, husk and kernel; what if our 'inner life' were better spoken of in terms of extension in time? the time it takes to understand?[2] My sense of the 'hiddenness' of another self is something I develop in the ordinary difficulty of conversation and negotiation. I don't follow; I don't know how to respond in such a way that what I want can be made clear and achieved. Conversation and negotiation are of their nature unpredictable, 'unscripted'; their outcome is not determined. Thus I develop the sense of the other speaker/agent as *obscure* to me: their motivation or reasoning is not transparent, not open to my full knowledge, but always waiting to be drawn out and clarified. In this process I develop correspondingly the sense of myself as obscure: I must explain myself if I am to attain what I want, and as I try to bring to speech what is of significance to me in such a way as to make it accessible to another, I discover that I am far from sure what it is that I can say. I become difficult to myself, aware of the gap between presentation and whatever else it is that is active in my acting. It is not surprising that I embody these things in the picture of one hidden self confronting another, both hampered by the inadequacy of language or shared conventions—with the result that we can then fall into the trap of supposing that there could be a self-presence without difficulty, a real or truthful apprehension of myself and another agent or agents, freed from the distorting effects of our imperfect linguistic or social tools.

In other words, we assimilate the difficulty of mutual understanding between two agents to the difficulty of two people speaking a different language; somewhere there are better tools, a speech in which we are more properly or honestly at home. But in fact the difficulty is not that experienced by two speakers, one or both of whom are working in an unfamiliar or problematic medium. The exchanges of conversation and negotiation *are* the essence of what is going on, not unsatisfactory translations of a more fundamental script. The difficulty is inherent in what is being done, and could not be removed by a more adaptable or familiar medium. Difficulty and what goes with it, the awareness of possible error (in how I hear and how I am heard) form the stuff of my awareness of what we commonly call the 'interior' life, mine and the other's. It thus becomes abundantly clear that my interiority is a construct that emerges through the labour of exchange—which is not to say that it is a reducible, secondary, epiphenomenal matter. Quite the contrary: what is lost in this analysis is not the ideal of a truthful self-perception but the myth of a truthful perception that can be uncovered by the redescription of the self's linguistic and social performance as the swaddling-clothes of a hidden and given reality—which, of course, divorced from the reality of performance, becomes formal to the point of emptiness.

The 'for-myself' and the 'for-another' of awareness and speech are thus not separable. Even when I try to formulate or picture my 'real' self, what I am in effect doing is imagining an ideal other, an ideal interlocutor and observer, a listener to whom I am making perfect sense. The danger, of course, is that this imagined other, the perfect listener, blocks out the actual, less perfect, less sympathetic hearers with whom I am actually and temporally doing business, so that my self-perception remains firmly under my own control. The proper logic of this recognition that my self-knowledge emerges from converse and exchange enjoins a consistent scepticism about claims to have arrived at a final transparency to myself. If it is converse that gives me a self to know, the continuance of converse means that I have never done with knowing. I do not cease to be *vulnerable* to other accounts of myself, to the pressure to revise what I say of myself at those points where I have to recognise a breakdown in the movement of exchange, the delay and obscurity that drives me back to ask, 'What *did* I mean?' The point at which I cease to ask or even understand such a challenge is, arguably, the beginning of mental sickness, the index of a pathology. And this vulnerability must also extend to my account of my own interest or 'good': I cannot assume that my good or my destiny is specified by the mysterious interior reality that is imagined to underlie the surface activities of language and negotiation. I shall discover what is good for me, I shall discover how to construe and articulate my interest, just as I construe everything else about my self-perception—in the processes of encounter and exchange, not in the excavation of a buried inner agenda.

2

This is the point at which substantive conflict seems to arise. Say that we are indeed in the process of constructing the inner life and the integrity that is believed to go with it in the processes of conversation or negotiation: this cannot deliver a vision of anything like a *common* good in itself. To discover what is good for me in the process of converse may well in the first instance mean discovering the need for resistance, the need to *deny* that my interest is specified for me by some other in a unilateral way. That there is an adversarial moment in the construction of the self and its knowledge of itself is, of course, the insight that fuels Hegel's entire discussion of the Lord and the Bondsman;[3] and in the complex political situation of our century, it sometimes appears to be the dominant motif in the discovery or appropriation of selfhood: I discover who or what I am by the discovery of myself as victim, stripped of my 'true' identity by some other. My interest must be articulated by denial and revolt, by a distancing from the other's definition of the linguistic field. Hence what we might call the 'separatist moment' in all twentieth century liberationist movements, racial, gender-based and so on. I/we am/are not what you have taught us to be and to believe; to be what *we* truly are, we must reject *your* account of reality and overturn what it privileges (European rationality, pale pigmentation, masculine bias in language, heterosexual coupling). Current debate about 'political correctness' in the United States and elsewhere is often clouded by a twofold misunderstanding (curable, perhaps, by the digestion of more Hegel): on the one hand, the separatist moment is absolutised in an insistence that self-definition, definition 'from within', is the most fundamental moral need in a situation of manifest and continuing inequity; on the other hand, objectors fail to see the significance of the recognition entailed here that language and negotiation are about *power*, and that the bestowal of power on the powerless requires the most unsparing interrogation of the processes by which groups, persons and interests are in fact, historically and socially, defined. The former ends up in the crudest kind of mythology about self-realisation on the basis of some mysterious inner essence, unpolluted by converse; the latter remains at a resolutely pre-reflective (and so essentially pre-political) stage of awareness. Both sides of the debate, insofar as they fall into one or other of these attitudes, explicitly or implicitly, assume there is no *difficulty*, to use the word yet again, about the discovery of interest, and no continuing agenda to lead us into questioning about *common* interest. They remain at the level of adversarial definition: interest is secured at the expense of another.

The problem to be faced and overcome, then, is one about how we move beyond rivalry; how we are to arrive at ethics properly so called, instead of a battleground between competing interests (I take it that ethics is nothing if not a discipline for evaluating and judging local or individual claims to know the good in the light of accounts of the good that are not purely local or individual). This leads us back to reflection on the processes of self-discovery already sketched in this essay. We learn how to 'speak' ourselves, how to 'utter' ourselves, in conversation, in the presence of an interlocutor. To imagine an ideal interlocutor, what I earlier called the perfect listener, the presence to which I am wholly transparent or to whom I make sense, is to imagine a presence with which I do *not* in the ordinary sense 'negotiate'; the capacity of the other for attention, an attention complete enough to assure me of unconditioned space or time to develop and discover what I am to be, is in such an ideal case not shadowed at all by the other's own particular agenda, by another set of interests comparable to mine. Yet to spell it out in these terms is to display the character of this ideal interlocutor as a fantasy. On the one hand, my language and self-presentation only acquire identity in the *contentions* of exchange with another, in a set of particular and historical encounters with those elements in the world of personal transactions that deny my illusions of control, my passion for 'scripting' the language used around me; I become a self only in the self-dispossession of discovering that there are things I cannot acquire, goals I cannot attain. On the other hand, to absolutise contention is to remain trapped in a stage of consciousness where the other is always liable to be apprehended as a threat or a rival. Thus I do not emerge into selfhood without concrete otherness; I do not discover my humanity in the absence of frustration, the resistance of the world to my will (if I can even be said to have a 'will' in the absence of the linguistic specificity that is developed in negotiation). But I do not recognize the convergence of my interest and the other's without a move beyond opposition and negotiation. In the crude terms of recent social debates, it is in a measure true that we do not grow without competition; but competition without mutual recognition and mutual need is barbarous and self-destructive.

The other who is concrete yet not a partner in negotiation, not engaged in a process of mutual 'adjustment', seems, then, to be what we look for and perhaps presuppose in the search for a way into ethical discourse. The concreteness of the other cannot be sacrificed; the ideal listener will not do, since this figure has no 'resistance', and is, ultimately, only at the service of my development; and an other purely instrumental to my specification finally collapses back into the chaos of my undifferentiated existence, into pre-consciousness rather than a conscious self-appropriation.[4] A concrete other of this kind would have to be apprehended as other *equally* to my own project and interest *and* to any specific other subject in the field of negotiation; neither competing with me for moral space, nor endorsing or protecting my moral space over against other subjects. In this sense, we can say that it must be articulated as that to which I and others are commonly answerable; it is what makes sense of me as a moral subject (i.e., as a subject not determined by my private calculation of my interest or good), and is therefore what I appeal to in making sense of my positions or policies. But, precisely because it is what makes sense of me in this way, questioning and reshaping my would-be private or partisan account of what is good for me, it is more than a static principle of legitimation for what I happen to decide. If I appeal to it in the struggle of negotiation, I do so in the acknowledgement that I as well as the other will be exposed to its challenge, and liable to be changed by it. Further, I can accept this situation as something other than simply the triumph of another will over mine in the battle for moral space, since this non-competitive other remains other as well to the specific 'rival' subject that confronts me at any given moment. The appeal either of myself or of a specific historical other to this presence with which neither of us can negotiate provides a ground for discourse about our human negotiation that is not immediately trapped in rivalry: a common discourse before a common other, to which I and the other are alike vulnerable or responsible.

If we can and do presuppose something like this in trying to formulate a moral discourse at all, that is, a discourse not determined by the tribalism of competing accounts of the good, a discourse of shared self-criticism, what exactly is it that we are talking about? We could say, as a good many would, that this is a necessary fiction if we are to find a Kantian 'tribunal' for the settling of moral dispute.[5] But as soon as the appeal to common answerability is defined as an instrumental construction, we are in danger of returning to our starting point: *really* human interests are conflictual, but it is more convenient to pretend otherwise, since social harmony is desirable. However, on such an account, it is desirable, presumably, because it is in *my* interest. I don't like being disturbed. And I assume that others have a similar distaste for being disturbed, and will to that extent co-operate in realising my desire. This passive and minimal version of the foundations of law remains vastly popular in the liberal North-Atlantic milieu, and—before it is too readily criticised—it must be said that there are worse accounts. The trouble with it is that it is inadequate to *adjudicate* anything, or to assist in the negotiation of conscientious matters rooted in a coherent moral worldview: hence the chaos of 'liberal' responses to the presence of Islam in the West; hence the violent bitterness that characterises the debate over abortion and the law, especially in the USA. The classical theological principle that what is just for me is bound up with what is just for my neighbour, and that my desire, if it is to be genuinely for a good beyond the private and local, must be a desire for the good of my neighbour[6] is not necessarily capable of being stated in the terms of mutual non-disturbance. A fictive or abstract account of shared answerability takes it for granted that what we first learn as human subjects is *private* desire, and that this remains a fundamental: the social ideal is to discover a means of securing maximal realisation of private desires, under a 'contractual' arrangement whereby certain of them are sacrificed so as not to interfere too severely with the private policies and goals of other individuals. We are, in fact, back with the priority of the private, of the inner life. This account of the situation is as problematic philosophically as it is practically.

If we are *not*, then, talking about a notional or contractual tribunal, must we be talking about the apprehension of an 'absolute' presence, a transcendent interlocutor? The temptation is to give a rapid 'yes' to this question, without noticing that this would still leave us with the problem of how the moral world is concretely learned. It is, notoriously, not enough to appeal to universal moral intuitions, an innate code; the supposed deliverances of anything like this are at best trivial, and fail to offer any method other than a majority vote for settling moral conflict. If we are serious about the material and temporal character of learning selfhood, we have to ask about the material and temporal processes whereby a sense and a practice of common answerability might be intelligibly generated. How might I or we historically be educated in a relation with something I cannot negotiate with?

One of the earliest attempts to give some moral substance to a notion of common human interest appears in Stoicism and Cynicism. The precise social background out of which these philosophical movements developed is difficult to analyse, but one can at least say that they both have something to do with disillusion about the possibilities of the conventional classical ethics of public life. In a period of endemic warfare between Greek states, there was much to be said for developing a foundation for ethics independent of the traditional civic context. Cynicism has its alleged origins in the fourth century BCE, and Stoicism enters its first major period of evolution in the century following, when the rise and disintegration of Alexander's empire had still further weakened the old civic patterns of virtue and raised the awkward questions of cosmopolitanism.[7] The idea of the human being (or at least the *free* human being) as a 'citizen of the universe'[8] initiates a tradition of reflection on the unity of kinship of human agents, and consequently a kind of egalitarianism (a *kind* of egalitarianism, since the theoretical allowance of equality is not in practice or, often, in theory, extended to slaves). The fundamental unifying factor is wisdom or the capacity to be taught it, and this wisdom is defined as living according to 'nature'. The difficulties of this were already being extensively discussed in antiquity:[9] philosophers had noticed that appeal to 'nature' was an unhelpful move when it came to specifics, and the critics of Stoicism in particular were unhappy with a double list of possible actions, those performed according to nature and those wholly indifferent, for which there could be no fully reasonable grounds. Both Stoics and Cynics also seemed to go no further with their universalism and egalitarianism than a strong commendation of attitudes to be shared by the non-civic community of the wise; they remained figures deliberately marginal to the public sphere.

Such a summary is, of course, a simplification of complex history, social and intellectual; but it is worth pondering in the light of the comparisons frequently drawn in recent New Testament scholarship between the recorded preaching of Jesus and the Cynic tradition.[10] It is easy, perhaps, to assimilate too glibly the universalism of Stoic or Cynic to the universalism of the Christian Church, without considering the difference between an ethic of shared attitudes among a fraternity of the wise and a specific social structure existing alongside the ordinary civic systems of the Roman Empire, in a perennially uncomfortable relation with them for several centuries. My point is that the earlier question of how a non-tribal ethic might be historically learned can be answered at one level by adducing the radical universalism of Stoic or Cynic; these ideas enter the moral vocabulary partly in reaction to a situation of moral scepticism in the context of a reshaping of social boundaries. But the ideas themselves have no clear embodying structures. To the extent that the Christian Church is an embodying structure for an ethic of shared accountability and common interest, it needs closer examination in this connection. In the next part of this essay, I shall be suggesting that the narrative (not simply the recorded teaching) of Jesus functions in such a way that it mediates historically the meaning of a non-negotiable and therefore non-competitive presence 'before' which ethical discourse is conducted; and that, when conducted systematically in that light, the character of ethical discourse itself is significantly affected.

3

There are two aspects of the narrative of Jesus that immediately establish the centrality of a 'non-competitive other' in the construction of an ethic capable of dealing with common interest or common good. The first and most evident is what the gospels present as Jesus' offer of access to God for all, including—and perhaps especially—those who could have no claim of moral or spiritual privilege. The God of Jesus is the God who sends rain on the just and the unjust; and this entails a community of God's people *not* defined by their prior satisfactory behaviour. It is what J. D. Crossan, in his important, if controversial, study of *The Historical Jesus*[11] refers to as an 'unbrokered' society—that is, one that does not rely for its workings upon control by some privileged class of the means of access to power or acceptability. In proclaiming, in action as well as words, that the welcome of God is like an invitation to a meal with no social rationale, no ritual for ranking guests and marking their various levels of wealth or importance, Jesus 'makes ... no appropriate distinctions and discriminations. He has no honor. He has no shame.'[12] In consequence, the God of the Gospels ceases to function as guarantor of a particular set of conditions for access to the holy and the transformative. This is a God who resists being used ideologically, or used as a criterion for the exclusion of the unsatisfactory and alien. To turn to a rather different intellectual milieu from that of recent New Testament scholarship, we may recall René Girard's observation: 'The Gospels deprive God of his most essential role in primitive religions—that of polarizing everything mankind does not succeed in mastering, particularly in relationships between individuals.'[13] Girard goes on to offer a reading of the parable of the talents in terms that make this 'deprivation' clear:

> The servant who is content to bury the talent that was entrusted to him, instead of making it bear interest, also has the most frightening picture of his master. He sees in him a demanding overseer who "reaps where he has not sown." What happens to this servant is, in the last analysis, in exact conformity with his expectations, with the image he has constructed of his master. It does not derive from the fact that the master is really like the servant's conception of him (here the text of Luke is the most suggestive), but from the fact that men make their own destinies and become less capable of breaking away from the mimetic obstacle the more they allow themselves to be fascinated by it.[14]

In their different idioms, both Crossan and Girard are, I believe, saying that the proclamation of Jesus makes concrete the presence of a non-competitive other: God is not to be approached through skilled intermediaries who will see to it that God's 'interest' is safeguarded in a transaction that, by giving privilege to us, may compromise the divine position. And, if God is conceived as needing to be conciliated so that violent reaction may be averted, as in the mind of the unprofitable servant in the parable, God is still within the competitive framework; God has a 'good', an interest, that is vulnerable. Whereas, if God's reaction can never be determined by a supposed threat to the divine interest, God's action and mine do not and cannot occupy the same moral and practical space, and are never in rivalry.

God's action is never, in this picture, *reactive*: it is always, we could say, *prior* to human activity, and as such 'gracious'—that is, undetermined by what we do. This in turn changes how I am to see my activity: what it can never be is any kind of bartering for a favourable or advantageous position vis-à-vis the universe and its maker. That God is never threatened by finite action entails that there is a level at which my own being is not capable of being threatened. It is simply established by God's determination as creator—that is, by God's will for what is authentically other to the divine being to exist. My behaviour does not have to be a defensive strategy in the face of what is radically and irreducible other, because the radicality of that otherness is precisely what establishes my freedom from the necessity to negotiate with it. There is no question here of saving the interest of diverse parties to a transaction. The traditional theological commitments to the timelessness of God, or at least God's non-participation in the same scheme of temporality as ours, and to the doctrine of creation from nothing are very far from being abstract and speculative matters for the believer, examples of the philosophical 'corruption' of theological reflection. They are ways of safeguarding the fundamental point of the proclamation of Jesus, that God's acts are undetermined by ours, and that therefore we can never and need never succeed in establishing our position in the universe.

If this is how we are to understand the nature and activity of the Christian God, and if, consequently, no failure or defeat within the human world can ultimately determine our standing before God, one further consequence is a change in how we understand our being-in-time. God's difference from our temporality leaves us with a time that can be seen as *given*, as an opportunity for growth or healing, since no disaster is finally and decisively destructive. The theological assurance about the future that is proclaimed in Christian discourse has to be read in this light. It is not a conviction that there is or must be a happy ending to any particular human story; this would be to make trivial (and often almost blasphemous) the doctrine of divine providence. Rather it is an assurance that time is always there for restoration; that we are never rendered incapable of action and passion, creating and being created, by any event. To be the object of God's non-historical regard is to be assured not only of a *status*, but also of an *involvement*: we are always 'addressed'. That is to say, our time can be apprehended by us as a question, or a challenge, as something to be filled. To sense my future as being a question to me is to sense that what I can receive, digest and react to is not yet settled or finished. What God's regard, as pronounced by Jesus, establishes is my presence as an agent, experiencing and 'processing' experience. I continue to be a self in process of being made, being formed in relation and transaction.

Here, then, is one way in which the gospel announced by Jesus, in separating out our action from the business of establishing a position in the universe, might be said to liberate ethics. What we are to say in evaluation of our behaviour is not to be determined, or even shadowed, by considerations of how this or that action succeeds in securing the place and interest of a particular subject or group vis-á-vis its environment. This vision of a convergent human good thus appears almost as a kind of by-product of the proclamation of indiscriminate divine welcome. If there is no anxiety of rivalry in our ethical reflection, no anxiety about the possible ultimate extinction of our interest in the presence of God, it follows that every *perceived* conflict of human interest represents a challenge to work, to negotiate. This can sound as though all conflicts are simply matters of error, and require better explication in order to be resolved; but such a utopian piece of ethical intellectualism would overlook the way in which (as outlined earlier) 'real' or 'true' interest is itself only formed in the process of engagement, inter-action. It is true that consciousness repeatedly mistakes itself, its nature and its good; but this is an error corrigible only within action and interaction that modifies the consciousness and changes its position.[15] But, as suggested in the first part of this essay, a commitment to what might be called, in a rather Hegelian phrase, the *labour* of ethics can emerge only as the social world is freed from the assumption of basic and non-negotiable collisions of human interest. To put it another way, the self is free to *grow* ethically (that is, to assimilate what is strange, to be formed into intelligibility) only when it is not under obligation to defend itself above all else—or to *create* itself, to carve out its place in a potentially hostile environment.

Theology has formalised the teaching of Jesus on the 'non-competitive difference' of God and God's indiscriminate welcome in terms of justifying grace; we are reckoned to have a right to be, by God's free determination. My basic argument has been that ethics is only going to *be* ethics if it assumes something like justification. However, if all we can say is that Jesus introduces into our discourse about the good a fruitful new idea, we are in danger of returning the whole discussion to abstractness. I turn finally then to the second aspect of the narrative of Jesus, to what lies beyond not only his recorded teaching but also his practice of hospitality and absolution. The practice of Jesus in his ministry is bound up with the formation of a community in which the acceptance and welcome of God is not negotiated into being, not 'brokered' by an intermediary or a system of administered conditions. As such, it might be simply an historical experiment, leaving an inspiring example. That it has *not* been understood in such terms is significant.

From the beginnings of Christian discourse, the community around Jesus in his ministry—the community of disciples and of others, including those who have received from him healing or absolution[16]—was held to be continuously present, so that to join the community was to become 'contemporary' with Jesus (this is what is taken for granted in numerous sayings, especially in the Matthaean tradition, such as Mt 18.20 and 28.20). How is it that the 'unbrokered kingdom' becomes more than an historical project dependent on the physical presence of Jesus, or the direct 'personal' inspiration of Jesus?

The narrative elucidates this by recording that the historical *failure* of the mission of Jesus, conceived as a call for the renewal of Israel in certain radical ways, is overridden. Jesus proclaims the indefeasible and indiscriminate and indestructible regard of God for all, regardless of merit and achievement; yet he falls foul of the religious and political authorities and is executed. But to proclaim that he has been raised from death is to say that both the proclamation and the practice of Jesus cannot be brought to an end by an authority, even one that has the power of life and death. What Jesus does is, in theological language, owned and vindicated by God as *God*'s proclamation and practice; as such, it is not ultimately vulnerable to history, in the sense that its continuance is never at the mercy of human will or the institutions of the world. Put another way, Jesus' action becomes recognizable as divine action when it is shown to be something that endures beyond the strongest rejection. Jesus remains as the focus of the new community, not as a memory but as a living presence. While this last formulation needs a great deal more elucidation, it expresses the sense in the first Christian documents of belonging to a community of interactive fellowship with Jesus, rather than a community founded by a figure in the past. The precise form of his ministry continues, in healing and absolution, in the introduction into new forms of prayer and intimacy with God, in the activity of extending the limits of God's people beyond the limits of the legally satisfactory. Gradually but inexorably, the practice of Jesus' continuing ministry in the community extends also beyond the boundaries of the ethnically and historically acceptable members of God's people—to the non-Jewish world. As I have argued elsewhere, this extension to the non-Jewish world is a major factor in the development of classical Christology, in that it carries the assumption that Jesus is 'free' to be heard and received throughout the human world, and to redefine the perceived will of God in respect of God's people by universalising the scope of God's call.[17]

The resurrection of Jesus can thus be read as the way in which God's indefeasible commitment to welcoming the human creation and constructing communion among diverse human beings appears as an historical phenomenon, as the *temporal* persistence of the action and the gospel of Jesus. That Jesus cannot be described, in Christian terms, as a *past* figure only means that what he is and does endures—through his own literal and material presence and so through all the ways in which who and what he is is obscured, betrayed or apparently historically defeated in the life of the Christian community as in the life of the entire human world. The theological *idea* of the indestructible regard of God, with all its implications for the possibility of reconciled community, is capable of being perceived and learned as an historical matter through the perdurance of Jesus' life in the life of the community and as the continuing source of *judgement* to which the community looks. We are not talking about an *identity* of Jesus and community; if we were, the distinctiveness of the claim that Jesus remains *active* in the community would be lost; his action would simply be initiating the activity of the community. The doctrine of the resurrection is, among other things, an attempt to distinguish between the emergence of the new community as an historical fact and the continuance of Jesus' activity in calling and forming the community. This latter is, of course, not available for historical inspection in the same way; but the early Church, in associating the resurrection with the empty tomb, insisted that the perdurance of the practice and proclamation of Jesus was not reducible to 'internal' shifts in the collective consciousness of the Church. This matter remains, I believe, problematic wherever the theology of Jesus' resurrection fails to separate out the changes in the Church's mind from the action of God in respect to the person of Jesus. The question of the empty tomb is not theologically indifferent.

What I have been attempting so far is not a natural theology, a digging-out of a conceptual space into which theological claims can be inserted. It simply seeks to identify a practical as well as conceptual problem in our world, a problem about the foundations of a non-tribal, non-competitive ethic, in such a way as to suggest that the Christian theology of justification, grounded in the narrative of Jesus' ministry, passion and resurrection, provides a structure and vocabulary for discussing this problem. Is it then an essay in apologetics? In a sense, yes. The claims made by classical Christian theology for the universal pertinence of the proclamation of Jesus, the claims to a decisive authority in shaping the human world, can only be given flesh by trying to see if, in fact, the narrative of Jesus *can* offer resources for an ethic and an anthropology with some ability to liberate us from the manifestly self-destructive spirals of human interaction. It is only in the unceasing and manifold generation of such attempts at seeing the world in the light of the gospel narrative that Christian theology can make *concrete* sense of its own convictions—not by winning a succession of arguments that 'prove' the inadequacy of secularism, but in displaying at least the confidence that our theological discourse has the ability to promise human transformation.

4

Thus a Christian theological statement has to be—at least—an invitation into a world of possible readings of the world in terms of the gospel, and possible responses to the given narrative of Jesus; not a provider of occult information, but, to borrow a famous phrase from Eliot on the metaphysical poets, a modification of sensibility. This in turn implies that the criteria for theological coherence and adequacy are going to be quite complex: general considerations of how hypotheses may be given plausibility by argument are not going to be obviously the best tools, nor will arguments about the explanatory force of doctrinal formulae (as making sense of odd phenomena) best address the significant issues.[18] We must ask about how we test a theology's force or comprehensiveness in consolidating a distinctive and resourceful perspective on the diverse narratives of human agents; we must consider whether a particular theological idiom or construct strengthens the sense of an integral fullness of perception and discernment in respect of human agency, whether it shrinks or extends the fundamental conviction about the transforming pertinence of Jesus' narrative and identity to all human situations. In the rest of this essay, I propose to look at aspects of the theological style of two elements in Christian scripture which are often supposed to be problematically diverse: the primary Pauline literature along with the disputedly Pauline letter to the Ephesians; and the gospel of Matthew. My aim will be to underline how Pauline and Matthaean theology alike approach what we might call ethics and spirituality by a twofold strategy, drawing out how Christian behaviour is to be interpreted in terms of the *manifestation* of God through Jesus Christ, and at the same time making it plain that this manifestation is not restricted to *successful performance*: the comprehensiveness of the structuring vision emerges in the way in which failure, recognised and accepted as such, entails a 'dispossession' that itself mirrors the divine gift as narrated in the history of Jesus. Only (I suggest) when we can trace this dual, ironic strategy can we properly assess the theological import of Paul (and deutero-Paul?) and Matthew, in relation to what we have already traced in the Jesus tradition at its most basic level.

Paul first: for him, being co-opted into the divinely chosen community, being in Christ, is inseparable from co-option into the divine action; and this action is not only God's active pursuit of reconciliation with the world, but also God's self-revelation. The Christian life is, from one perspective, the repetition or recapitulation of the act and the narrative of God, primarily but not exclusively in the incarnate Christ: this we could draw out of, for example, the meditation in II Cor about the ministry of reconciliation (II Cor 5.11 ff.). We find many other passages in the Pauline corpus where the imitation of God in Christ is a central theme. We are not to consider our own interests above those of others, for Christ did not so consider himself (Rom 15.2–3); rather, we are to welcome or accept each other as Christ has accepted us (15.7). We are to give generously to each other—Christ became poor for our sake, and made others rich by that voluntary poverty (II Cor 8.9). We are to offer our lives as a sacrifice to the Father, as Christ did (Eph 5.1), and to follow the pattern of self-emptying or non-grasping embodied in Christ, pre-incarnate and incarnate (Phil 2.1–11). And so on: but the argument does not stop simply with an appeal to what Jesus has done. It is significant that such passages repeatedly move towards a further level of 'grounding' the appeal when they go on to speak of 'glory' as the goal or product of certain sorts of action. This is particularly clear in Rom 15: the mutual forebearance of believers, their acceptance of each other, issues in God being glorified—not simply through the voice of the community's praise, though that is a significant part of the meaning of Rom 15.6, but also surely through the manifestation of the character of God that is involved. If we accept each other 'for the glory of God' (15.7), this is part of a display of God's self-consistency (15.8), which issues finally in the joy and gratitude of the non-Jewish world. That is to say, the Gentiles don't rejoice only because they are granted a spectacular privilege, but also because the glory of God is made plain to them. Indeed, the gift is inseparable from the delight: here as elsewhere, 'the glory of God' functions as a rationale for certain styles of action (e.g. I Cor 10.31, II Cor 4.15, 8.19). Generosity, mercy and welcome are imperatives for the Christian because they are a participation in the divine activity; but they are also imperative because they show God's glory and invite or attract human beings to 'give glory' to God—that is, to reflect back to God what God is. Giving glory is practically identical with rejoicing—rejoicing 'in' God, being glad that God is God, not merely that God is well-disposed towards us.

Thus, the imperative changes its character: we are to act in such a way that the nature of God becomes visible, in the way it was visible in the life and death of Jesus. The further rationale for acting so as to manifest the nature of God is ultimately that the nature of God is that which provokes joy, *delectatio*. The point of the whole history of divine action which our acts imperfectly recapitulate is that there should be cause for rejoicing. This, I believe, is the sense in which Paul's ethic carries the dimension of 'contemplative fruition': our final purpose is to enjoy seeing something of what God eternally is. II Cor 9 puts this very plainly in recommending financial generosity so that there may be an overflow of thanksgiving to God (9.11–14): the beneficiaries of the Church's generosity do not rejoice simply because their needs are met, but because it makes plain the divine and fundamental character of gift itself; because God has become manifest. Or, to put it in more tendentious terms, the Pauline ethic has a powerfully *aesthetic* foundation: delight in the beauty of God is the goal of our action, what we minister to each other and to the human world at large. In some passages, like Rom 15 and II Cor 9, Paul even seems less interested in the receiving of God's mercy by the Gentiles than in the fact that the bestowal of this mercy calls forth praise—presumably not exclusively from believers.

If this is correct, then the writer to the Ephesians is closer to a central Pauline theme than he is sometimes assumed to be. Ephesians makes much of the manifestation of God's long hidden purposes, God's longing to exhibit the full range and depth of the divine liberty to give and recreate (1.5 ff., 12,

2.7, 3.10–12, 16–21). God does what God does so that the divine glory may be known, praised and enjoyed—and I take the three words to be necessarily interlinked. I should want to add that the believer's knowing is 'intellectual', in the scholastic sense in which intellect is itself a participation in the reality understood, so that the mind's reception of what God is believed to have done becomes another channel for the divine reality to manifest itself. The Christian's thinking is a vehicle of 'glory', an occasion for praise and thanksgiving.

Ephesians uses very freely the language of 'mystery' to describe what is shown in Christ, in the preaching of Christ and in the living of the believing life; the word is more frequent in this epistle than anywhere else in the Christian scriptures. It is, as I have indicated, connected with the idea of God revealing hidden purposes. But it is actually in the undoubtedly Pauline literature that one finds a use of the word that links it more clearly to the themes we have just been considering. Paul, in I Cor 4.1, famously refers to himself as a 'steward' of God's mystery, the person who handles or administers or conserves the narrative of the divine purpose. This usage, however, follows immediately upon a sharp polemical discussion of the divisive issue in Corinth concerning the authority and status of the various missionaries: Paul's conclusion is that the preacher of the gospel is bound to point away from himself or herself, to divert attention from any simply individual skill, power or fluency. The preacher is not there to impose a personal philosophy, but to introduce people to the fullness of God's work in Jesus; this is accomplished when preachers put themselves at the disposal of the hearers. 'All things are yours,' says Paul: through the preacher's self-deliverance into the hands of the hearers, the hearers are 'delivered' into the possession of Christ and thus into divine ownership (or, better perhaps, divine 'owning', divine acknowledgement of responsibility for us). This is what leads on immediately to the image of the apostle as *oikonomos* of the divine mystery. The apostle's stewarding role becomes manifest, it seems, when the apostle is *dispossessed* of individual power or expertise, the kind of power that comes from the successful deployment of rhetoric. The divine purpose, as Paul is constantly repeating in these early chapters of I Cor, is realised in the vulnerability and awkwardness of the human voice proclaiming it.

Could we then go a step further, admittedly beyond the explicit words of Paul, to suggest that the mystery that is the purpose of God is in some way rooted in a perception of God as naturally self-dispossessing or self-giving? There is a kind of convergence between the idea of a *practice* of generosity as sharing in and making visible the character of the generous or welcoming God, and the experience of an 'anti-rhetoric' of human inarticulacy and unskilledness in verbalising the nature and purposes of God. The practice of the ethical life by believers is a communicative strategy, a discourse of some sort; and equally the speech of believers is an ethical matter, morally and spiritually suspect when it is too fluent, too evidently grounded in the supposedly superior quality of the speaker. A form of religious persuasion that insists upon its right to possess or control its own outcome, whether by appeal to status or privilege (in Paul's terms, especially the status of ethnic and/or legal 'purity') or by insistence upon its own excellent performance fails to communicate its intended matter, which is the action and nature of God. If the substance of the gospel has to do with God's giving up possession or control—in Paul's language, the Father giving up or giving over the Son to the cross, or Christ giving up his 'wealth', security, life for the sake of human beings—then the speech appropriate to this must renounce certain kinds of claims and strategies. This is why (a point we must face candidly) Paul's correspondence is characterized by a sense of moral danger: Paul himself is walking the tightrope of Christian persuasion with something less than total success as far as the renunciation of possession and control are concerned. He can be bullying and manipulative, even in the very passages where he most plainly articulates his own ethic of preaching. Perhaps this is why generations of Paul's readers, including those who framed the liturgical offices for the feast of his conversion, have found the agonized contradictions of II Cor 11–12 very close to the heart of his theology and ethics; as if here he is recognizing that his very failure to observe his own prescriptions for the rhetoric of the gospel is turned to persuasion by its recognition of its own failure and folly. 'When I am weak, then I am strong': not only the 'weakness' of stumbling language or confused argument, but the scandal of the self-acknowledged moral crassness of Paul's appeal to authority and experience.

What follows or might follow from this is the problematic agenda of Christian theology for some centuries after Paul. In the first place, the idea of a self-dispossessing witness being transparent to a self-dispossessing God, the idea (to borrow a significant insight from the *Contra Arianos* of Athanasius) of a God whose essential life is the generation of difference that is still conceivable as communion or continuity, is built into the slowly evolving model of God as Trinity. To say that Paul, or any writer in the corpus of Christian scripture, simply enunciates a 'trinitarian ethic' is, of course, anachronistic and over-simple. But it is always worth asking what it is that the language of Christian scripture *prompts*, makes thinkable, gestures towards. At this level, it is not nonsense to suggest, I believe, that a trinitarian structure for discourse about the eternal life of God offers the fullest explication of Paul's moral rhetoric. But secondly, there is a particularly sharp (perhaps rather distinctively Protestant?) paradox implied if this is pursued in reading Paul. The self-forgetting of God, God's putting the divine life 'at the disposal' of what is not God, becomes manifest precisely in the acknowledged inadequacy, the fractured and failed character, of all Christian rhetoric, whether in word or in deed. What in the created order mirrors the giving-away of God is not simply the practice of concrete generosity—which remains of focal importance, of course—but the practice of penitent irony about the misapprehensions of the life and speech of faith. If I may here pick up a notion I have very briefly touched on elsewhere, we understand the truth of the Christian God in the very apprehension of our own *misapprehensions*;[19] our spiritual conformation to the life of the trinitarian God involves, among a good many other things, a scepticism, both relentless and unanxious, about all claims to successful performance in our life and our discourse.

Matthew and Paul have regularly been represented as—at best—tensive, if not contradictory poles in Christian ethical discourse:[20] Matthew is interested in Jesus as a second Moses, Paul is interested in a new creation to which the law, even in intensified or interiorised form, is marginal. But the Matthaean ethic is in fact as concerned as the Pauline to avoid an ideal of the self-construction of the righteous agent by successful performance. There are *appropriate* kinds of performance, but what is constitutive of fundamental identities is a relation with God that is shaped not by the pursuit of consistent moral policies but by that puzzling mix of disposition and circumstance sketched in the Beatitudes. The commendatory rhetoric converges surprisingly closely at certain points: ethics is about manifestation. The Sermon, when it appeals to the correlation between human and divine forgiveness (Mt 6.14–15), when it exhorts the believer to a perfection consisting in indiscriminate love (5.43–48), when it implicitly grounds the constants of human generosity or responsiveness in divine willingness to give, faintly imaged in human dispositions (7.7–11), nudges us in precisely the same direction as Paul: Christian virtue is there to display a reality that will cause thanksgiving and delight, that will cause people to give glory to the Father (5.16).

What is more, the external situations in which 'perfection' is to be realized are almost all circumstances of discomfort or disadvantage. Christian 'excellence' is in significant part a matter of how we are to deal with our powerlessness or dispossession, just as the conditions listed in the Beatitudes are conditions of vulnerability or conditions metaphorized as vulnerability ('hunger and thirst' in the cause of justice).[21] We'd better notice carefully what this does and doesn't say. There is no commendation of passivity as such, no simple advice to the systemically powerless that they accept their lot: the counsels are being given to people who have expectations of exercising power but are placed in circumstances where they lose it or have it undermined. When I am injured, I have the means of possible redress; I have power to restore the balance that has been upset (I can retaliate, I can go to court or whatever). But I also have, as a believer, the freedom to alter the terms of the relation: I can decline to see it as a challenge to equalize the score, and opt to display positively the sovereign liberty of God not to retaliate or defend an interest. In other words, I can either attempt to close off my vulnerability or I can so work with it as to show the character of God. If we come to the Sermon looking either for an ethic of passive obedience to external authority or an ethic of resistance and liberation as conceived in our own age, we shall be disappointed. Matthew's Jesus is a more teasing character than either model would suggest; and the Sermon ought to be read with great patience and nuance before we try to derive a political ethic of the right or the left from it. But more of this later.

So the substance of the Sermon seems to direct us, as does Paul, towards the focal point of a renunciation of certain kinds of defence or safety as itself an imaging of the divine character suitable for provoking gratitude or glorification directed towards God. This may be reinforced if we look, secondly, at the rhetoric of 'inwardness' that appears as a unifying theme in much of the Sermon. Our contemporary intellectual climate, as we noted at the beginning of this essay, has taught us to be wary of interiority—the privileging of motive, the search for authority or integrity or authenticity in an 'inner' identity unsullied by the body or history, the essentialism in various doctrines of human nature that arises from a preoccupation with the hidden and true 'centre of the self'. Nietzsche's denunciations of Christian moral discourse frequently return to this point, to the poisoning of the wells of human life by encouraging scepticism about appearances. The Sermon has, it seems, a lot to answer for, if this is its progeny.

Well, yes, it does; we have to grant the ways in which a rhetoric of interiority which Christianity has consistently fostered has had philosophical and moral and cultural consequences that have been corrupting. But if we jump to hasty conclusions here, we shall have missed something of the Matthaean ethic; it is not developed with the conscious and extravagant irony of Paul, but it suggests its own ironies. Matthew does indeed take it for granted that integrity belongs in an inner realm and that it is not to be constructed or construed in terms of patterns of action alone. But if he privileges truth in the inward parts, it is not, as in most of the more modern varieties of discussing interiority, so as to allow the inner to be *deployed*. If the interior is the place of truth, it can *never* be deployed; you cannot use it to win arguments, to ground anything about your or anyone's identity, to establish sincerity or good intentions. The inner life, in this context, cannot be *spoken*; it silences moral defence and debate. If you do what you do to be seen by human eyes, you have your reward; your moral 'audience' is the Father *en tō kruptō*, the one whose habitat is secret places. Because of the Father's secrecy, the divine judgement, the only one actually of any truthfulness or final import, remains beyond anyone's power of utterance. It is not an *esoteric* truth—which is what the appeal to interiority has so regularly become—but an inaccessible truth. In short, the appeal to the inner world is another strategy of disempowerment for the Christian moral agent.

Hence, of course, the injunctions about not judging. There is no secure access to the inner life of another, and if you judge by external standards, you may expect to be open yourself to equally shallow and unmerciful judgement. When Matthew's Jesus uses the word 'hypocrite', as he so freely does in the Sermon, we must not think immediately of a disjunction between inner and outer, of a problem about *sincerity*, but of the moral or spiritual weakness of someone who expects to be judged on external performance: in ch. 6, 'hypocrites' are not necessarily people who don't mean what they do, or who are trying to conceal inner unfaithfulness; they are simply (as the Greek word implies) 'actors', agents who consciously construct themselves in the process of performance. The word's negative resonance of deceit or simulation arises from the fact that, if selves cannot really be so constructed, the self that is evolved in patterns of behaviour is in some way false. The 'hypocrite' has not learned that the self is not a sort of possessed object, to be refined or matured by conscious practice; the 'hypocrite' has to recognize the uncomfortable truth that the self's standing, the self's adequacy or excellence or attunement to God ('blessedness'), is out of the agent's control.[22] Matthew foreshadows here the later Christian paradoxes explored in Gregory of Nyssa and Augustine, paradoxes concerning the systematically unknowable character of the self. But he has given this theme a more clearly defined moral edge by linking it with the proscription of judgement or, more exactly, of offering oneself for judgement by humanly perceptible criteria.

Of course Matthew's general rhetoric in the gospel is liberally strewn with judgement and with hostility towards the outsider, the non-believer, the unconverted Jew; this is a still darker aspect of the legacy of the first gospel. This should not, however, lead us to a simple rejection of the ethic of the Sermon, or even an accusation of 'hypocrisy' in the modern sense. Matthew, like Paul, is exploring an area of moral danger, and the riskiness of the discourse is exhibited, as with Paul, though less self-consciously, in the failures of consistency. The challenge is still audible: can the moral agent relinquish the centrality of an image of herself or himself *as* moral agent? So long as we are, so to speak, polishing the image of the agent, what our actions show is a successful will; the *meaning* of the actions terminates in the will's success. If we let go of that image, the meaning of what is done is grounded in God, the act shows more than the life of the agent: it shows the character of the creator. But to get to that point, the discipline that the agent has to undergo is attention not to performance but to an interiority that is not to be possessed. It is visible and judgeable only by God. So that, finally, for Matthew, Christian excellence is what it is for Paul: the manifestation of the divine reality in such a way as to provoke thanksgiving and delight. Externally focused morality is unacceptable not because it encourages insincerity, but because it is in grave danger of always terminating in itself, in the successful will, not in the life of the creator. And successful wills do not provoke contemplative joy, on the whole.

5

In the last part of this reflection, I want to look rather sketchily at the sorts of moral practice and moral critique that might emerge from these considerations.

Scepticism, penitence, irony about performance, the dissolution of the solid moral self built up by good actions—all of this could issue in a morality that is profoundly individualized, incapable of thematizing ethical questions or of providing a critical edge to the believer's engagement with the wider culture. A sophisticated Protestantism in particular lends itself to some such style, and its literary heritage would be interesting to explore, across a spectrum ranging from John Updike to Antonia Byatt or Iris Murdoch. There are times, too, when this kind of moral scepticism (i.e. scepticism about the attainability, but not the reality, of virtue) is a welcome relief from the deafening new rhetoric of common virtue secured by the balancing of rights and the reparation made for offence. This is a proper concern in reflecting on the conditions of justice, but a poor substitute for the discourse of virtue. Whatever the attractions of this sceptical and reticent ethic, it is not finally a fruitful basis for ethical talk, to the extent that it concentrates upon the realm in which no negotiation takes place, no public risk, no common policies; and it certainly represents only a sliver of the moral world of the writers we have been looking at. I want to propose three elements of the ethic outlined here that might have bearing on the contemporary language of public or common moral practice and speech.

(i) The sceptical or reticent principle, in the context of Christian scripture as a whole, is the negative side of a positive insight. The controlling question of much, if not most, of our New Testament is about who belongs among the community of the friends of God, formerly identified exclusively with the people of Israel. Paul and the evangelists build on the clearly remembered practice of Jesus, for whom the friends of God are those who are content to accept the assurance of Jesus that their willingness to trust God's word through him is the sole basis of belonging with God's people. To hear and accept that word is not to perform a task (there is no satisfactory answer to the rich man's question as Matthew records it, 'What good *deed* must I do to have eternal life?'), but to enter into the sharing of Jesus' company, foreswearing any other kind of *claim* to God's favour than the assurance given by God of an unearned and prior favour freely offered. Virtue in this new community of the friends of God thus comes to be bound up with the steady critique of all practices that reinstate or try to reinstate claims on the love of God grounded in achievement. Positively, this casts light on the way in which Paul, especially in Rom and I Cor treats ethics, questions of specific behaviour, as governed by the principle of 'edification': good acts are those that build up the Body of Christ. Virtue thus rests upon the fundamental process of curing the delusion that I have an interest or good that I alone can understand, specify and realize. It is essentially to do with the definition of an interest that is both mine and the other's, since what we most basically share is the assurance of being equally valued or welcomed by God. What I think I possess is there to be given for the sake of that newly envisioned common interest. When Paul deplores 'boasting', and he so frequently does, it is to undermine the nonsense of any language about claims within the Christian community.

Christian ethics thus suggests a nuanced approach to some of those issues of justice or reparation touched on earlier. On the one hand: the Church has or should have a quite disproportionate interest in how mechanisms of exclusion work in human societies, in what sort of things are deployed so as to make claims that allow this person or group in and shut that one out. Christian 'bias to the poor' is not simply a doctrine that God likes poor people better than others, and that is all there is to it. It is, rather, a persistent critical concern about how claims to do with security and legitimation are made, both in and out of the Church. It is a 'bias' in the sense that the Christian begins with a non-negotiable commitment to basic egalitarianism.

On the other hand: Christian ethics can never be happy with a model of justice that is solely or even primarily reparative. The good or interest of the excluded matters not in itself but as the indispensable and unique contribution it constitutes to the good of all. The language of 'rights' is an important *dialectical* moment in ethical discourse, but becomes sterile when it is divorced from a proper conception of the human good that has to be worked on in conversation with others. In this sense, strange as it may seem to put it thus, Christian ethics is relentlessly political, because it cannot be adequately expressed in terms of atomized rights invested in individuals or groups, but looks beyond to the kind of community in which free interaction for the sake of each other is made possible. That means adjustment and listening; it means politics.

(ii) When ethics ceases to be about securing claims, it is free to rethink itself as something like the reading of a particular language; that is to say, it can concern itself with what acts mean or communicate, not what they contribute to a tally of successful performances and whatever results may accrue from that, nor how acts correspond to a scale of rightness and wrongness constructed in the abstract. The crucial question that has to be asked in the Christian moral evaluation of act or character is, does it speak of the God whose nature is self-dispossession for the sake of the life of the other? of the commitment and dependability of the divine action towards the creation? of the divine relinquishment of 'interest' and claim as embodied in the life and death of Jesus? These are not, I think, issues that leave us with an individualized or uncritical ethic. They are matters capable of being raised in the context of sexual ethics as much as the ethics of business or international relations. And it may be that something like this is rather badly needed as the discourses of Christian ethics polarize increasingly between legalism based on the injunctions of the text and a vacuous experientialism, appealing to precisely the wrong sort of interiority for its criteria. It might allow us to recognize that the actions of Christians are constantly called upon to manifest God so that God may be glorified, and yet are enacted in a world where circumstances oblige us to choose between more and less damaging (and therefore, in respect of God, more and less opaque) options; where this happens, where the tragic dimension of the moral world impinges, what gives glory is—if we have been reading Paul (and even Matthew) correctly—the candid acknowledgement of powerlessness, in grief, not in complacency, because this in its way models the divine dispossession.

(iii) Finally, let me be allowed one more use of that annoying word, 'paradox'. The kind of interiority that seems to be evoked in the Sermon on the Mount points not to an undervaluing but to a revaluing of the *bodily* agent in our ethical thinking: a paradox. If the interiority in question is the 'secret place' where God lives, then, as we have seen, it is not a higher and better sphere of performance: motive and intention cannot be elevated above practice or treated as sources of authority or legitimation. The challenge is to move entirely out of the performance-oriented world. External achievement does not secure status, but neither does intensity, sincerity, or good will. The inner sphere belongs to God's judgement and is not available. What *is* available is action: judged not according to how it serves to secure a position before God and others, but according to its fidelity to the character of God, its 'epiphanic' depth. This allows us to pick up the sound Aristotelean point that doing worthy acts is a way of becoming a worthy person, in the sense that options may be evaluated by their possible transparency to God, not by their presumed correspondence to a hidden good (or otherwise) will: the inner may well follow the outer, as far as the actual processes of transformation go. But the basic point remains: of course, I cannot *become* a worthy person in any sense that would presume to make me worthy *of* God's regard. But attention to the degree to which my choices might be read as open or not open to God's glory might help to free me from the tyranny of both motivation and achievement. If this at all recalls Luther's notion in chapter 27 of *The Liberty of the Christian* that the believer, like Christ, acts in charity because a given (not attained) reality is simply expressing itself in his or her life, that is no accident. If it also recalls Eliot's transcription of the Gita on detachment from 'action and the fruits of action', doing what corresponds to truth and wisdom for its own sake, not because of a clear calculation of results, that is no accident either.[23]

NOTES

1 Walter A. Davis, *Inwardness and Existence. Subjectivity in/and Hegel, Heidegger, Marx, and Freud* (University of Wisconsin Press 1989), p. 105.
2 See Rowan Williams, 'The Suspicion of Suspicion: Wittgenstein and Bonhoeffer', in Richard H. Bell (ed.) *The Grammar of the Heart. New Essays in Moral Philosophy and Theology* (San Francisco: Harper , 1988), pp. 36–53, especially pp. 48–9.
3 *Phenomenology*, 133–50.
4 This would be my central criticism of 'non-realist' accounts of theological discourse, in particular the work of Don Cupitt; see, for example, his *Creation Out of Nothing*, (SCM Press, 1990), *What is a Story?* (SCM Press 1992), etc.

5 See Kant's First Critique, Ch.1, section 2 of 'Transcendental Doctrine of Method' on this idea of the universal tribunal; cf. my own discussion of this in 'Doctrinal Criticism: Some Questions,' Sarah Coakley and David Pailin (eds), *The Making and Remaking of Christian Doctrine. Essays in Honour of Maurice Wiles*, (Oxford University Press 1993), pp. 239–264, esp. pp. 258 ff.

6 Cf. Augustine, *de trinitate* VIII (esp. vi. 9) on the connection between love of the good and love of justice (since loving the good means desiring that the good be present in all subjects).

7 Diogenes, the 'patriarch' of Cynicism, flourished in the middle of the fourth century BCE, and was thus contemporary with Alexander; Zeno established the Stoa at the end of the same century.

8 Diogenes, as reported by Diogenes Laertius 6.63; see John M. Rist, *Stoic Philosophy* (Cambridge University Press 1969), p. 59, for a good discussion of the meaning of this phrase.

9 Rist, op.cit., pp. 62–3, 68–80.

10 See especially F. Gerald Downing, *Christ and the Cynics: Jesus and Other Radical Preachers in First-Century Tradition* (Sheffield Academic Press, 1988); John Dominic Crossan, *The Historical Jesus. The Life of a Mediterranean Jewish Peasant*, (San Francisco: Harper, 1990), esp. pp. 72–88.

11 See n. 10; this book is a valuable essay in comparative anthropology, and makes a strong case for the affinities of Jesus with Cynic teaching. It is weakest in its highly speculative reconstructions of the history of the gospel tradition, especially the passion narratives.

12 Crossan, op.cit. p. 262.

13 René Girard, *Things Hidden From the Foundation of the World* (Athlone Press, 1987), p. 185.

14 Ibid., p. 189. The term 'mimetic obstacle' refers to the way in which a desired object possessed by another subject occasions frustration; the possessor has what I want, and is therefore what I want to be like, what I desire to imitate, but his/her possession of what I want is not only the occasion but the obstacle of my desire.

15 This is brought out very finely in the work of Gillian Rose on Hegel; see particularly *Hegel Contra Sociology* (Athlone Press, 1981); and *Judaism and Modernity* (Blackwells, 1993), especially the Introduction.

16 This is how Mary Magdalene is introduced in Lk 8.2, as one of a number of female followers alongside the Twelve, distinguished as those who have been healed by Jesus.

17 Cf. Rowan Williams, *Mission and Christology. The J.C. Jones Memorial Lecture* 1994 (Church Missionary Society Welsh Council, 1994).

18 Cf. the essay cited above, n. 5; also Bruce D. Marshall, 'Absorbing the World: Christianity and the Universe of Truths,' in Bruce D. Marshall (ed.), *Theology and Dialogue. Essays in Conversation with George Lindbeck* (University of Notre Dame Press, 1990), pp. 69–102, on the 'assimilative power' of theological utterance and Christian discourse in general as a (long-term) criterion of adequacy and truthfulness.

19 See Rowan Williams, 'Between Politics and Metaphysics: Reflections in the Wake of Gillian Rose', *Modern Theology* 11.1 (1995), pp. 3–22, esp. 11–12, 17–18.

20 A significant recent exception is Dan O.Via, Jr., *Self-Deception and Wholeness in Paul and Matthew* (Fortress, 1990). This book converges at several points with my argument here, and I am glad to acknowledge my debt to it.

21 See Via, op.cit. pp. 112–127 on the Beatitudes as presenting the dialectical character of a present blessedness conceived in terms of present 'emptiness'.

22 Ibid., pp. 92–98, on hypocrisy as self-deceit.

23 Sections 1 and 2 of this paper have appeared as *Ethik und Rechtfertigung* in *Rechtfertigung und Erfahrung*, ed. M. Beintker, E. Maurer, H. Stoevesandt and H.G. Ulrich, Gütersloh 1995, pp. 311–327. Much of the remainder was prepared as a response to a still unpublished manuscript by Ellen Charry on ethics and spirituality entitled (provisionally) *By the Renewing of Your Minds. The Salutarity of Christian Doctrine*, discussed at a symposium in March 1995 at the Divinity School of Duke University on ethics and the New Testament. I must acknowledge my great indebtedness to Professor Charry for insights contributory to the present essay.

MYSTICAL THEOLOGY REDUX: THE PATTERN OF AQUINAS' *SUMMA THEOLOGIAE*

A. N. WILLIAMS

One of the curious features of ecclesial existence in the late twentieth century is the quiet breakdown of the marriage between what we call theology and spirituality. The fact that we now possess quite separate terms to designate each field is one of the signs of estrangement. Another and more important indication of the shift is the fact that in our time, it is widely assumed that each discipline can operate fruitfully in isolation from the other.

Spirituality has seized cultural attention in our time to an extent that few other religious phenomena could claim. This popularity is evident not only in bookstore shelves closely packed with titles on angels, meditation and spiritual growth, or in the constant outpouring of magazine articles on such subjects, but also in the frequency with which one hears declarations that spirituality is important to people's lives, often people who have no connection to any organised religion and are indeed often contemptuous of such organisations. The books, the articles, the testimonials, all exhibit a common characteristic: they use 'spirituality' to designate any number of forms of religiosity undifferentiated with respect to their doctrinal foundations. One may adopt Native American prayer forms, the teachings of a Zen master and Julian of Norwich, making use of all simultaneously.[1]

Part of the impulse behind such syncretism is traceable to the spirit of the Enlightenment that continues to pervade the culture despite the death certificate which Postmodernists keep issuing for it. Where the spirit of toleration once meant that we allow freedom of religious expression to all without discrimination, it now seems to mean that we express all religious

Dr. A. N. Williams
Department of Religion, The University of Puget Sound, 1500 North Warner, Tacoma, WA 98416-0460, USA

sensibilities indiscriminately. One does not so much tolerate differences as ignore them, compiling a personal anthology of those notions and practices one likes, regardless of their provenance or the compatibility of their underlying assumptions.

The growth of such a popular spirituality accounts in part for the separation of theology and spirituality; theology is an inconvenience for an eclectic spirituality and as spirituality becomes increasingly dissociated from rigorous thought, theologians seem wary of being tainted by its anti-intellectualism. In distancing themselves from the intellectual vapidity of much contemporary spirituality, however, theologians have also severed themselves from the past.

The separation of theology from spirituality has three deleterious effects: on spirituality, on theology, and on the church. If Christians continue to appropriate forms of religiosity informed by any and all belief systems, or indeed none at all, we risk separating prayer from scholarship, creed, proclamation and worship—unless, of course, we are willing to empty these also of specifically Christian content. We need not fall into the trap of which the ghosts of the Enlightenment warn, a bigoted denunciation of all non-Christian forms of religious expression. We need only assert more clearly the anthropological foundation of a Christian understanding of faith: that Christianity is not a religion of the soul and its destiny, but a religion of the person, a composite of body, mind and soul.[2] This anthropological principle dictated to early Christians that embodiment is a fact of human spiritual life, not a hindrance to it, and to our time it announces that the mind cannot be separated from the soul. Certainly, we do not proclaim a rationalistic faith that engages the mind alone—a danger so lamentably far from real that there should be no need to warn against it—but neither is Christianity a faith which considers we can jettison the mind, focusing on the soul or spirit alone. Spirituality that is authentically Christian must be plausibly and intelligently tied to foundational understandings of God, humanity and the purpose of human existence that are also authentically Christian. If we take seriously the notion of *lex orandi, lex credendi*, then we must realise that the relation between theology and prayer runs in two directions: our prayer is the form and sign of our belief, but prayer also teaches belief and forms us in faith. Using prayers from traditions with different views of God, of humanity, of the divine-human relation, necessarily affects belief and can only declare either the inadequacy of Christian doctrine or a schizophrenic divide between what we teach and what we pray.

If spirituality emptied of theological content suffers, so does theology when it fails to recognise its grounding in concerns that are ultimately those of the spiritual life. Wherever one locates oneself on the spectrum from apophatic to cataphatic theology, the foundation of any speech about God is the acknowledgement of the one who has not only called us into being but also into relation. If, as some modern Western theologians would maintain, we cannot speak of the immanent Trinity as distinct from the economic, and if, as the East would claim, we cannot know the divine Essence but only the divine energies, then the God we know and whom theology describes is specifically the God who engages us. That engagement is not only the foundation of all theology; it is equally the reason for all theology. Unless we would have theology exist as an end unto itself, an absorbing game for academics, then surely we must say we contemplate God in order to know the One we profess to love, to understand the One whom we follow and serve. The beginning and the end of theology is thus essentially a spiritual concern.

In the end, however, it is the church that must suffer the most when the bond between theology and spirituality is severed, for it is the church that must proclaim theological teaching and help its members incorporate that teaching into their lives. It is the church that must help its members to view their world and their lives theologically, as derived from God, ever dependent on God and finding their only enduring fulfilment in God. This task is never easy, but it can be rendered only more difficult when the connections between theology and spirituality are obscured by their proponents and practitioners. For the sake of Christian theology, then, for the sake of a genuinely Christian spirituality and for the sake of all the ministers of the church, both clergy and lay, we must find a way back to the integration of theology as a discipline both systematic and contemplative.

I

It is the past, now in danger of being buried in our embarrassment over the present, that indicates that the separation of theology from spirituality need not be, and indeed was not, until relatively recently. The Fathers knew no distinction between the various branches of theology, nor even between theology and spiritual discipline.[3] That is why students of patristics read Cassian's *Conferences*, intended as monastic spiritual directives, as a source in the doctrine of grace, for example. While the Middle Ages are sometimes taken as the *terminus ab quo* for the division of theology into discrete branches,[4] well into the medieval period we find a fluid mingling what we now call theology and spirituality. Bernard of Clairvaux's sermons on the Song of Songs, for instance, may be read as much as a Christological treatise as biblical exegesis or a testament to mystical experience. Jean Leclercq, while claiming a distinction between monastic and scholastic theology in the Middle Ages, nevertheless maintains the difference is one of emphasis rather than a fundamental divergence of goals.[5]

We may, with the benefit of hindsight, perhaps find the first cracks foretelling a later rift between theology and spirituality in the Middle Ages, but the actual rupture seems, not surprisingly, to be a product of a modern mentality. The *New Catholic Encyclopedia* seems to trace the divide to the seventeenth century, by which time not only spirituality was separated from theology, but spirituality itself had divided into the mystical and ascetical.[6] In our day, the divide is so pronounced that the term 'mystical theology' seems like a contradiction in terms; 'mystical' enjoys almost exclusive usage as the adjective corresponding to 'mysticism', and mysticism is commonly regarded as the revolutionary among religious phenomena, knowing none of the constraints of dogma or communitarian concerns.

What I would like to suggest is that we need to revitalise the notion of mystical theology and that it is precisely to older theology that we should look for guidance in finding our way back to a unified and integrated discipline. To understand why and how this might be the case, we need first to define this term that permits usage in several senses. Mystical theology, in the sense in which the term will be used here, may be described as theology concerned with the conditions of the possibility of union with God.[7] It is not concerned specifically with mystical experience—visions, revelations, ecstasy and such—not only because these are products of union rather than its theological underpinning, but also because these heights of mystical experience have always been the province of the very few. Mystical theology is, like all theology, concerned to state what is true of all the people of God, not to recount individual experience, much less to universalise it. Because mystical theology is ultimately concerned with the union of God and humanity, its first question is not 'How?' but 'Who?' It seeks first to describe the two parties to this union, to portray God and human persons. It is from this description that the 'How?' of union follows. In the Christian view, we are brought into intimate relation with God not in the first place by the practice of extraordinary spiritual feats, but because of who God is and who God has created us to be. The heart of mystical theology lies in the relationship between God and humanity, not from the perspective of what specifically human practices may foster right relatedness, but from the perspective of God's creative intentions for us. A mystical theology thus of its nature integrates theological and spiritual concerns.

II

Fortunately, we do not entirely lack models for what such an integrated theology should look like, although we perhaps do not know we possess them. I want to suggest that Thomas Aquinas, in particular, will furnish an example of how one may write a theology that is not only inspired by concern to articulate the nature and possibility of the union between God and humanity, but which is also in itself, in its structure and method, prayer. I am proposing that we look at one of the greatest of all systematic theologies, Thomas' *Summa Theologiae*, as both an exhortation to contemplation and an act of contemplation.[8]

Thomas' *magnum opus* has often been construed not only as a systematic theology, but even a philosophical work. Scholarly attention has so focused on its philosophical foundations and implications that the *Summa*'s other qualities have tended to recede into obscurity, creating the widely-held impression of Thomas as a hairsplitting philosopher. While there are any number of individual articles that confute such a characterisation (on alms-giving, gluttony, the relative merits of the active and the contemplative life —scarcely purely abstract questions) the most fundamental sense in which the *Summa* functions as a mystical theology can be appreciated only by looking to the broader patterns of its structure, for the mystical character of the *Summa* is most immediately determined by its systematic impetus.

We may see the mystical themes of the *Summa* in four operative principles: the theoretical, the theological, the anthropological and the Christological. These themes specify the precise way in which Thomas articulates the union of God and humanity. Each principle defines the basis on which this union may take place and thus each principle constitutes a mystical theology in miniature. The theological, anthropological and Christological principles broadly correspond to the *Summa*'s three parts. The Prima Pars primarily treats the doctrine of God, theology narrowly speaking; the Secunda Pars deals chiefly with anthropology and the Tertia Pars with Christology. Conventional wisdom alone indicates that the Tertia Pars deals with a divine-human union and the Secunda Pars deals in large measure with what are clearly matters of sanctification, such as virtue and grace. The mystical intent of the Prima Pars becomes evident as one appreciates how Thomas' description of divine nature relentlessly portrays a God intent upon union with humanity. Nevertheless, while the mystical-theological underpinning of the theological, anthropological and Christological principles are in some respects more obvious, the true nature of the *Summa*'s mystical theology is best illustrated by the theoretical principle and so it is there that we will focus. The theoretical principle operates diffusively rather than being concentrated in a single part, gathering up and holding together several strands of the *Summa* whose connection to one another might not be readily apparent unless we take the work as a mystical theology.

III

The theoretical principle as understood here is composed of two elements which at first glance, and especially by the lights of modern theology, seem to be completely unrelated. The first element concerns the method and purpose of the *Summa*, as stated in the opening questions of the First Part. The second concerns the notions of beatitude and contemplation as delineated in the Second Part. The reason for uniting these apparently disparate themes lies in the way they are all connected in the notion of *theoria*. In the context of Greek thought, both classical and Christian, *theoria* means contemplation. Theological method, prayer and beatitude are all concerned with how the human mind encounters the divine: with, then, the means and end of contemplation. The theoretical principle thus describes how the union of God and humanity may be understood as taking place in the act of contemplation, and indeed as taking place in that act in a way surpassed only by the Incarnation itself.[9]

As Thomas will show us, in a genuinely mystical theology it is precisely the impetus to understand the union of God and humanity that links theology to prayer. Contemplation, which in modern parlance is taken simply to designate a form of prayer, in fact carries a more complex burden of meaning. In Thomas' work the word 'contemplation' functions on the basis of a productive ambiguity, so that individual usages might almost always refer either to theological reflection or to prayer. As we explore his understanding of both the nature of theology and of prayer, we will come to see how closely tied they are in Thomas' thought.

We can measure both the depth of mystical focus in the *Summa* and the distance between Thomas' theological assumptions and those of our day by noting the function of his discussion of method. Like most modern systematic theologies, the *Summa* opens with a statement of the nature of theology. If one reads it as a systematic theology *tout court*, one would take the first question as merely the obligatory methodological prologomenon, stating the author's assumptions and warrants. Part of Thomas' concern in the *Summa*'s opening question is undoubtedly to lay down the principles which will guide the construction of his theology: the respective roles of revelation, tradition and reason or philosophy. If one approaches the text as a mystical theology, however, the first question appears rather differently, and the connection of method to the questions of beatitude and prayer become clearer.

The impetus for the whole work emerges clearly in I.1,1 as Thomas describes the nature of theology: God has destined us for a goal that lies beyond the grasp of reason and the attainment of this goal is necessary to our well-being. God, indeed, is the culmination of all theology: "Man's whole salvation, which is in God, depends upon knowledge of this truth" (I.1,1 resp.).[10] Lest there be any doubt that Thomas has described the science (*scientia*) of theology as no less than the apprehension of God which brings blessedness, let the reader turn to the second article. Here Thomas declares that the teaching of God, the revelation which is to be the foundation of theology, is based on premises known by the light of a higher science, God's own knowledge of himself, shared with the blessed in heaven (I.1,2 resp.). Thomas suggests, then, that theology is a form of reflection deriving from a kind of active participation in God's self-knowledge, which is no less than God's own self. If we consider this statement in light of doctrine which Thomas later develops, it appears quite a radical statement, for according to the doctrine of divine simplicity, God's knowledge is not an attribute of God, something separate and distinct from God's own being, but that very being itself. Theology is thus construed not so much as a human task, but as a divine self-giving, the means by which we are drawn into God's own existence.

Thomas presses this point as he expands upon the nature of theology in the articles that follow. Theology constitutes a single, unified science, he claims, because it has one main subject-matter, God, with everything else treated as beginning and ending in God (I.1,3 ad 1; cf. I.1, 7 resp.). The very shape of theology is determined by the object of its contemplation. Here we begin to see how the theoretical principle sheds light on the *Summa*'s structures. Just as the beginning of all theological concern is God, so the first part of the work is theology proper, the doctrine of God; as the end of all theology is God, the Tertia Pars concerns the God-Man, God Incarnate who brings us to God. The movement of the Secunda Pars reflects this larger structure, beginning with the goal of human life and ending with considera-tion of the ways of life, the means by which each one of us finds our way to God.[11] Thomas, in other words, has structured his work to mirror what he claims about theology in his methodological prologomenon, and the purpose of both method and structure is to direct the mind towards the contemplation of God and show how humanity is united to God through contemplation.

The oneness of theology's object also determines a second kind of unity in the discipline: the lack of distinction between pure and applied knowledge. The nature of God's self-knowledge means that in knowing himself he also knows all he has made (I.1,4 resp.). God's own self-knowledge is not bifur-cated, radically separating self-knowledge from knowledge of creation. As theology is a participation in divine self-knowledge, it does not distinguish between discourse about Love on the one hand and directives regarding how one should love one's neighbour by giving alms, for example, on the other. Thus even in its most practical moments, the *Summa* is to be read as an act of contemplation whereby we are united to the mind of God.

However, although theology may thus be considered contemplative even when it attends to mundane matters, Thomas does not avoid the conclusion that the discipline is on the whole more pure than applied (I.1,4 resp.[12]). Once again his reasoning is instructive. Theology is in the end more concerned with God than with human behaviour, because it treats the latter as the means of achieving that perfect knowledge of God which constitutes eternal bliss (I.1,4 resp.). In other words, Thomas is telling us that even when he discusses the most practical of human affairs, he is still essentially concerned with the contemplation of God, because it is in contemplation and ultimately only in contemplation that our happiness lies. In two distinct ways, then, all theology, may be taken as a transformative envisioning of God.

Thomas forges the clearest link between theology and sanctification in the last article of Question One. Here he draws an analogy between the mind's engagement by God and the broader transformation of the human person. Reason is to faith, he says, as grace is to nature (I.1,8 ad 2). Just as the natural inclination of the will serves charity, so reason serves faith. The significance of this analogy lies in the thoroughness with which Thomas integrates theological reflection into the general pattern of humanity's journey to God. Nature's fulfilment by grace now appears as the paradigm by which we are to understand the mind's reflection on God, a reflection that both makes use of our natural capacities and transforms them by God's gift of self. Just as the infusion of charity perfects but does not obliterate the need for the natural motion of the will, so the gifts of revelation and faith work in tandem with a mind whose natural endowments equips it to engage revelation and reflect upon faith. The impetus to understand God, then, forms part of the larger process whereby God draws humanity towards himself: the gracing of nature that we may come to glory.

The description of theology as a form of contemplation in I.1 is what points toward the description of beatitude at the opening of I.II.1. The first question Thomas answers at the beginning of his theology is 'Why do we contemplate God?'; the very same question motivates the beginning of his anthropology. He opens his discussion with consideration of beatitude no doubt in part because of his Aristotelian proclivity for regarding ends as determinative of character; to describe beatitude as the end of human existence is therefore in the first place simply to designate the definitive quality of human existence. This obvious and important purpose is not Thomas' only intent in the opening questions of the Secunda Pars, however. He is also describing contemplation, recapitulating and expanding upon what he said in the Prima Pars.

Thomas begins by defining beatitude. What we mean by being happy, he says, is our way of attaining the goal for which we were made. The goal must be God, the ultimate goal of all. The precise content of being happy and attaining to God consists of no more than coming to know and love God. Throughout the *Summa*, Thomas draws on the Augustinian insight that knowledge necessarily precedes love—you cannot love what you do not know. In I.II.1 he relates this principle to beatitude. Here, however, he does not simply identify knowledge as love's precondition; knowledge itself is part of beatitude. Theology, therefore, not only attaches humanity to God in the sense of absorbing the mind by the consideration of the things of God; it also constitutes part of the joy we associate with union with God, the bliss of paradise.

Thomas does not use the term union in these articles, but as the Secunda Pars progresses, it becomes clear that he is thinking of beatitude in terms of a particular kind of union. He begins by stating his governing assumption: that since humanity is not the supreme good, our fulfilment must lie outside ourselves (I.II.2,8 resp.[13]). Happiness, then, can only be found by attaching ourselves to something that is not-us. One of Aquinas' main concerns in these articles is to emphasise that the union he is envisaging is not an ontological melding, the absorption of one party into the other, or their joining to form a *tertium quid*. Rather, he is thinking in terms of a union in which two distinct entities are brought into a lasting relation that destroys neither. Accordingly, he can claim that our happiness is from one perspective un-created and from another created (I.II.3,1); it is at once the Uncreated whom we attain, and the joy we have as a result of union, a joy which is a part of us and therefore created as we are.

Our beatitude can thus be considered from two distinct but interrelated perspectives. On the one hand, our happiness is not less than God *ipse* (I.II.2,8 ad 2[14]). On the other hand, this happiness is a share in the divine happiness and something God creates in us (I.II.3,1 resp.). This created hap-piness is a life of human activity in which human powers are ultimately fulfilled (I.II.3,2). Since, however, these are not two separate kinds of hap-piness, but one happiness considered from two different perspectives, Thomas is claiming that human beings not only become what they are meant to be only in union with God, but that specifically human activities are a form of participation in divine beatitude, in God's own self. Again, Thomas assumes a kind of synergy: these activities entail the exercise of human powers, but for them to lead us to beatitude they must be perfected by grace. Since knowledge of God and the use of the mind specifically fall into this category of activity according to I.II.1,8, we may safely deduce that theology itself may be a form of sharing in God's happiness, a form of union with God.

What is implicit at the beginning of I.II.3 becomes more and more clear as the question progresses. By the second article, Thomas is explicitly utilising the language of contemplation. Here he specifies the relationship between contemplation in this life and the beatific vision of the next. The contem-plative ideal may be found only in the next life, but contemplation in some form is available in this, and Thomas clearly sees a connection between the ideal and the less-than-ideal: "In that state of happiness [heaven] man's mind will be united to God by one continual, everlasting operation. But in the present life, in as far as we fall short of the unity and continuity of this operation, so do we fall short of perfect happiness. Nevertheless it is a parti-cipation of happiness: and so much the greater, as the operation can be more continuous and more one" (I.II.3,2 ad 4). Thus, while the contemplation of this life and that of the next seem to differ, Thomas also forges a seamless link between them so that contemplation in this life is distinguished from contemplation in the next only in that it is less than constant.

At this point, twentieth-century readers, precisely because we have been lulled into assuming a sharp distinction between theology and spirituality, may question whether this contemplation akin to the beatific vision could really be described as theology rather than as a form of prayer, but Thomas dispels this notion decisively. In the Second, Third and Fourth Articles of I.II.3, Thomas defines beatitude as an operation of the intellect whereby the mind is united to God in knowing God.[15] This 'knowing' might of course be taken as a direct apprehension of God in prayer, but Thomas says nothing to indicate he is thinking exclusively in such terms and his definition is broad enough to include any variety of theological reflection. Indeed, because he identifies this operation as an act of understanding rather than willing (I.II.3,4, s.c.), his definition leans more towards the side of theological reflection than, say, some form of mystical rapture, as least as such experiences are commonly described in the writings of the mystics. The notion that contemplation is a matter of mind rather than heart reveals not some fastidious disdain of the emotions, but follows upon the principles deeply embedded in the *Summa*'s structure. For Thomas, our highest activity must be one that engages our highest power with its highest object (I.II.3,5 resp.); since intelligence is our highest power and God our highest object, contemplation must be the intellect's absorption in God, and this highest of activities is therefore necessarily intellectual, a conclusion decidedly at odds with contemporary notions of both happiness and spirituality.

Thomas' conception of contemplative union differs from many modern notions of spirituality in a second respect, in that he is not equating beatitude with human satisfaction per se, not even intellectual satisfaction. He is thinking specifically of union and not merely solipsistic personal fulfilment. What the mind is capable of knowing in and of itself cannot provide the beatitude that is our destiny. That beatitude can come only from knowledge of truth, and Aquinas differs from Socrates in not regarding the truth as lying in ourselves, but in a person whom we encounter as Other. Because truth is God alone (I.II.3,7[16]), contemplation is both apprehension of the Other and union with the Other. Prayer and theology are both theocentric activities and eccentric activities: means by which we are drawn towards God and beyond ourselves. Neither is a means of 'finding' ourselves in the contemporary sense, and certainly not means of 'finding the god within'.

Third, the Thomistic notion of contemplative union differs from contemporary spirituality in that Thomas naturally couples varieties of experience which in our time are almost wilfully divorced. In I.II.3,8 he portrays complete happiness as the mind's knowing the first cause of anything and as a union with God. To the contemporary mind, these are quite different sorts of activities, the one intellectual in a rather grim and sterile sort of way, the other appealingly emotive. That Thomas can speak of contemplation in both ways within the same article suggests that for him there exists no such dichotomy, no appropriation of intellectual apprehension to one sphere and union to another. By the time the reader has reached the end of the *Summa*'s discussion of beatitude, it should be clear that not only does Thomas regard contemplation as an intellectual activity, and as the only activity that can bring complete human fulfilment, but that he also regards this intellectual activity as a form of union with God.

The questions on beatitude in the Prima Secundae, in their discussion of contemplation, look towards a third part of the *Summa* where we find evidence of the theoretical principle: the sections on prayer and forms of life. As we have seen, in the Prima Secundae, Thomas distinguishes between the contemplation of this life and the perfect contemplation of the next (I.II.3,2). Yet he not only distinguishes between them, but also deems the contemplative life the most perfect way of life to be had on earth: "the active life ... has less of happiness than the contemplative life" (*Ibid.*). In the discussion of forms of life in the Secunda Secundae, he maintains this position and expands upon it.

He opens his discussion of ways of life in II.II.179 by distinguishing between the two styles of life, the active and the contemplative. While he views the active life as necessary and good (and even in some respects as superior to the contemplative life), he also clearly allies the contemplative life with the kind of beatific contemplation he described in the Prima Secundae. Thus, he makes explicit what was earlier implicit, defining contemplation as the simple act of gazing at the truth (II.II.180,3 ad 1), seeking the principle which is God (II.II.180,4 *s.c.*, citing Gregory[17]). In these questions, though, he also clarifies some of the ideas only implicit in the questions on beatitude. Thus, he indicates that his habitual distinction between the intellect and the will is not intended to portray these as existing in some sort of tension or opposition: "the contemplative life, as regards the essence of the action, pertains to the intellect, but as regards the motive causes of the exercise of that action it belongs to the will, which moves all the other powers, even the intellect, to their action" (II.II.180,1, referring back to I.82 and I.II.9,1). Again, we sense that Thomas' conception of the intellect is more comprehensive than the usual notion operating in the twentieth century, a respect in which he resembles the breadth of vision of the Fathers, and our discomfort with both is perhaps symptomatic of the extent to which we have unnecessarily viewed head and heart as being at war with one another. Thomas, after all, can quite naturally cite Gregory's view as the basis of his own notion of contemplation: the contemplative life is identified with the love of God inflaming us to gaze on God's beauty (II.II.180,1[18]). The contemplation he has described as primarily an act of the mind is now taken as also encompassing love and the perception of beauty.

This wholeness of vision emerges above all in Thomas' treatment of prayer, in II.II.82 and 83. As strongly marked as the *Summa* is by the Augustinian insight that one cannot love what one does not know, it is equally influenced by the Dionysian principle that love is a unitive force, that union is above all constituted by love. Thus, in II.II.82,2, Thomas states: "It belongs immediately to charity that man should give himself to God, adhering to Him by a union of the spirit" (I.II.82,2 ad 1[19]). It would seem, then, that here he has appropriated union wholly to the side of love, and therefore to the will rather than the intellect. Thomas nevertheless never vacillates between Augustine and Denys, much less chooses between them. The strength of his mystical theology lies in the synthesis he forges. What motivates us to love God, to attain union in Denys' terms, is the contemplation of God: "Matters concerning the Godhead are, in themselves, the strongest incentive to love and consequently to devotion, because God is supremely lovable" (II.II.82,3 ad 2[20]).

Note that at this point, Thomas differs from many writers who might better be described as mystics than as theologians. It is not reflection on one's own experience of God's goodness, or the intense awareness of God's presence or absence that motivates unitive love, in Thomas' view, but mediation on God's nature. These articles on prayer thus provide us with a gloss on the Prima Pars. The careful, often technical, discussion of divine simplicity, goodness, perfection and all the rest, may now be viewed as a form of meditation which is meant to incite the love that leads to union. If the ultimate supremacy of love in Thomas' vision indicates that our knowledge of God leads to union only inasmuch as it reaches completion in love, the necessary precedence of knowledge indicates that Thomas envisages no spiritual experience which is not fully a human experience, and therefore the experience of a composite being. The Aristotelian framework of the *Summa*, with its insistence on the foundation of human knowledge in sense experience, may now be taken as the logical complement to the pattern of humanity's attachment to God which Thomas sketches. The foundational importance of the senses in the *Summa* simply reduces to the acknowledgement of human nature as composite and our apprehension of God as composite. If we are led to God by our senses as well as by our minds and our hearts, it is because we are embodied, a recognition which is in the first instance God's rather than Aristotle's. We are drawn into participation in God's life through body, mind and soul. Neither our physicality nor our intellect bars us from union with divine; rather, our senses and our minds lead us to God, the finite knowing the Infinite, the created contemplating the Uncreated, that the two may be joined in love.

Perhaps the most complete expression of the theoretical principle may be found in a locus where Thomas discusses neither theological method nor prayer, however. In I.12, he treats the knowledge of God and it is here that he expresses many of the themes we have already seen at work, bringing them together concisely. We may usefully conclude our exposition of the theoretical principle by considering this article. Thomas begins by acknowledging the ontological divide and its consequences, granting that the supremely knowable is not necessarily knowable to all lesser intellects (I.12,1 resp.). Nevertheless, humanity possesses a natural desire to know, and in particular, to know causes (*Ibid.*). We are therefore caught in a predicament: endowed with a yearning to know causes, our minds are incapable of attaining the First Cause. Thomas makes clear that the impossibility of knowing God lies in the limitations of the human mind, not in any inherent unknowability of God's (*Ibid.*); nevertheless, because our ultimate happiness consists in our highest activity, which is the exercise of our minds (*Ibid.*), we would seem to be doomed to lead frustrated existences. "If the intellect of the rational creature could not reach so far as the first cause of things, the natural desire would remain void" (*Ibid.*), Thomas admits. God, however, is not only the object of our understanding, but also the source of our ability to understand (I.12,2 resp.). The mind can be raised by God's grace (I.12,4 resp.) and the result of this gracing is a shared likeness of his primordial intelligence (I.12,2 resp.[21]). Our power of sight is this likeness to God which enables us to see God. This 'seeing', Thomas hastens to clarify, is not a matter of sense perception (I.12,3 resp.), for God, having no body, cannot be sensed or even imagined, but only understood (*Ibid.*[22]). The language of sight in these articles, then, denotes an act of the intellect, and the gift of grace which enables sight effects a union of intellects: "When any created intellect sees the essence of God, the essence of God itself becomes the intelligible form of the intellect" (I.12,5 resp.[23]). While even the reason with which we are endowed by nature is a share in God's light (I.12,11 ad 3), something more than nature is needed to predispose us to the sublimity of seeing the divine substance, and this *donum superadditum* is the light of glory (I.12,5 resp.[24]).

This light makes the creature like God (I.12,6 resp.[25]), and the increase of light that brings about the greater ability to see God is connected to a prime attribute of God, namely love: "The more light there is in the mind, the more perfectly the mind sees God. And those who have greater love have more light" (*Ibid.*). Again, Thomas emphasises vision and intellectual apprehension only to link them to love. That loving contemplation is clearly taking place in this life, inasmuch as Thomas is still speaking in terms of nature and grace rather than glory; nevertheless, the contemplation he envisages brings us to an earthly beatitude that is apparently not much different from the heavenly: "God ... is the fount and principle of all being and of all truth. He would so fill the natural desire of knowledge that nothing else would be desired, and the seer would be completely beatified' (I.12,9).

The theoretical principle thus brings together three themes that might appear to the modern reader not at all an inevitable trio: theological method, prayer and beatific union. The common denominator among them is contemplation. Contemplation is conceived in the *Summa* not as a particular method or variety of prayer, but as that activity whereby our attention is absorbed in God, and in virtue of this attentiveness, we are bonded to God. The activity is broadly conceived and can thus encompass both the contemplation that is theological reflection and the contemplation that is prayer. Because Thomas in his treatment of prayer prescribes little in the way of techniques (and for this reason alone we would not call the *Summa* an ascetical theology) one would be hard pressed to determine where the difference lay between theological reflection and prayer. Both activities are motivated in the first instance by the constitution of the human person: we are intellectual creatures who can know happiness and fulfilment only by knowing the highest object our mind can entertain: God. The gift of grace that is God's self-disclosure, the basis of all theology as well as of all prayer, means that not only are we not frustrated in our desire to know what lies infinitely beyond us, but we are drawn to a destiny we could not of our own accord have even envisaged. Both theology and prayer are forms of that envisioning, and means by which we are united to our goal.

IV

We turn from the theoretical principle to consider briefly the three other principles that articulate the mystical concerns of the *Summa*. The theoretical principle differs from these three in that it centres on an activity, contemplation, while each of the others focuses on the conditions of the possibility for union. There is a formal parallelism, however, in these different bases for union. The theological and anthropological principles stipulate divine and human nature as ordered, by the divine will in each case, towards the mystical union of God and humanity. The theoretical and Christological principles stipulate what one might call the means of union: in the case of the Christological principle, the means of nature, in the form of the hypostatic union and in the case of the theoretical principle, the means of grace. The theoretical principle is articulated in the *Summa*'s first two parts, showing how the natures inclined to union may be united by the grace of God's self-disclosure and invitation to communion; the Christological principle articulated in the Third Part shows how the natures are united in the person of Christ, the hypostatic union thus representing the ontological actualisation and culmination of the principles of union described in the first two parts.

In the Prima Pars, the union is grounded in the divine intention to bring into being creatures ordered towards union, and in portraying God as desiring union with what he has made, Thomas grounds his mystical theology in divine nature. Thus, the Five Ways (whether or not they are intended as proofs of God's existence) each in its own way suggests not only God's actual connection to creation, but a divine desire to be connected to it. The First Mover voluntarily moves something; the Efficient Cause voluntarily causes something; awareness of our own contingency leads to the conclusion of a Necessary Being who freely gave being to all else that exists; the gradation of being implies the Highest Being's sharing of goodness and perfection with the lesser beings; and the Divine Intelligence's ordering of the universe presumes God's will to move nature towards its divinely ordained end. Obviously, from one perspective, God is being portrayed as the source and end of all because Thomas has begun by looking at creation for signs of the Creator. Yet in the heat of the debate over the value of natural theology, we have overlooked that each of the Five Ways is also a description of God, hence the antiphon at the end of each to the effect that 'this everyone understands to be God.' The purpose of the Five Ways seems not only to find evidence of God's hand in creation, but to portray God as the source and end of all, the one who desires to create and to unite creation to himself.

This connection between God's nature and God's relation to humanity may seem tenuous, but as one progresses through the Prima Pars it becomes more and more evident as Thomas constantly presses the mystical implications of his doctrine of God. The treatment of divine goodness, for example, both identifies God as alone good by nature (I.6,4) and as the pattern, source and goal of all goodness (*Ibid.*). Thomas does not therefore treat this important attribute of God solely from the perspective of what God is in and of himself. He uses the assertion of divine goodness additionally to claim God's intention to attract humanity to himself. The treatment of perfection similarly both distinguishes God from creation by stressing the difference between divine perfection and any other variety of perfection and yet connects God to creation by describing the divine perfection as the cause and realisation of all other perfection. God, in other words, being distinct from creation, need not invite creatures to share his life, and yet he does. The fact that we can see some form of perfection in creatures is a testament to God's invitation to humanity to share his life, God's desire for union.

In the Secunda Pars, on the other hand, union is grounded in the structure of the human person. Thomas modifies the traditional account of the *imago Dei* by showing it to inhere in humanity at three levels: nature, grace and glory (I.93,4 resp.). Thomas portrays these as a continuum, so that grace builds upon nature without destroying it, and glory without obliterating nature and grace perfects them. The human person is described not only as by nature oriented towards God, but as constituted for continual growth towards God. Glory is thus in a sense the intended (though by no means inevitable) outcome of nature. As the theological principle operative in the Prima Pars shows God as the One who desires union, so the anthropological principle of the Secunda Pars shows the human person as ordered towards union with God.

That the theological and anthropological principles should unite in the Christological principle of the Tertia Pars might seem no more than one would conventionally expect. The *Summa*, however, transcends the commonplace in its very systematic impetus. Thomas begins from the patristic maxim 'God became human that we might become divine' (III.1,2, citing Augustine), and proceeds to link the suggested union to principles established in both the Prima and the Secunda Pars. Thus he speaks of a personal union of divine and human nature as the consequence of God's goodness (III.1,1 resp., drawing on Denys), hearkening back to the treatment of divine goodness in I.6. He also links the hypostatic union to creation's return to the divine and sanctifying source: "The mystery of the Incarnation ... [was completed] through His having united Himself to the creature in a new way, or rather, having united it to Himself" (III.1,1 ad 1[26]). The corrective clause indicates that Thomas views the hypostatic union not so much as God's descent as the foundation of humanity's exaltation. Christ is described as establishing and confirming faith, lifting hope and enkindling love, and by the example of his life, bringing us to beatitude and a share of his divinity (III.1,2). Here Thomas hearkens back to the Secunda Pars, which opens with the discussion of beatitude and continues on to describe human gracing above all as the infusion of the theological virtues of faith, hope and charity. The Christological principle thus grounds the transformative character of the Incarnation in the character of the two natures that comprise the hypostatic union: the one creating for the purpose of union, the other for that purpose created.

V

The very systematic impulse of the *Summa*, the dense web of connections amongst its various parts, points to the union of God and humanity. If, then, systematic and mystical theology need not be opposed, and indeed, if they can productively co-exist, one difficulty lying in the way of a twentieth-century appropriation of mystical theology has been cleared: we need not fear that by asking that theology orient itself toward contemplation and union that it must necessarily become unsystematic in the sense of being incoherent, or incomplete. Nor, the *Summa* demonstrates, need it become forgetful of its philosophical underpinnings. While one may deem Thomas' Aristotelian suppositions as inappropriate or outmoded for adoption in our time, his work shows that at least some varieties of philosophy are no more incompatible with 'spirituality' than they are with theology itself. Indeed, we should have to ask what use a philosophical framework is to Christian theology if it rendered theology incompatible with prayer, worship and the practice of Christian life. The first use of the *Summa* for modern theology, then, is simply to show that a mystical theology can be rigorous, 'real' theology in the sense that the twentieth century has chosen to define 'real'.

The *Summa* can do more than just establish the possibility of a remarriage between spirituality and systematic theology, however; it can also provide guidelines for effecting the reconciliation. The guidelines fall into two broad categories, which we can label teleological and unitive. The teleological invite us to consider God and beatific vision as the end of both humanity and of all theology; the unitive invite us to see the unity of human existence and the unity of God and humanity as the proper assumptions of any Christian theology.

As we have seen, the *Summa* is concerned in all its parts with God as the telos of human existence. Thomas never denies, and indeed the structure of his thought strongly implies, that we can somehow consider God *in se*, rather than *pro nobis*. He never loses sight of theology's human dimension, both in that it is subject to the constraints of human conceptuality and language, but also in that its end is in one important sense human: theology describes God and the things of God, not for God's sake but for ours, that we may be transformed by contemplation of τὰ θεία.

This realism about theology's human dimension nevertheless differs strikingly from the anthropocentric quality of much contemporary theology and spirituality. The contemplation of God is not, as Thomas engages in it, an activity generated principally by the desire for human satisfaction. To be sure, he envisages no other activity that humanity will find ultimately satisfying, but he does not advocate theology as a path to self-fulfilment. On the contrary, his theology is relentlessly theocentric, even in its anthropology: grace is given that we might be made deiform. Our transformation is not into better or happier human beings, but into partakers of God's own life. The theocentric focus of his theology thus invites the twentieth century reader to abandon the notion that the purpose of religion is self-satisfaction. Love, as Denys and Thomas remind us, is a unitive force, one that draws us beyond ourselves, toward an Other.

Thomas' teleological focus acts not only as a corrective to an inverted spirituality but also as a corrective to an anthropocentric theology, a theology whose end is fundamentally human. It serves both as a caution against apologetic and against a sterile intellectualism—ironically, both qualities that have often been attributed to Thomas himself. Despite the frequency with which it is read as apologetic, the *Summa* is seldom concerned with making Christian belief plausible to those who have not already accepted it. It is concerned with the transformative possibilities of the contemplation of God: how the believer may not only assent to the propositions of faith but may be joined to God through faith. When one acknowledges the *Summa's* contemplative dimension, the implausibility of focusing on its apologetic elements becomes clearer. One contemplates, not in order to make God welcome where he would otherwise not be, but in order to make oneself present before the face of transforming glory. The communal and communicative dimension of theology does not disappear, but becomes the consequence of spiritual transformation. We do not speak in order that others will be persuaded; we speak because we *have been* transformed. Likewise, Thomas does not treat God as an awkward or intriguing metaphysical problem to be solved or dismissed, but in his detailed and exacting discussion of the divine attributes alludes to a spiritual significance: we know God as good and perfect not for the sake of sustaining traditional claims about God, or making interesting new ones, but to seek the One who has first sought us. Theology is thus for Thomas categorically distinct from other forms of human inquiry. It may indeed be a form of *scientia*, but it is not simply one more science among others. We engage in theological reflection in a sense for our own sake, as we have noted, but the ultimate purpose of theology is neither some means to intellectual satisfaction nor a form of personal self-realisation. We engage in theological reflection not to satiate our own or others' intellectual hunger, but to join our minds to God.

Thomas' teleological focus reminds us also that this world is not an end in itself. Liberation theology's ringing denouncement of theology that uses the

Christian hope of paradise as a warrant for indifference to the actual condition of society is necessary and good, and liberation theologians have not in
general advocated ignoring Christianity's eschatological dimension, nor its
proclamation of human consummation as union with God.[27] Nevertheless,
contemporary interest in political theologies of all varieties has tended to
create an atmosphere in which an eschatological focus can be portrayed
as masking an indifference to the urgent social issues of our time. While
Thomas could not be categorised as a political theologian, the teleological and
theocentric focus of his work by no means prevents him from attending to
matters that immediately affect human relations and human societies: for
example, hatred (I.II.29 and II.II.34), fear (I.II.41–44), anger (I.II.46–48), war
(II.II.40) and justice (II.II.57–80). What Thomas' work suggests is that we
seek the good of others for the same reason that we seek individually to
grow closer to God's purpose: because already in this life, we seek union
with God and therefore, transformation into God.

Thomas' teleological focus is compatible with the cry for justice on earth
precisely because his spirituality is not individualistic. We are not, in his
vision, solipsistically seeking the satisfaction of our spiritual needs, nor are
we seeking experience for experience's sake. Because his mystical theology
focuses not on the extraordinary experience of the spiritually accomplished,
but union with God as the end of all people, he avoids the greatest pitfall
of any spirituality: the self-absorbed preoccupation with one's own soul.
In other words, it is precisely because his spirituality is not marred by the
individualism of much spirituality, both classical and contemporary, that it
is also compatible with political theology's demand for justice in this life.

By incorporating concern for justice with a relentless focus on justice's
Source, Thomas avoids the trap into which social concern and political theology can easily fall: of mistaking means for ends, of disconnecting the search
for justice in this world from the consummation of the next. If focus on the
eschatological promise of the gospel is not a mandate for ignoring societal
need, rightly attending to humanity's needs must equally not degenerate
into a de facto materialism which suggests that the task of the church lies
primarily in feeding, housing, clothing, educating and inoculating those who
have been denied these basic necessities. Remembering that Christianity
simultaneously preaches the goodness of matter *and* the emptiness of materialism has become especially important in the United States in the late
twentieth century, when political leaders are calling for the church to provide services that have long been considered the responsibility of society as
a whole. If the church falls into the trap of accepting responsibility for
binding the wounds created by a society riddled with social injustices, it will
effectively have consented, for the most compassionate reasons, to become a
relief organisation that addresses primarily material needs, and is thereby
distracted from its mission to attend to spiritual ones. The anthropological
principle that grounds Christian discourse is, as has already been stated, the

primacy of the person, a composite of body, mind and spirit. Just as we cannot neglect the body, no more can we neglect the spirit by seeking nothing more than material well-being and thereby, despite our best intentions, effectively proclaiming a gospel of materialism.

Second, Thomas' work suggests a unitive principle should guide all Christian theology. This unitive principle encompasses both a new way of understanding the systematic impulse behind Thomas' work and a way of conceiving the theological task based on the pattern he employs. We need to begin by understanding the nature of the *Summa*'s systematisation, the impetus for which is not to be sought solely in historical factors such as the propensity of medieval theologians to write *Summae*. Thomas identifies and forges connections between his theological method, doctrine of God, anthropology and Christology not just to create a vast yet tidy system. As we have seen, the inner connections of the *Summa* point to and make manifest the unity of God and humanity and the unity of all human existence before God.

The most important lesson we can learn from Thomas is to foster and sustain these two kinds of unity in our own theological reflection. In the first instance, the unity of theology indicates that theologians must press the spiritual significance of the claims they make. If their spiritual significance cannot be identified, then perhaps we should ask what constructive purpose they serve. Such an approach certainly raises questions about some forms of apologetic and philosophical theology, although it by no means banishes them as authentic forms of Christian inquiry. Indeed, asking the question of spiritual significance might well be beneficial: one reaffirms that the reason for explaining Christian belief to those who do not share it is not that Christians may look respectable in the public square but that others might be drawn to God; we analyse the nature of religious discourse not to vanquish those who think it absurd, but to make sense of the discourse that is theology, preaching and prayer.

In recalling that no part of human existence is theologically insignificant, we are reminded that theology addresses and describes the human *person*'s relationship to God and that person is a composite who consists, by definition, of more than any one part of the composite. In recent years, theologians have recognised that the early church's struggles with the question of matter did not exhaust the issue and the result has been a renewed and fertile theological reflection on the human body, the natural environment and the material needs of God's people, and the inclusion of such issues within the compass of systematic theology. We need now to demand the inclusion of the whole field of sanctification, and not solely the treatment of grace and the sacraments. Systematic theology must, if it is to be truly complete, attend to prayer, worship, spiritual discipline and experience, and above all, the relation between the transformation that occurs in this life and the consummation of the next. Eschatology cannot be solely the discussion of salvation; it must also speak to beatitude. Systematic theologies that are not shy of discussing the environment should be equally willing to explore the theological foundations and implications of fasting; those who call for political action should be just as prepared to discuss the efficacy of prayer.

The problem is not so much that such questions currently receive no attention; it is that they are almost invariably treated as distinct from larger theological visions, and consequently are easily marginalised and ignored. Such a claim might inevitably appear to question the value of ad hoc theology, theology not connected to a system. Can one give adequate theological consideration to spiritual questions *only* in the context of a systematic theology? I would say no, but that in the current climate, we urgently need systematic theologies that address the questions of spirituality. For a time, at least, we need not integrate spirituality into theology as a whole, and not only to treat its concerns in opuscula separated from a comprehensive theological vision.

Such sustained and disciplined theological reflection on the whole of Christian life will inevitably result in theological systems that express the second kind of unity we see in Thomas' work: the unity of God and humanity. Resolutely seeking the spiritual dimension of theology will mean that we do not treat the doctrine of God as connected to theological anthropology only through such means as Christology, but as intrinsically connected by God's desire to draw humanity into divine life. One does not thereby lessen the systematic importance of Christology, but restores its original patristic significance: God became human that we might become divine. This patristic maxim not only grounds the ancient idea of deification in Christology, but also in divine intention. The purpose of the Incarnation was that we might be drawn into the most intimate union with the One who made us for himself. Those who therefore accept Christ as divine and human, those who seek to articulate Christ's significance, must also necessarily be concerned with the divine intention of which the Incarnation is the fullest pledge: God's desire to draw humanity into mystical union.

Theologies which thus express the telos of both theology and human existence itself, and which testify to the unity of human experience and the unity of God and humanity will succeed, as Thomas' *Summa* does, in not only speaking of theology and contemplation, but engaging in theology contemplatively. They will be, as Thomas surely is, true to Evagrius' maxim: "To be a theologian is to pray truly and to pray truly is to be a theologian."

NOTES

1   For a more detailed description of a spirituality divorced from a recognisable doctrinal foundation, see the account of Thomas Moore's *Care of the Soul* in L. Gregory Jones' essay in this volume.
2   The appeal to the human person as a composite here and throughout this essay is not intended to make any claim regarding the metaphysical status of the soul, but only as a convenient way of designating the variety of ways in which God engages the human person.

3   Cf. Andrew Louth, *The Origins of the Christian Mystical Tradition: From Plato to Denys*, (Oxford: Clarendon, 1981), p. 199, and *Discerning the Mystery: An Essay on the Nature of Theology*, (Oxford: Clarendon, 1983) pp. 3–4, 136. Yves Congar notes that for both Maximus and Evagrius Ponticus, theology is the most elevated of degrees of life, being that perfect knowledge of God which is identified with the summit of prayer (*A History of Theology*, Tr. and ed. Hunter Guthrie, [Garden City, NY: Doubleday, 1968], p. 31).

4   Congar locates the beginning of the divide at the rise of Nominalism and the 'subtle scholasticism of the late Middle Ages', both of which effected a separation of the intellectual from the religious (*op. cit.*, p. 145; cf. also p. 166). John Welch concurs, locating the divide between spirituality and theology around the beginning of the fourteenth century ("Mystical Theology" in the *New Dictionary of Theology*, ed. Joseph A. Komonchak et al., [Wilmington, DE: Michael Glazier, 1987], pp. 692–94). The unnamed author of the article on mystical theology in *The HarperCollins Encyclopedia of Catholicism* (General ed. Richard P. McBrien, [San Francisco: HarperSanFrancisco, 1995], p. 900) locates the beginning of the separation of experience and intellectual knowledge in the Middle Ages, a separation which supposedly became final in the nineteenth century, when mystical theology became a discipline concerned with the higher reaches of contemplation. The same author also notes: "Contemporary theologians reject such distinctions [between mystical and dogmatic theology] and favor a reintegration of spirituality with doctrinal and moral theology" (*op. cit.*, p. 900). Sadly, this pronouncement seems more like a laudable wish than a realistic appraisal of the current state of the discipline. Congar also takes a benign view of the contemporary situation, seeing in it not a disintegration, but the result of a normal (and apparently good) process of development (*op. cit.*, p. 275).

5   Cited in Bernard McGinn, *The Growth of Mysticism: Gregory the Great through the 12th Century*, p. 367. (Vol. II of *The Presence of God: A History of Western Christian Mysticism*. [New York: Crossroad, 1994]).

6   "Spiritual Theology" in v. 13 (New York: McGraw-Hill, [1967]–1989), p. 588.

7   This definition is consonant with some standard definitions of the term, but differs from others. Some definitions tend to tie mystical theology specifically to mystical experience, being primarily concerned to distinguish mystical from ascetical theology, infused from acquired contemplation (for example, Aug. Poulain in the section on mystical theology, pp. 621–22 of "Theology" in v. 14 of the *Catholic Encyclopedia*, ed. Charles G. Hebermann et al. [New York: Robert Appleton, 1912]). John Welch, in the *New Dictionary of Catholicism*, modifies this view only slightly, broadening the scope of the discipline beyond reflection on the experience of those we would term mystics by defining mystical theology as systematic reflection on "the experience of a loving knowledge of God" (*op. cit.*, p. 692). While this broadened definition certainly makes mystical theology of greater significance to all the faithful, it does little to distinguish mystical theology from any variety of theology whatsoever. The *New Catholic Encyclopedia* uses the term 'spiritual theology' to designate both mystical and ascetical theology, claiming that it is the study of the application of Christ's redemptive work to the individual soul and the manner by which each soul receives and cooperates with it. Its task is "to establish the true nature of Christian perfection and to determine the means, both in general and in particular, that are used in the soul's advance on the way to perfection" (v. 13, p. 589). However, this article also acknowledges that for 'older authors' mystical theology was "a knowledge of God and of divine things acquired by the soul in the highest form of contemplation" (*Ibid.*), a description that may not emphasise the specifically theological component of mystical theology as much as the one given here. Most recently, the *HarperCollins Encyclopedia of Catholicism* defines mystical theology as systematic reflection on the deepest levels of human experience of God (p. 900). The definition I give here most closely resembles that of Congar, though it is by no means identical: "All of theology, because of the connection its practical elements have with the speculative, appears normative and has ... 'life value'. ... asceticism and mysticism find their place in theology, not as special parts added to a moral itself separated from dogma, but as elements organically integrated in the scientific study of the revealed mystery of God beatifying. This is theology" (*op. cit.*, p. 263).

8   Although the point is not elaborated, the *New Catholic Encyclopedia* singles out Thomas as an example of a thinker who treated theology holistically (v. 13, p. 589). Edward Farley, while distinguishing between theologians who thought theology was a discipline (*scientia*)

and those such as Bonaventure who saw it as the mind's road to God, acknowledges that Thomas belongs to the first group, but never abandoned the idea of theology as a cognitive state (*Theologia: The Fragmentation and Unity of Theological Education* [Philadelphia: Fortress, 1983], p. 35). Congar also describes Thomas' theology in terms compatible with the analysis which follows: "The sacred doctrine inasmuch as it is a science reproduces as far as possible (but in an order of ascent to the principle) the vision of God's science. Its goal is to bind everything to God Himself in His mystery both necessary and free" (*op. cit.*, p. 96).

9   While Bernard McGinn does not, as far as I can determine, define the word 'mystical theology' in *The Growth of Mysticism*, he does identify *theologia mystica* as *contemplation* (p. x).

10   Quotations from the *Summa* follow the Dominican Province translation (Westminster, MD: Christian Classics, 1911, rev. 1920, rpt 1981).

11   This claim about the mystical import of the *Summa's* structure of course resembles Marie-Dominique Chenu's well-known observation that the work follows an *exitus-reditus* pattern (*Toward Understanding Saint Thomas*, Tr. A. M. Landry and D. Hughes, [Chicago: Regnery, 1964]). Note, however, that the claim can survive quite happily outside of a specifically Neo-Platonic context.

12   "Magis tamen est speculativa quam practica."

13   "Ex quo patet nihil potest quietare voluntatem hominis, nisi bonum universale. Quod non invenitur in aliquo creato, sed solum in Deo."

14   "Si ergo beatitudo hominis consideratur quantum ad causam vel obiectum, sic est aliquid increatum: si autem consideretur quantum ad ipsam essentiam beatitudinis, sic est aliquid creatum."

15   Because happiness is something created, existing within us, it is an operation (I.II.3,2 resp.). It does not consist in a sensitive operation (I.II.3,3 s.c.). It is an operation whereby our mind is united to God (I.II.3,3 resp.). This act of the intellect is identified with knowledge of God in I.II.3,4 s.c. and contemplation of truth in I.II.3,2 ad 4: "The active life, which is busy with many things, has less of happiness than the contemplative life, which is busied with one thing, i.e. the contemplation of truth [circa veritatis contemplationem]."

16   "Solus Deus sit veritas per essentiam."

17   "In contemplatione principium, quod Deus est, quaeritur."

18   "Et propter hoc Gregorius constituit vitam contemplativam in *caritate Dei*: inquantum scilicet aliquis ex dilectione Dei inardescit ad eius pulchritudinem conspiciendam."

19   "Ad caritatem pertinet immediate quod homo tradat seipsum Deo adhaerendo ei per quandam spiritus unionem."

20   "Quod ea quae sunt divinitatis sunt secundum se maxime excitantia dilectionem, et per consequens, devotionem: quia Deus est super omnia diligendus."

21   "Et cum ipsa intellectiva virtus creaturae non sit Dei essentia, relinquitur quod sit aliqua particpata similitudo ipsius, qui est primus intellectus."

22   "Unde nec sensu imaginatione videri potest, sed solo intellectu."

23   "Cum autem aliquis intellectus creatus videt Deum per essentiam, ipsa essentia Dei fit forma intelligibilis intellectus."

24   "Cum igitur virtus naturalis intellectus creati non sufficiat ad dei essentiam videndam, ut ostensum est, oportet quod ex divina gratia superaccrescat ei virtus intelligendi."

25   "Facultas autem videndi Deum non competit intellectui creato secundum suam naturam, sed per lumen gloriae, quod intellectum in quaedam deiformitate constituit."

26   "Incarnationis mysterium non est impletum per hoc quod Deus sit aliquo modo a suo status immutatus in quo ab aeterno non fuit: sed per hoc quod novo modo creaturae se univit, vel potius eam sibi."

27   Indeed, several Latin American liberation theologians have called explicitly and forcefully for the reunification of theology and spirituality. See especially Gustavo Gutiérrez, *We Drink from Our Own Wells The Spiritual Journey of a People*, tr. Matthew J. O'Connell, (Maryknoll, NY: Orbis, 1985) and Jon Sobrino, *Spirituality of Liberation: Toward Political Holiness*, Tr. Robert R. Barr (Maryknoll, NY: Orbis, 1988). Nevertheless, liberation theology seems to suffer from the same malady as other contemporary theology: while it sees the problem of the separation of theology and spirituality, it no more successfully bridges the divide. In the two works mentioned above, spiritual concerns or attitudes appear more in theory than in practice. In this respect, however, liberation theology is no less effective than other theology; it is merely no *more* successful.

JULIAN OF NORWICH—
INCORPORATED

F. C. BAUERSCHMIDT

We often speak of the individual and the social as though of inner and outer, but in reality, the inner, too, is social. Luigi Sturzo[1]

Introduction

Julian of Norwich's day was a long time in coming. The modern popularity of the fourteenth-century anchoress and the author of *A Revelation of Love*[2] follows upon several centuries of neglect, during which copies of her book were rare, and there was little or no scholarly or popular interest in it. When the first printed edition of her book was published in 1670 (just less than 300 years after the visionary experience that occasioned the book), it was by no means greeted with universal accolades. The Anglican bishop Edward Stillingfleet saw it as an example of "the Fantastic Revelations of distempered brains"[3] so highly regarded by the Roman Church—a Church that forbade the reading of scripture, yet commended "the blasphemous and senseless tittle tattle of this Hystorical [sic] Gossip."[4] Times certainly have changed. Since the turn of this century, there have been three editions of Julian in her original Middle English, at least seven modernizations, and countless collections of excerpts.[5] The choice of Edmund Colledge and James Walsh's 1978 modernization, *Julian of Norwich: Showings*, as the inaugural volume in the series *Classics of Western Spirituality* indicates not only its current status as a "classic", but also its popularity with a wide audience. Even Stillingfleet's Anglican Church seems to have come around: a shrine to her has been built at St. Julian's Church in Norwich, where she was enclosed and from which she took her name, and recent years have seen the foundation of the Order of Julian of Norwich in the American Episcopal Church.

Dr. F. C. Bauerschmidt
Department of Theology, Loyola College in Maryland, Baltimore, MD 21210-2699, USA.

Such interest should give one pause, particularly in its more "popular" manifestations. Though Julian's summary of the meaning of her revelation— "Learn it well: love was his meaning"[6]—seems simple enough, her thought is in fact complex and, in a number of places, quite obscure. Apart from the probably unresolvable question of what written sources, if any, lie in the background of her text, she clearly draws upon a host of medieval theological conventions with which most of her modern readers are unfamiliar. In some ways her piety is typical of late medieval affective devotion, with its emphasis on the human sufferings of Christ and the royal majesty of God, themes that seem distinctly unfashionable today. The central image around which her visions cluster—the crucifix that is placed before her and which she sees bleed copious amounts of blood—seems excessively morbid when compared with the contemporary religious iconography of Western Europe and North America.

Nor is the point of attraction the events of Julian's life. Whereas many who do not particularly care for or about Augustine's theology are still captivated by the life story of the sinner turned saint, Julian offers us no such narrative. We know virtually nothing about her except the meager information that she herself gives us: born probably in early 1343, she fell ill in May of 1373 and was the recipient of a series of sixteen visions, or "showings", upon which she meditated for at least the next twenty years of her life. We know from the texts that have been preserved that she wrote at least two accounts of the visions, the "short text", which was written at some point before 1388, and the greatly expanded and theologically more developed "long text", which was written at some point after 1393, and perhaps as late as the early fifteenth century.[7] Apart from a few external witnesses who tell us that she had been enclosed as an anchoress by 1393, served at least on occasion as a spiritual guide to those who sought her out, and was still alive in 1416, this is about all we know.[8]

The ability of such an obscure and alien figure to garner relatively wide popularity today is at least in part related to modernity's construction of the category "mysticism" and Julian's location under that rubric. Such a positioning brackets Julian's historical situatedness in all its medieval and anchoritic peculiarity and gives to her a universal availability. However, this availability is bought at the cost of isolating Julian from the concrete beliefs and practices that shaped her thought, with the result that her theology is "depoliticized" by being removed from any particular tradition, constituted by actual social practices. It is my purpose in this essay to reconstrue Julian's work, not as an instance of a putatively universal and ahistorical "mysticism", but as a particular reading of the Christian tradition that seeks to imagine and commend a specific form of human social existence, characterized by a compassion that mirrors in history the divine sociality of Father, Son and Spirit.

An Unincorporated Fellowship

Arthur Edward Waite, doyen of the Hermetic Society of the Golden Dawn, wrote in 1906, "I have no personal doubt that true mystics of every age and country constitute an unincorporated fellowship communicating continually together in the higher consciousness."[9] Waite was an eccentric figure— a high church pantheist with a devotion to both the Holy Eucharist and the Holy Grail—but his image of the "unincorporated" nature of the fellowship of "true mystics" is indicative of an understanding of "mysticism" common among those less eccentric writers of the late nineteenth and early twentieth centuries who have determinatively shaped our current understanding of mysticism. These figures range from professional philosophers like William James to interested amateurs like Evelyn Underhill. They offer at times quite different understandings of the phenomenon of mysticism, but certain features seem to remain constant. In particular, all share an image of the mystics as forming, in Waite's terms, an "unincorporated fellowship". However they delineate the phenomenon of mysticism, what seems clear is that it stands in opposition to or, at best, benignly alongside more embodied forms of institutional religion. To these writers mysticism seems to offer a spiritual alternative in an era in which, as Waite puts it, "[t]he official formulæ of religious doctrine and instruction have passed ... under a ... cloud of limitation."[10] Recourse to a more "inward" form of religion seeks to provide some refuge from the scientific erosion of such Christian beliefs as the Garden of Eden, the virgin birth and the bodily resurrection. The attractions of "an unincorporated fellowship", the members of which share what is essential behind the decorative trappings of diverse religious traditions, are obvious.

While not all writers on mysticism at this time were explicitly anti-institutional in their orientation,[11] the persistent tendency since the late nineteenth century has been to present mysticism as an experience or range of experiences that receive subsequent articulation in specific religious or philosophical traditions. In fact, such a presumption frequently guides the very composition of many of the classic modern works on mysticism. As is well known, William James circumscribes his topic at the outset of *The Varieties of Religious Experience* in such a way as ultimately to exclude institutionally determined "over-beliefs" from the essence of religion. Though James claims that his restriction of his discussion to the sphere of "personal religion" is in a sense an arbitrary one, it becomes clear that it is in fact intrinsic to a project that attempts to salvage religion via pragmatism. He wishes to "reduce religion to its lowest admissible terms, to that minimum, free from individualistic excrescenses, which all religions contain as their nucleus, and on which all religious persons may agree."[12]

In a similar way, Evelyn Underhill's depiction of the unincorporated fellowship of mystics in her classic work *Mysticism* is guided by a similar circumscription. While her anti-institutional bias is not as strong as James', and she is more willing than he to specify the object of mystical experience as "God", Underhill shares with James a tendency to speak of theological doctrines as a "symbolic wrapping" around an essentially ineffable experience. Writing to a friend who was translating parts of Eckhart for her (since Underhill herself could not read German), she offers the following instructions:

> Would you either translate or send a note of anything that strikes you as specially fine? I want most passages in metaphysical rather than definitely Christian language: i.e. references by name to Our Lord, the Blessed Virgin etc. or bits flavoured with scraps of Scripture aren't much good: but those in which the same things are called the Eternal, the All, the Divine Love, etc. etc. will be useful. The book is not going to be explicitly theological as I want to make a synthesis of the doctrine of Christian & non-Christian mystics—so no 'over-beliefs' are admissible.[13]

While it may be tempting to accuse Underhill of a self-serving distortion of her sources, she actually believed that "definitely Christian language" *was*, in fact, an instance of "over-beliefs" obscuring the phenomenon to be studied. If the language of Christian theology is but a "wrapping," it not only can, but *must* be discarded in order truly to appreciate the gift contained within. Doctrines that have passed under a cloud of limitation, and the institutions that bear them, need not be excessively fretted over. What counts is the experience. Even in her subsequent revisions, which under the influence of Baron Friedrich von Hügel moved away from doctrinally dubious formulations that implied union without distinction between the soul and God, Underhill does not follow von Hügel's more positive appreciation of institutional religion.[14]

It was in this milieu that the modern recovery of Julian of Norwich occurred. The first book-length treatment of Julian, Robert Thouless' *The Lady Julian: A Psychological Study*, published in 1924, embodies many early twentieth-century presumptions about the nature of mysticism. Thus he distinguishes "the religious mystic from the ordinary religious person" by "the fact that [the mystic] experiences certain peculiar mental conditions in which he feels that he comes into real and convincing contact with spiritual objects."[15] As in William James, mysticism is a "mental condition", a certain type of *experience*, a particular mode of *consciousness*. For the purposes of "scientific" investigation, the reality of what is experienced can be bracketed: "Looking at them with cold scepticism from the scientific viewpoint, we may decide to believe that these inner convictions are illusory; but, at least, we must recognize that they are psychological realities" (pp. 18–19). Not unlike James, Thouless gives the study of religion (not, one should note, theology) a scientific status by focusing on the "fact" of religious experience.

In many ways Thouless' is an admirable work that seeks to approach its subject sympathetically but without undue credulity. He attempts to let

Julian speak for herself by quoting liberally from Grace Warrack's modernization, though he recognizes that even such selections are no substitute for an encounter with the original, which he commends to the reader (p. 5). However the model of religious experience as a particular kind of "mental condition" haunts his work, often thwarting his best insights. Thus while he puts forth a salutary understanding of doctrine as intellectual formulations "crystallised out of the experience of a community," he denies that Julian's mystical experience can be assigned doctrinal significance, since it is an "individual experience whose value lay rather in its rich feeling content than in anything which could remain to it after its intellectual formulation" (pp. 10–11). Here we see not only the classic modern antinomy of individual and social, but also of feeling and thought. And while he notes that "Julian was an orthodox daughter of the Holy Catholic Church, and inherited a body of belief which reacted on her mystical revelation" (p. 94), these beliefs seem merely to have "influenced the form of her revelations" (p. 95), in a subsequent shaping of an essentially amorphous emotive experience. It is almost as if Julian's revelation undergoes a "fall" from the pristine realm of experience into the dark value of thought and language.

Thouless claims that "those familiar with the writings of the mystics will have no difficulty in recognising in Julian's work the characteristic features of mystical expression" (p. 21). Just as William James claims that the experience of the mystic is self-authenticating and undeniable for the mystic himself, yet possesses no authority for others, Thouless denies Julian's visions, and her reflections on them, any communal significance. "Julian's hope [that all shall be well] is merely a dogmatic assertion on the strength of a mystical insight which can carry no intellectually grounded conviction to anyone who does not share that experience of insight" (p. 75). Yet this seems to fly in the face of Julian's own assertion that her visions are not her own private possession, but are given to be shared with her fellow Christians: "In all this I was greatly stirred in charity to mine even-christians, that they might see and know the same that I saw: for I would it were comfort to them. For all this sight was shewed general" (VIII. 19). In fact, Julian notes that her visions may be of more benefit to others than they are to her: "Because of the shewing I am not good but if I love God the better; and in as much as ye love God the better it is more to you than to me" (IX. 20). Similarly, Thouless claims that Julian's visions bear an undeniable authority for her based on their immediacy, and as a result of this authority, "[s]he does not doubt or argue, and she speculates very little" (pp. 21–22). Yet while Julian does ascribe an undeniable authority to her revelation, this authority is a source of genuine *intellectual* anguish she experiences over the idea that "all shall be well" and that God does not blame us for sin. She writes:

> But in this I stood beholding things general, troublously and mourning, saying thus to our lord in my meaning with full great dread: Ah! good

lord, how might all be well for the great hurt that is come by sin to the
creature? And here I desired, as far as I durst, to have some more open
declaring wherewith I might be eased in this matter (XXIX. 60).

Julian must continue to meditate on her visions, and produce two quite
different accounts of them, precisely because she doubts, argues, and
speculates.

By locating individual experience as the proper realm of Julian's revelation, Thouless effectively "disincorporates" her, both by removing her from
her own time-and-place situated historicity, and by severing any connection
between the revelation and those for whom Julian believed it was intended,
her "even-christians," the Body of Christ "in which all his members are
knit," in which "he is not yet fully glorified nor all impassible" (XXXI. 63).
Locked in the prison of an experience that is incommunicable except through
a fall into signification, a fall into exteriority, a fall into history, Julian's
revelation seems to come from nowhere in particular and is addressed to
no one in particular. Thus we may read it as addressed to *us*, whoever
"we" may be. Julian joins the ranks of those who make up Waite's "unincorporated fellowship communicating continually together in the higher
consciousness."

Thouless' study is not widely cited in contemporary works on Julian, yet
the same interpretive frame is operative in many of them, particularly the
more theologically-oriented ones, and more particularly those aimed at a
popular audience. To take one example, Karen Armstrong anthologizes
Julian in her book *Visions of God: Four Medieval Mystics and Their Writings*. In
her introduction, Armstrong presents a view of "religion" and "mysticism"
remarkably similar to Waite, James, Underhill and Thouless, though with a
woolliness unmatched by any of them (with the possible exception of Waite).
She begins with the historically dubious proposition that "[u]ntil recently,
each of the great religions of the world developed independently and had
little contact with each other."[16] From there she moves on to the claim that
with the advent of modern communications, we have "begun to learn ... the
almost uncanny universality of religious experience" (p. viii). Any difference
between religious traditions is merely the diverse expression of an essentially identical religious experience. This is particularly the case with "mysticism". While Armstrong, like Thouless, acknowledges that "[m]ystics often
have different beliefs, and these inevitably affect their experiences," behind
this difference is a profound sameness.

[T]he actual experience of all mystics is strikingly similar: All encounter
a reality in the depths of the self that is, paradoxically, Other and
irrevocably separate from us. All emphasize that this ultimate reality,
which gives meaning and value to human life, is ineffable, transcending
our limited words and concepts (p. ix).

Also consistent with James and Thouless is Armstrong's belief that it is precisely as a state of consciousness that "mysticism" can gain a hearing in the court of science, which is the realm of "facts". "However one chooses to interpret it, the mystical experience has been a fact of life ever since human consciousness had developed to a particular point" (p. ix). One need not believe in God to accept, on the basis of evidence, the existence of mystical experience, what Armstrong calls, in terms reminiscent of Waite, "higher states of consciousness" (p. x). The subjectivization of religion in general and mysticism in particular ironically prepares them to be the formal objects of scientific investigation; mysticism may or may not be about God or Nirvana or Ultimate Reality, but it is clearly about the self, the existence of which is assured. The "inner journey to a God found in the depths of the self" (p. xvi) can be appreciated and studied on the "factual" basis of the self, if on no other. On this basis religion, like art, "is an imaginative and creative attempt to find meaning and value in human life" (p. xxiii).

Armstrong is aware that Julian does not quite fit into the picture she has painted of mysticism. Thus she says that Julian is "perhaps, more like a prophet who brings a message of God to mankind than a mystic" (p. 172). As a part of this she recognizes Julian's concern for her "even-christians": in the case of prophets, as opposed to mystics, "God does not send these revelations for their own edification but for the sake of their people" (p. 175). At the same time, whether prophet or mystic, Julian is depicted by Armstrong, again in a manner not unlike Thouless, as the recipient of an experience which, if communicable, is not *rationally* communicable: "Julian's solution [to the question of sin and evil] does not make rational sense, but it does reverberate emotionally with an important dimension of the Christian religion of love, which sometimes gets lost in the more cerebral doctrinal formulations of the faith" (p. 177). Beyond this, however, Julian represents a version of Christianity particularly useful for modern people who feel keenly the cloud of limitation hanging over Christian doctrines: "In recent years people have found the doctrines of Christianity increasingly difficult, but a visionary like Julian penetrates the cerebral crust of the religious experience, which has little to do with logic and reason, to reach its core" (p. 177). Armstrong seems to ignore Julian's professed concern for Church teaching, as well as the rigorous intellectualism already noted. The intellectual apprehension of doctrine is not, for Julian, a "crust" over religious experience; rather it is like a knife she wields to prune and probe her revelation.

Armstrong's construal of Julian might be criticized from numerous angles. There are clear scholarly lapses in her presentation of Julian, though these are perhaps forgivable in an avowedly popular book.[17] What I wish to do here is simply point out the way in which her presentation of "mysticism" as what William James called the "root and centre" of religious experience[18] profoundly depoliticizes Christianity. Like James and Waite and Underhill and Thouless, she defines mysticism as a space of interiority, and she proceeds to immure Julian in that space. No doubt Armstrong sees herself walling Julian up for her own good, placing her in a protected sphere of *interiority-self-affectivity-experience*, safe from the forces of *history-politics-intellect-doctrine*. The conclusion of Armstrong's introduction is highly instructive:

> Today we have less confidence than before in the power of more external, socially oriented ideologies to change the world. We have watched the demise of enthusiasms like nationalism, Marxism, and Thatcherism, which promised a salvation of sorts. Many people feel that a deeper solution is necessary and seek the interior transformation of psychotherapy or counselling. In the late twentieth century, therefore, people may find the mystical experiment, which also urges the adept to look within himself for the truth and warns against the danger of simplistic ideas and projections about God, to be a more attractive form of religion than the more conventional and dogmatic types of faith (p. xxv).

Leaving aside the question of whether a faith that is "more attractive" to late twentieth century people is in fact inoculated against "simplistic ideas and projections about God," we might do well to question the simple dichotomies that Armstrong sets up between inner and outer, individual and social, mysticism and politics. Christian belief in the incarnation of God—the "incorporation" of God in the unique person Jesus Christ and in his Body the Church—sunders all such dichotomies. What Christ establishes is not the possibility of individual redemption, but the possibility of restored communion: the communion of human beings with God and a communion of human beings with each other. In other words, salvation is social; it is incorporation into the polity defined by the incarnation of Christ and the Gospel he proclaimed.

Thus Christian faith is less like a therapy of the inner life and more like the "external, socially oriented ideologies" which Armstrong mentions. As such, it is frequently (though not necessarily) in conflict with other social ideologies. One cannot divide human existence into the inner mystical sphere and the external political sphere and declare a truce or division of labor between them. The attempt of Armstrong and most other modern writers on mysticism to relegate the "mystics" to a putative inner sphere tends to result, whether wittingly or unwittingly, in a Christian exit from the stage of history, leaving its inhabitants prey to the wolves of "nationalism, Marxism, and Thatcherism". The ultimate task of theology is reflection upon and explication of the social practice of the Gospel, precisely so as to enact it anew in diverse circumstances. In the remainder of this essay I shall argue that Julian of Norwich offers a specific, though not necessarily detailed, vision of the common life, one grounded in the Gospel narratives of Jesus (particularly the passion narrative) and which centers upon her understanding of the nature of Christ's body. Rather than presenting us with, as Armstrong claims, an "imaginative approach to religion [that] shows a possible way forward" for those moderns who "have lost the will to create a faith for themselves" (p. 178), Julian in fact offers nothing less than an "external, socially oriented" ideology in which the "incorporated fellowship" of Christ's body the Church is brought into conformity with the appearing of divine love in the crucified body of Jesus.

A Bodily Sight

Julian's *A Revelation of Love* resists any "unincorporated" reading because of its resolutely *corporeal* nature. Recent scholarship, particularly the work of Caroline Walker Bynum, has dealt a mortal blow to the old canard that medieval piety was marked by a suspicion, even a hatred, of the body.[19] Though body is clearly subordinate to soul, it is also true that for much medieval piety, as Bynum puts it, "body is not so much a hindrance to the soul's ascent as the opportunity for it. Body is the instrument upon which the mystic rings the changes of pain and delight."[20] Likewise, Christ's body, both as represented in art and as present in the Eucharist, was perhaps *the* central object of religious devotion in late medieval Christianity. It was central both to individual piety and to the identity of Christendom as a whole, which saw itself as the *Corpus Christianum*. Whether the body was that of the devout seeker or that of Christ, corporeality was central to medieval religious practice.

In this regard, Julian was very much a woman of her day. Near the outset of her account of the revelation she says, "I desired a bodily sight" (II. 4), and she receives that for which she asked: her revelation is thoroughly embodied. I will focus on three senses in which corporeality is central to Julian's visionary experience and the theology that grows out of it. First, Julian's vision is of the body of Jesus, crucified and risen. This body is the "text" that she must interpret. Second, Julian understands Christ's saving work as reuniting our "substance" and our "sensuality"—complex terms that indicate respectively the higher and lower aspects of the human soul, but that also extend "upwards" to participation in the divine life and "downward" to redemption of all that is bodily, material, and historical. Finally, Julian's revelation is intended for her "even-christians", her fellow members of Christ's body who suffer still on earth. It is in the realm of this body, not the realm of interiority, that God is encountered through the imitation of Christ's compassion. I treat each of these in turn.

1) Christ's Body as Text

Julian recounts that when she was thirty years old she fell ill with what everyone, including her, presumed was a fatal illness. Her visionary experience is initiated when the priest who has been called to attend her dying places a crucifix before her face, saying, "I have brought thee the image of thy maker and saviour. Look thereupon and comfort thee therewith" (III. 6).[21] As she looks at the cross, she begins to feel her life flow away and believes herself to be at the point of death. Then her pain suddenly leaves her. She asks God "that my body might be fulfilled with mind and feeling of his blessed passion. For I would that his pains were my pains with compassion, and afterward longing to God." But she notes that "in this I desired never bodily sight nor shewing of God, but compassion, such as a kind[22] soul might have with our lord Jesus, that for love would be a mortal man: and therefore I desired to suffer with him" (III. 7). Nevertheless, "suddenly I saw the red blood trickle down from under the garland, hot and freshly and right plenteously, as it were in the time of his passion when the garland of thorns was pressed on his blessed head, who was both God and man, the same that suffered thus for me" (IV. 8).

Julian says that in seeing this "suddenly the Trinity fulfilled my heart most of joy" (IV. 8). She then goes on to state the basic theological/hermeneutical presupposition of *A Revelation of Love*: "where Jesus appeareth the blessed Trinity is understood, as to my sight." This triune God revealed to Julian in her vision of Jesus is not, as Armstrong et al. would have it, a human projection or construct, imposed on the ineffable reality of God; it *is* the reality of God. As she puts it: "the Trinity is God, God is the Trinity." And this Trinity that is "our maker and keeper," that is "our everlasting lover,[23] everlasting joy and bliss," is so "by our lord Jesus Christ" (IV. 8). In other words, the corporeal, suffering humanity of Jesus, in all its categorical particularity, is not simply a symbolic wrapping around an ineffable, transcendental experience, but is the actual appearance in history of the triune life of God, the mutual indwelling love of Father, Son, and Spirit.

Another way to put this is that Julian approaches Christ's body as a "text" from which she must "read" the divine nature. Images of Christ's body as text can be found in several medieval English sources, particularly in descriptions of what was called the "Charter of Christ", the charter of humanity's freedom from the thralldom of Satan, written by Christ in his own flesh on the cross.[24] A fourteenth-century English preachers' manual speaks of how "Christ, when his hands and feet were nailed to the cross, offered his body like a charter to be written on. The nails in his hands were used as a quill, and his precious blood as ink."[25] Likewise, Richard Rolle (c. 1300–1349) writes,

sweet Jesu: Your body is like a book entirely inscribed in red ink, (which is) compared to your body because that is entirely inscribed with red wounds. Now, sweet Jesu, send me grace to read this book again and again, and to understand something of the sweetness of that reading; and allow me the grace to grasp something of the matchless love of Jesus Christ, and to learn from that example to love God in return as I should do ...[26]

For Rolle, the purpose of "reading" this text of Christ's crucified body is not so much discerning a meaning as arousing a response in the reader, which leads to greater conformity to Christ. Intellect and affect blur together as the reader is assimilated to the text in the very act of reading it.

Julian does not explicitly invoke the image of the Charter of Christ. However, when one asks precisely *what* is revealed in Julian's showings, one must say that it is Christ's body that is revealed and must be read. This text shares in the fundamental interpretive ambiguity and indeterminacy of any text; it must be interpreted. Nicholas Watson has noted that what was shown to her in May of 1373 was not any sort of detailed message or scene, but rather "a disparate series of glimpses of Christ's Passion, strung like beads along her life saving gaze at a crucifix, and interspersed with other, more abstract sights, as well as with a few pregnant words passed from Christ to her and sometimes back again."[27] By comparing the earlier short text with the later and more theologically-developed long text, one can see that Julian has elaborated her account of the showings in such a way that the line between vision and subsequent "reading" of that vision is blurred, if not obliterated. Drawing an analogy with Biblical exegesis, Watson writes:

> It is as though the Biblical text in the centre of its manuscript page were literally to 'overflow' and to merge with the surrounding apparatus; or, to put the same point the other way around, as though the apparatus were to merge with the text, annexing its divinely-inspired status and authority, and forming a layered, composite text which engages in its own exegesis.[28]

Thus the revelation consists not only in what occurs during her sickness, but also in her interpretive process growing out of that experience. To interpret this revelation, to "read" it, is to be conformed to it. Just as text merges with commentary, so too Julian is united with Christ through the process of interpretation.

This interpretation process is not simply discerning meaning but, because "Love was his meaning," it involves assimilation to the text through participation in the compassion of Christ displayed on the cross. At one point, after describing in minute detail her showing of the dying agony of Christ, she writes, "The which shewing of Christ's pains filled me full of pain ... And in all this time of Christ's pains I felt no pain but for Christ's pains" (XVII. 39). This is a real union with Christ, but it is not so much a union without distinction—of which theorists of mysticism are so enamored—but a union of incorporation into Christ through a bodily sharing in his passion and compassion. The experience of the pain of Christ's passion conforms Julian to the compassion that Christ displays on the cross, thus uniting her with him. This incorporation into Christ is thoroughly *social*, for in the cultivation of compassion toward one's fellow Christians, union with Christ is deepened: "I saw that each kind compassion that man hath on his even-christians with charity, it is Christ in him" (XXVIII. 59).

We have no reason to think that Julian's "mystical experience" was an instance of "higher consciousness" or a glimpse of some such abstraction as "Ultimate Reality". Rather it was a revelation in which both the medium and the message is the love of God taking flesh in the crucified humanity of Jesus. The seemingly simple "meaning" of the revelation—love—can only be understood when it remains inextricably bound to the image of love seen in the cross of Jesus. This is why, in a key passage, Julian describes how her eyes were fixed on the cross before her when she had "a proffer in my reason" that said, "Look up to heaven to his Father." To this Julian "answered inwardly with all the might of my soul, and said: Nay; I may not: for thou art my heaven." She goes on to say:

> Thus was I learned to choose Jesus to my heaven, whom I saw only in pain at that time. Meliked no other heaven than Jesus, which shall be my bliss when I come there. And this hath ever been a comfort to me, that I chose Jesus to my heaven, by his grace, in all this time of passion and sorrow. And that hath been a learning to me that I should evermore do so, choose only Jesus to my heaven in weal and woe. (XIX. 42).

The suffering Jesus in all his corporeal particularity is not something that Julian seeks to move beyond. She rejects the kind of apophaticism commended by a work like *The Cloud of Unknowing* in favor of something that seems at first more akin to the humbler spirituality of affective piety, which focuses on the humanity of Jesus. But this is not simply recoiling from the deep mysteries of God into the refuge of the more familiar humanity of Jesus; Julian's revelation is in its own way profoundly apophatic. The conventional images of the crucified Jesus are stretched and exaggerated through Julian's extended meditation on the infinite divine love seen in them. As Vincent Gillespie and Maggie Ross note: "Signs are not rejected or despised; they are exalted by being transfigured. The emptiness of the ineffable and the apophatic becomes occupied, filled, and fulfilled 'in fulhede of joy' ... by the love of God."[29] Thus Julian offers us neither imageless contemplation nor affective meditation on the humanity of Jesus, but rather an interpretive practice focused on the "apophatic image" (to use Gillespie and Ross' phrase) of the crucified Jesus.

Spiritualities that claim an undisciplined apophaticism can too easily collapse into a narcissism in which, through the process of negation of concepts and images, the self that negates grows fat. Thus Karen Armstrong's portrayal of Julian as one who urges her readers to "reach through the dogmas and intellectual propositions, which can never do justice to the ineffable mystery of the divine, and touch the heart of faith" turns, as we have seen, into a call for them to "create a faith for themselves" (p. 178). Yet Julian, in her resolute focus on the image of the crucified Jesus, liberates "religious experience" from the prison of the self in which so much modern piety is locked. Robert Thouless, though in many ways prey to the solipsism endemic to the modern discourse of "mysticism", was quite perceptive in his comments on the significance of Julian's focus on the suffering Jesus. He writes: "The love which seeks the sky may too easily be lost in the self. Christ in agony on the cross is the object calling out in sympathetic pain all the love of Julian, thus saving her from the dangers of self-love" (p. 61). In choosing Jesus for her heaven, in seeking God in Christ's tortured human body, Julian takes a step toward a God who is truly "other", and not simply a higher modality of the self's consciousness. In her participation in the passion and compassion of Christ on the cross, Julian is initiated into a true dispossession of the self.

2) Substance and Sensuality
Julian notes that in the moment that she "chose Jesus to my heaven, by his grace, in all this time of passion and sorrow," she simultaneously regretted or "repented" of her choice, because of the intensity of Christ's pain that she shared. She ascribes this simultaneity of contraries to a duality within the self:

> Repenting and willing choice be two contraries which I felt both in one at that time; and these be two parts: the one outward, the other inward. The outward part is our deadly flesh-hood which is now in pain and woe, and shall be in this life, whereof I felt much in this time, and that part it was that repented. The inward part is an high, blissful life which is all in peace and in love, and this was more inwardly felt; and this part is in which mightily, wisely and with steadfast will I chose Jesus to my heaven (XIX. 43).

These two "parts", the outward and the inward, she later describes in terms of "substance" and "sensuality", explicitly identifying these terms with the phenomenon she describes in chapter XIX (see LV. 134). This distinction names the persistent tendency, which we saw in Armstrong and others, to divide life into the inner, spiritual realm and the external realm of history. However for Julian the separation of these two is an effect of the Fall and not something which justifies the abandonment of the external. The terms "substance" and "sensuality" are used by Julian both to mark a fundamental cleavage within the self which accounts for the pain and blindness of the fallen human condition, and to describe the saving work of Christ who heals this cleavage by coming to dwell within our sensuality.

The substance-sensuality distinction is not, as it might first appear from Julian's description of its two elements as "outward" and "inward", a distinction between soul and body, but rather a distinction within the soul. Julian writes, "our substance and our sensuality, both together may rightly be called our soul" (LVI. 135–136). A bipartite division of the soul into "higher" and "lower" was common in the Middle Ages;[30] however, Julian's anthropology and her use of terms in describing it are distinctive. Her contemporary, Walter Hilton (c. 1343–1396), makes a distinction between "reason" and "sensuality", but his usage is somewhat different from Julian's. For Hilton, sensuality is "the carnal feeling through the five senses which is common to man and beast." In other words, it is simply the capacity for sense perception. "Reason" is a distinctively human capacity, which is further divided into a higher and lower part—the former being oriented toward the intelligible and the latter toward the sensible.[31] In Julian's usage, "substance" corresponds roughly to Hilton's higher part of reason, while "sensuality" seems to encompass both the lower part of reason as well as the capacity for sense perception that human beings share with animals.[32] Even beyond this, "sensuality" seems to extend for Julian to the point of including corporeality itself. Julian says that it is in the "knitting" of soul to body that "we are made sensual" (LVII. 138). Thus sensuality seems to be both spiritual and somatic.

The self, for Julian, is stretched between these poles of substance and sensuality. Our substance is intimately associated with God's substance, though she carefully notes that God's substance is uncreated and ours is created: "And I saw no difference between God and our substance, but as it were all God, and yet mine understanding took that our substance is in God: that is to say, that God is God, and our substance is a creature in God" (LIV. 130–131). While maintaining the crucial distinction between creature and creator, Julian's language seems to brush up against an identification of the soul and God.[33] It is with reference to our substance that Julian makes her rather startling remarks about the "godly will":

> For in every soul that shall be saved is a godly will that never assented to sin nor ever shall; right as there is a beastly will in the lower part that may will no good, right so there is a godly will in the higher part, which will is so good that it may never will evil, but ever good; and therefore we are that which he loveth, and endlessly we do that which him pleaseth (XXXVIII. 76).

At the opposite pole, sensuality is characterized by mortality, bound up as it is with "weight of our mortal flesh and darkness of sin" (LXXII. 176). The realm of sensuality, in its isolation from our substance, has become the realm of change, sin, and suffering that characterizes our life on earth: "man is changeable in this life, and by frailty and overcoming falleth into sin; he is weak and unwise of himself, and also his will is overlaid. And in this time he is in tempest and in sorrow and woe, and the cause is blindness, for he seeth not God" (XLVII. 99). Because the duality of substance and sensuality is not one that neatly divides between soul and body—the sin and suffering of sensuality is an affliction of the soul as much as the body—Julian conveys a strong sense of rupture within the self, to the point that the self is hidden from itself: "our passing life that we have here in our sensuality knoweth not what our self is" (XLVI. 96). Fallen humanity is characterized by a separation of substance and sensuality, rendering the self, as Nancy Coiner puts it, "doubled and split, ... familiar and yet hidden from itself."[34] Thus Julian can both "choose" the crucified Jesus and "repent" of that choice in the same moment, for "in our substance we are full, and in our sensuality we fail" (LVII. 138).

This duality in the self sets the stage for the dilemma with which Julian struggles in attempting to understand her revelation. To the doubled self there corresponds a double judgement: God's judgement (which she refers to as the "higher doom"), made on the basis of our substance, whereby God assigns no blame for sin, and human judgement (which she refers to as the "lower doom"), made on the basis of our sensuality, whereby sinful acts are worthy of divine wrath (XLV. 94–95). And just as substance cannot override the reality of sensuality, so too the higher judgement does not trump the lower. This lower judgement is "of the common teaching of holy church in which I was afore informed and grounded" and Julian steadfastly maintains that "by the shewing I was not stirred nor led therefrom in no manner of point, but I had therein teaching to love it and find it good" (XLVI. 97). But this presents Julian with two seemingly irreconcilable truths:

> And thus in all the beholding methought it was needful to see and to know that we are sinners, and do many evils that we ought to leave, and leave many good deeds undone that we ought to do, wherefore we deserve pain and wrath. And notwithstanding all this I saw soothfastly that our lord was never wroth nor ever shall be, for he is God: good, life, truth, love, peace; his charity[35] and his unity suffereth him not to be wroth; for I saw truly that it is against the property of his might to be wroth, and against the property of his wisdom, and against the property of his goodness. God is the goodness that may not be wroth for he is not but goodness; our soul is oned to him, unchangeable goodness, and between God and our soul is neither wrath nor forgiveness in his sight (XLVI. 97).

The same revelation that shows no wrath in God, that shows that wrath would mar God's perfection, also tells Julian to hold fast to the faith of the Church, which teaches the reality of God's wrath.[36] Just as there is a fissure within the self, there is a fissure within Julian's revelation. And just as the healing of the self involves a reconciliation of substance and sensuality, so too comprehension of the revelation involves a reconciliation of these two judgements. "Then was this my desire: that I might see in God in what manner that which the doom of holy church teacheth is true in his sight, and how it belongeth to me verily to know it; whereby the two dooms might both be saved;[37] so as it were worshipful to God and right way to me."

Julian goes on to say, "And to all this I had none other answer but a marvellous example of a lord and of a servant" (XLV. 95).

The "example" of the lord and servant is the hinge on which the long text of Julian's *A Revelation of Love* pivots. It is the puzzling solution offered to the problem of reconciling substance and sensuality, higher and lower judgements. Julian's description and exegesis of this example are one of the most striking of the additions to the short text, taking up all of the lengthy fifty-first chapter in the long text. She describes this as a "shewing full mistily" (LI. 107) by which she indicates that the significance of this example was unclear to her (which perhaps accounts for its omission from the short text). Her contemplation does not issue in an answer as much as it sketches and reproduces within the self the contours of the drama of cosmic redemption which reaches its denouement only with God's final reconciling deed at the end of time. Even as Julian composes the long text, she both presents the example of the lord and servant as an answer to her desire, and notes, "yet I stand desiring, and will unto my end" (XLV. 95).

As Julian describes it, she sees a lord sitting "stately in rest and in peace" and a servant standing before the lord, ready to do his will. The lord sends the servant on a task, and the servant "runneth in great haste for love to do his lord's will." But the servant falls into a ravine and is hurt: "And then he groaneth and moaneth and waileth and struggleth, but he neither may rise nor help himself by no manner of way." Julian looks to see whether the servant has fallen through any fault of his own, but can see only his good will. And the lord, looking at the servant, says:

> Lo, lo, my loved servant. What harm and distress he hath taken in my service for my love, yea, and for his goodwill! Is it not fitting that I award him [for] his affright and his dread, his hurt and his maim and all his woe? And not only this, but falleth it not to me to give a gift that be better to him and more worshipful than his own wholeness should have been? Or else methinketh I should do him no grace (LI. 109).

Julian says that there then "descended" into her soul the understanding that the lord, because of his great goodness and for his own sake,[38] must ("it behoveth needs to be") reward the servant "above that he should have been if he had not fallen."

Then, "at this point the shewing of the example vanished, and our good lord led forth mine understanding in sight and in shewing of the revelation to the end." What Julian seems to mean by this is that even though the "shewing" vanished, the revelation continued as God guided her reflections on its significance. As noted above, Julian makes no clear delineation between the "text" of the showing and her interpretation of it. She is able to distinguish the initial revelation from her subsequent "inward learning", and both of these from what she calls "all the whole revelation from the beginning to the end, that is to say, of this book," but she also says that "these three are so oned, as to my understanding, that I cannot, nor may, dispart them." She goes on to say that for the next twenty years she had "teaching inwardly", meditating on the image in accordance with God's command: "It belongeth to thee to take heed to all the properties and conditions that were shewed in the example though thou think that they be misty and indifferent to thy sight" (LI. 110). She was to scrutinize the example in all its details, yet, she notes, "notwithstanding all this forth-leading, the marvelling over the example went never from me; for methought it was given me for an answer to my desire, and yet could I not take therein full understanding to mine ease at that time."

Julian's chief puzzlement concerns the identity of the servant, whom she takes at first to be Adam. Yet in the servant she sees "many diverse properties that might in no manner of way be assigned to single Adam" (LI. 110). In particular, the servant seems to fall out of zeal for the lord's will, whereas Julian knows from the teaching of the Church that humanity fell out of willful disobedience, and thus is worthy of wrath and blame.[39] Also, in the standard medieval view sin has left the will, as Augustine put it, "half-wounded, struggling with one part rising up and the other part falling down."[40] Julian, however, sees the servant's will as essentially undamaged, though, as she notes earlier, it is "overlaid" by sin (XLVII. 99). Still, the chief effects of the fall seem to regard human power and wisdom, not will. Once fallen, the servant "was hurt in his might and made full feeble; and he was stunned in his understanding, for he turned from the beholding of his Lord. But his will was kept whole in God's sight; for his will I saw our lord commend and approve" (LI. 111). This last, the "godly will", is most puzzling to Julian; as she noted earlier: "I knew by the common teaching of holy church and by mine own feeling that the blame of our sin continually hangeth upon us, from the first man unto the time that we come up unto heaven; then was this my marvel, that I saw our lord God shewing to us no more blame than if we were as clean and as holy as angels be in heaven" (L. 106).

The resolution to Julian's puzzlement lies in her realization of the dual identity of the servant: "In the servant is comprehended the second person in the Trinity; and in the servant is comprehended Adam, that is to say, all-man" (LI. 116). Julian draws on Paul's Christ-Adam motif but gives to the relationship of Christ and Adam a striking ontological density by grounding it not only in our redemption, but in our very creation. The creation of humanity is, from God's eternal perspective, enfolded in the creation of the human nature of Christ. Human nature "first was prepared to his own Son, the second person. And when he would, by full accord of all the Trinity, he made us all at once; and in our making he knit us and oned us to himself" (LVIII. 142; cf. LIII. 129). In saying this, Julian describes an eternal union between God and humanity in the hypostatic union of the divine and human natures of Christ, which is willed by God from all eternity: "in his foreseeing purpose that he would be man to save man in fulfilling of his Father's will"

(LI. 117). The *totus Christus* of head and members is God's eternal intention. Likewise she sees that, from God's perspective, the fall of humanity into sin and the "fall" of Christ into this world of suffering are coincident:

> When Adam fell, God's Son fell: because of the rightful oneing which had been made in heaven, God's Son might not from Adam, for by Adam I understand all-man. Adam fell from life to death into the deep of this wretched world and after that into hell. God's Son fell with Adam into the deep of the maiden's womb, who was the fairest daughter of Adam, and for this end: to excuse Adam from blame in heaven and in earth; and mightily he fetched him out of hell (LI. 116).

Adam and Christ fall "together" because of the eternal bond between God and the exemplary humanity of Christ, and because of this same bond they are raised together.

Throughout the example of the lord and servant, the servant is always both Christ and Adam, the fall into the ravine is always both humanity's fall into sin and Christ's mission from the Father. This dual identity of the servant helps us to understand several of Julian's more puzzling claims. Humanity has a "godly will" because that will is "whole and safe in our lord Jesus Christ" (LIII. 127). God does not look with wrath upon fallen humanity, because in looking at the servant God sees the Son who has fallen out of zeal to do the Father's will; thus "our Father nor may nor will more blame assign to us than to his own Son, dearworthy Christ" (LI. 117). One might say that the relationship between God and sinful humanity is transformed through Christ's "economic" taking of a human nature so as to reflect the "immanent" relations of Father, Son, and Spirit.

At the same time, the higher significance of the example does not void the lower meaning. Julian, while believing that sin is quite literally "nothing",[41] does not think it can be ignored. In the sufferings of Christ on the cross, Julian sees not only the revelation of divine love, but also "a figure and likeness of our foul deeds' shame that our fair, bright, blessed lord bare for our sins" (X. 23). Therefore one must hold in tension the reality of the damage inflicted by evil and God's capacity to triumph over evil through the gracious "forthspreading" (LIX. 149) of the trinitarian relations.[42] In one place, Julian describes this tension in terms of the different tasks of humanity and God with regard to sin: "it belongeth to man meekly to accuse himself, and it belongeth to the proper goodness of our lord God courteously to excuse man" (LII. 125). The lower judgement cannot simply be negated by the higher, but must be reconciled with it. The example of the lord and servant is revealed to her in answer to her question as to how these two judgements might be "saved" (XLV. 95).

As we have seen, the dual judgements are related to the dual aspects of humanity: substance and sensuality. The reconciliation of the two judgements, therefore, is inextricably bound up with the saving work of Christ revealed to Julian, by which he reunited substance to sensuality in taking our sensuality upon himself. Just as the two judgements are "accorded and oned" (XLV. 94) in heaven, so too are substance and sensuality in the incarnation: "for our nature that is the higher part is knit to God in the making; and God is knit to our nature that is the lower part in our flesh-taking; and thus in Christ our two natures are oned" (LVII. 138). This atonement involves the reunion of "inner" substance and "outer" sensuality whereby "the inward draweth the outward by grace, and both shall be oned in bliss without end by the virtue of Christ" (XIX. 43). Rather than a retreat into the interior, Julian's revelation foretells a reunion of inner and outer graphically shown in Christ's body, radically exteriorized in its opening on the cross, but which ultimately, in one of Julian's most striking images, draws the creature into his crucified side. Yet this interior of Christ's body is not an enclosed, constrained space, but "a fair delectable place, and large enough for all mankind that shall be saved to rest in peace and in love" (XXIV. 51). This blurring of interior and exterior is enacted in Julian's text by the way in which she switches between speaking about humanity's dwelling in God and God's dwelling in humanity: "Our soul is made to be God's dwelling-place, and the dwelling-place of the soul is God, which is unmade" (LIV. 130).

While the union of divinity and humanity in Christ exists eternally from God's perspective, this must never be seen as relaxing the tension by which this union is unfolded as a drama in history. Though humanity is ordained by God from eternity to be "his own city and his dwelling-place" (LI. 113) and from the eternal perspective "God is never out of the soul in which he dwelleth blissfully without end" (LV. 133), from the perspective of our sensuality the fall of Adam makes humanity "not all seemly to serve in that noble office." However, rather than abandon humanity, God waits "till what time by his grace his dearworthy Son had brought again his city into the noble fairness with his hard travail" (LI. 113). This city into which God comes to dwell in the incarnation is not simply the "higher" aspect of our humanity, but includes our sensuality: "in the self point that our soul is made sensual, in the self point is the city of God, ordained to him from without beginning; into which seat he cometh and never shall remove it" (LV. 133). The humanity that Christ redeems as God's dwelling place is a thoroughly sensual, *incorporated* humanity. In this sense, Christ's redemption of sensuality is a healing of that realm characterized by bodiliness and change and the suffering of evils—that realm that we call "history". It is in this realm that Christ comes to dwell as "highest bishop, most majestic king, most worshipful lord (LXVII. 167). The reconciliation of higher and lower judgements, of substance and sensuality, of inner and outer, involves nothing less than a healing of the rupture between eternity and history by Christ coming to dwell in that history both as the exemplary servant of God and as history's sovereign ruler.

3) The Body that Suffers Still

For Julian the lower judgement of humans passed on the basis of our sensuality is, as noted earlier, inextricably bound up with the teachings of the Church. What is at stake in the reconciliation of higher and lower judgements is not, however, a simple desire for orthodoxy. Rather, Julian believes that the teachings of the Church must be "saved" through reconciliation with God's higher judgement because it is the visible bounds of the Church that form the arena within which one lives with one's "even-christians". More than a "crust" that hardens over experience, "the common teaching of holy church" and its rituals and sacraments are for Julian the necessary "means"[43] by which one lives a common life of mutual participation in the compassion of Christ. Julian desires neither an individual relationship with God, nor a faith of her own, but rather seeks incorporation into the suffering and generative body of Christ.

While Julian's concern that her vision conform to the teachings of the Church no doubt contains some element of fear of persecution as a heretic, her primary motivation is her desire not to single herself out from the body of her even-Christians: "if I look singularly to myself I am right nought; but in general I am in hope, in oneness of charity with all mine even-christians" (IX. 20).[44] The teachings of the Church, which are "common" both in the sense of "not extraordinary" and in the sense of "shared", constitute the bond which holds that body together. It is for this reason that Julian makes strong claims for the Church:

> God shewed full great pleasance that he hath in all men and women that mightily and meekly and with all their will take the preaching and teaching of holy church; for it is his holy church; he is the ground, he is the substance, he is the teaching, he is the teacher, he is the one taught, he is the meed for which every kind soul travaileth (XXXIV. 70).[45]

Rather than being a mere "symbolic wrapping" that obscures, the Church's doctrine presents us with the God who is its "ground" and "substance".

This should not, however, be taken as the naïve claim that there is some simple relation of correspondence between doctrines and the God of whom they speak. The tension that Julian sees between the higher and lower judgements, between her revelation and the common teachings of the Church, make it clear that she is not subscribing here to any sort of doctrinal positivism, which sees God as a kind of object to which doctrines might refer. If the truth of doctrine were referential in this sense, then either Julian's revelation or the teaching of the Church would have to be wrong. But Julian quite clearly wishes to maintain the truth of both, and to understand how both are true in the eyes of God (L. 106). The complexity of this relationship, like the complexity of the relationship of substance and sensuality, provides the shape of the Body in which Christians are incorporated through imitation of Christ's compassion. Christians as a body share in the sufferings of

Christ, and, like Christ, this corporate body will not finally be overcome. In this way, the Church as Mother is the sacramental presence of Christ our Mother:

> And he willeth that we take us mightily to the faith of holy church and find there our dearworthy mother in solace of true understanding, with all the blessed common; for one single person may oftentimes be broken as it seemeth to himself, but the whole body of holy church was never broken, nor never shall be, without end. And therefore a sure thing it is, a good and a gracious, to will meekly and mightily to be sustained and oned to our mother, holy church, that is, Christ Jesus; for the food of mercy that is his dearworthy blood and precious water is plenteous to make us fair and clean. The blessed wounds of our saviour be open and enjoy to heal us; the sweet gracious hands of our mother be ready and diligently about us; for he in all this working useth the office of a kind nurse that hath nought else to do but to give heed about the salvation of her child (LXI. 154–155).

Just as Julian is given the full reality of the Godhead in the crucified Jesus, so too the crucified Jesus is given over in the teachings and sacramental life of the Church. The Church as the Body of Christ serves to extend in history the suffering love that Christ enacted in an exemplary fashion on the cross. In this sense, as the sacrament of restored human unity, the Church participates in Christ's atoning work. It is through the practice of the Christian life as presented by the Church that "we be his helpers, giving to him all our attending, learning his lores, keeping his laws, desiring that all be done that he doeth, truly trusting in him." (LVII. 140). For Julian, this atoning work entails suffering. Just as "he that is highest and worthiest was most fully made-nought and most utterly despised" (XX. 44), so too "we be all partly noughted, and we shall be noughted following our master Jesus till we be full purged" (XXVII. 56). Julian says, "God's servants, holy church, shall be shaken in sorrow and anguish and tribulation in this world as men shake a cloth in the wind" (XXVIII. 57). But this suffering, like the sufferings of Christ, is a "noughting" that makes possible compassion, a sharing in others' suffering, by freeing the self from disordered affections. The noughting of suffering has as its reverse side the noughting of compassion: "That same noughting that was shewed in his passion, it was shewed again here in this compassion" (XXVIII. 59).

Julian recounts Christ saying to her, "I shall wholly break you of your vain affections and your vicious pride; and after that I shall together gather you and make you mild and meek, clean and holy, by oneing to me" and immediately she adds, "And then I saw that each kind compassion that man hath on his even-christians with charity, it is Christ in him" (XXXVIII. 59). Just as the body of the incarnate Christ was broken so as to be raised as a body of compassion, so too God breaks Christ's body the Church, in order to regather it as a community of compassion. And this compassion is nothing less than the participation of "his body in which all his members are knit," and in which is "he is not yet fully glorified nor all impassible," in Christ's desire, his "spiritual thirst," for the salvation of humanity (XXXI. 63–64). The community of Christ's lovers must find their identity in Christ's body, which is broken and transgressed on the cross both by love and violence because *this* is the icon of God's desire by which "all shall be well." The crucified body, as the site of the encounter between our "foul black deed" (X. 24) and the infinite thirst of Christ, becomes a body whose boundaries are crossed and recrossed by the compassion of God, a yearning body that opens itself to sinners, a body in which borders become not barriers but frontiers of encounter. It is in a sense a body that has no interior, because it is at every point of its existence "exteriorized" by participation in the infinite divine compassion revealed in Christ, a compassion enacted in visible practices of forgiveness and vulnerability.

It is in this context that we might begin to think about Julian's putative "universalism". Julian realizes that her revelation that "all shall be well" seems to call into question the Church's teachings on eternal damnation, which she affirms on the basis of the "lower doom". Thus it is clear that on one level Julian does not affirm that all shall be saved.[46] Yet those who see in Julian an impulse toward universal salvation are not, I think, mistaken. Because her revelation is of a body in which the divide between interior and exterior is overcome, she offers us an image of sociality in which boundaries of exclusion and denial can only be seen as penultimate. The city of God's dwelling is ultimately a city without defensive walls, defined not by its boundaries but by the king who dwells at its center. And this king is the servant of God, who from all eternity thirsts for humanity's salvation. To claim to know with certainty the salvation of all is to claim to know too much, but to claim to know with certainty of anyone's damnation is likewise overweening: "scarcely we know of our self or of our even-christian in what way we stand" (LII. 123). What *can* be known is that God "is ground in whom our soul standeth and he is mean that keepeth the substance and the sensuality to God so that they shall never dispart" (LVI. 135).[47] By focusing upon the crucified heart of the body, Julian leaves open its boundaries.

Conclusion

The discourse of "mysticism"—by which I mean the modern discourse *about* "mystics" and not necessarily the discourse of those whom we today have named as such—may be thought of as a procedure that attempts to construct a space that is protected from the necessary coercion and violence that characterizes "politics". There is a certain sense in which the two categories, in their modern construal, are parasitic upon each other. Mysticism becomes a way of locating a haven in a heartless world, the invulnerable space of interiority that makes tolerable the apparatus of the modern state. In providing a space for retreat, it serves to "secularize" the political, which in fact means to remove it from the sway of Christ's reign, leaving it to be ruled by other gods.

Mysticism is thus the refuge into which we recoil as we become progressively disillusioned by the various "external, socially oriented ideologies" of modernity. However, if I am correct in the reading of Julian of Norwich sketched here, she provides a vision that is both "external" and "socially oriented". *A Revelation of Love* is Julian's rendering of God's invitation to enter into Christ's crucified side, an invitation made to all of God's lovers, an invitation to be broken and regathered into union with God, to become the city in which Christ may reign. Salvation appears as the incorporation of humanity into a new polity, initiated by Christ's self-gift upon the cross and defined by practices which respond to that gift by reenacting it: feeding the hungry, giving drink to the thirsty, welcoming the stranger, clothing the naked, caring for the sick, visiting the imprisoned. As such, salvation is a task to be accomplished in history through the participatory *mimesis* of Christ's compassion, which reveals in history the perfect sociality of the Father's love for the Son in the Spirit.

Perhaps at least in part Julian's modern appeal is *not* the perennial appeal of an unincorporated mysticism, but the appeal of Christ's invitation to discipleship through incorporation into his body. For those today who resist being immured in the anchorhold of the self, what Julian presents is a sociality eternally realized in the mutual indwelling of the Godhead but which is yet to reach its completion in history by the Church's repetition of Christ's exemplary enactment of it upon the cross. A pilgrim city whose boundaries are always frontiers and never walls, the Body of Christ treads the path of his compassion through suffering to glory. It is this Body that Christ offers us in Julian's revelation, and that we are invited to perform.[48]

NOTES

1 Luigi Sturzo, *The True Life: Sociology of the Supernatural*, Barbara Barclay Carter, trans. (London: Geoffrey Bles, 1947), p. 40.

2 Julian herself seems never to have given a title to her book, and it is referred to by various names. I will refer to it as "A Revelation of Love," in part because this is how Julian herself characterizes the work at the outset of the first chapter of the long text: "This is a revelation of love ..."

3 Edward Stillingfleet, *A Discourse Concerning the Idolatry Practiced in the Church of Rome and the Hazzard [sic] of Salvation in the Communion of it: In Answer to Some Papers of a Revolted Protestant. Wherein a Particular Account is Given of the Fanaticisms and Divisions of the Church*, 2nd ed. (London, 1672), p. 224.

4 *Ibid.*, p. 226.

5 For a bibliography of editions and translations up to the year 1984, see Christina von Nolcken, "Julian of Norwich," in *Middle English Prose: A Critical Guide to Major Authors and Genres*, A. S. G. Edwards, ed. (New Brunswick, NJ: Rutgers University Press, 1984). Since then, Georgia Ronan Crampton has edited a students' text for the Consortium for the

Teaching of the Middle Ages, *The Shewings of Julian of Norwich* (Kalamazoo, MI: Medieval Institute Publications, 1993) and at least two modernizations have appeared: M. L. Del Mastro, *The Revelation of Divine Love in Sixteen Showings: Made to Dame Julian of Norwich* (Tarrytown, NY: Triumph Books: 1994) and Father John-Julian, O.J.N., *A Lesson of Love: The Revelations of Julian of Norwich* (New York: Walker, 1988).

6   Chapter LXXXVI, p. 202. Unless otherwise noted, quotations are taken from *Revelations of Divine Love, Recorded by Julian, Anchoress at Norwich, Anno Domini 1373*, Grace Warrack, ed. (London: Methuen and Co., 1901). Further citations will be made in the text with a Roman numeral indicating the chapter, followed by a period and an Arabic numeral indicating the page number in Warrack's edition. Warrack's modernization is on the whole quite judicious, keeping as close to the language of the Sloane manuscript as possible, while making the changes necessary to make the text comprehensible to a modern reader unfamiliar with Middle English. I have in most instances omitted Warrack's bracketed explanatory expansions, so as to preserve fruitful ambiguities in the text. Warrack also tends to capitalize terms that the manuscript leaves uncapitalized; therefore I have changed capitalization and punctuation to conform to Marion Glasscoe's edition of Sloane MS 2499, *A Revelation of Love*, 3rd rev. ed. (Exeter: University of Exeter Press, 1993). I will note any other deviations I make from Warrack's rendering. Quotations from Julian's original Middle English are taken, unless otherwise noted, from Glasscoe's edition. They shall be cited with an Arabic numeral indicating the chapter, followed by a period and an Arabic numeral indicating the page in Glasscoe's edition. Readers might note that pagination in the third edition differs from earlier editions.

7   On the dating of these texts, see Nicholas Watson, "The Composition of Julian of Norwich's *Revelation of Love*," *Speculum* 68 (July, 1993).

8   The dates of 1393 and 1416 are taken from wills that mention Julian, which are described in Colledge and Walsh's edition of the "Paris" manuscript (Bibliothèque Nationale MS Fonds anglais 40), *A Book of Showings to the Anchoress Julian of Norwich* (Toronto: Pontifical Institute of Medieval Studies, 1978), pp. 33–35. Our witness to Julian as spiritual counselor is the always provocative Margery Kempe. See *The Book of Margery Kempe*, Sanford Brown Meech and Hope Emily Allen, eds. (Oxford: Oxford University Press, 1940), pp. 42–43.

9   Arthur Edward Waite, *Studies in Mysticism and Certain Aspects of the Secret Tradition* (London: Hodder and Stoughton, 1906), p. 10.

10 Waite, *Studies in Mysticism*, p. 51.

11 A notable exception in this regard is Friedreich von Hügel who, while appreciative of much of William James' work, was critical of his neglect of the institutional aspect of religion. See James Luther Adams, "Letter from Friedreich von Hügel to William James," *The Downside Review* 98 (July 1980), pp. 214–236.

12 William James, *The Varieties of Religious Experience* [1902] (New York: New American Library, 1958), p. 380.

13 Evelyn Underhill, letter of November 4, 1908 to Margaret Robinson, quoted in Christopher J. R. Armstrong, *Evelyn Underhill: An Introduction to her Life and Writings* (Grand Rapids, MI: William B. Eerdmans Publishing Company, 1975), p. 104.

14 See Christopher Armstrong, *Evelyn Underhill*, pp. 134–135.

15 Robert Thouless, *The Lady Julian: A Psychological Study* (London: S.P.C.K., 1924), p. 19. Subsequent references in the text.

16 Karen Armstrong, *Visions of God: Four Medieval Mystics and Their Writings* (New York: Bantam Books, 1994), p. vii. Subsequent references in the text.

17 For example, she describes Julian's visionary experience as occurring "in about 1372" (p. 174) while Julian clearly dates it to May, 1373 (II. 3). Likewise, she says that Julian's sixteenth revelation took place "in a dream" (p. 174). Julian clearly states that while she experienced a demonic attack during a dream, she was awake for the final revelation (LXVI. 166).

18 James, *Varieties*, p. 292.

19 See Caroline Walker Bynum's now classic *Holy Feast and Holy Fast: The Religious Significance of Food to Medieval Women* (Berkeley CA: University of California Press, 1987) and the essays collected in *Fragmentation and Redemption: Essays on Gender and the Human Body in Medieval Religion* (New York: Zone Books, 1991).

20   "The Female Body and Religious Practice in the Later Middle Ages," in *Fragmentation and Redemption*, p. 194.

21   For some reason, Warrack reads "Master" for "maker".

22   The Middle English word "kynde" has the sense both of the modern meaning of "kind"—affectionate or loving—as well as the meaning of the modern word "nature" or "natural". Thus in Julian's usage "unkynde" could mean either "cruel" or "unnatural", or could possibly carry both meanings, as when she says that "as sothly as synne is onclene, as soth[l]y is it onkinde" (63.103). One might note that Warrack modernizes this "as verily as sin is unclean, so verily is it unnatural," making a clear interpretive choice. In the present case, the meaning is ambiguous. Colledge and Walsh translate it as "the compassion which I thought a loving soul could have for our Lord Jesus" (*Julian of Norwich: Showings*, Edmund Colledge and James Walsh, trans. [New York: Paulist Press, 1978], p. 181) while Clifton Wolters has "Such compassion as a soul would naturally have for our Lord Jesus" (*Revelations of Divine Love* [Hardmondsworth: Penguin Books, 1966], p. 66).

23   Warrack reads "everlasting love and …" for "everlasting lover."

24   For a brief overview of the motif of the Charter of Christ, see Miri Rubin, *Corpus Christi: The Eucharist in Late Medieval Culture* (Cambridge: Cambridge University Press, 1991), pp. 306–308.

25   *Fasciculus Morum: A Fourteenth-Century Preacher's Handbook*, Siegfried Wenzel, ed. and trans. (University Park: The Pennsylvania State University Press, 1989), p. 213.

26   Richard Rolle, *Meditations on the Passion* (Longer Meditations) in *Richard Rolle: The English Writings*, Rosmund Allen, ed. and trans. (New York: Paulist Press, 1988), p. 114.

27   Nicholas Watson, "The Trinitarian Hermeneutic in Julian of Norwich's *Revelation of Love*" in *The Medieval Mystical Tradition in England: Exeter Symposium V*, Marion Glasscoe, ed. (Cambridge: D. S. Brewer, 1992), p. 84.

28   *Ibid.*, p. 93.

29   Vincent Gillespie and Maggie Ross, "The Apophatic Image: the Poetics of Effacement in Julian of Norwich," in *The Medieval Mystical Tradition in England*, p. 68. Cf. Denys Turner, *The Darkness of God: Negativity in Christian Mysticism* (Cambridge: Cambridge University Press, 1995), where he notes that the "unknowability of God is approached through the 'excessive' variety of our language of the Trinity which bursts its own bounds in a kind of self-negating prolixity" (p. 257).

30   See Augustine, *De Trinitate*, Book 12 for the *locus classicus* of this distinction.

31   Walter Hilton, *The Scale of Perfection*, J. P. H. Clark and Rosemary Doward, trans. (New York: Paulist Press, 1991), pp. 213–214.

32   For a comparison of Hilton and Julian on this point, see Tarjei Park, "Reflecting Christ: The Role of Flesh in Walter Hilton and Julian of Norwich," in *The Medieval Mystical Tradition*, pp. 17–37.

33   For a highly intelligent discussion of this passage, see Turner, *The Darkness of God*, pp. 159–162. He points out that in Julian's case, "[l]anguage fails to mark the distinction [between created and uncreated] not because there is none but because the gulf is too wide" (p. 161).

34   Nancy Coiner, "The 'Homely' and the *Heimlich*: The Hidden, Doubled Self in Julian of Norwich's Showings," *Exemplaria* 5.2 (Fall, 1993), p. 311.

35   Warrack has "Clarity" here, though Glasscoe, Crampton, and Colledge and Walsh all read the manuscript as "Charity".

36   She makes this point often, e.g. XXXIII. 68, XLII. 88, LXI. 154.

37   This term means "reconciled", though the soteriological overtones of "saved" are appropriate.

38   Sloane MS 2499, from which Warrack's version is taken, reads "stonding his grete and his own worship," while the so-called Paris manuscript reads "standyng his grett goodnes and his owne wurschyppe" (Colledge and Walsh, *A Book of Showings*, p. 518). The Paris manuscript seems the better reading in this case.

39   The contrast between what Julian sees and the standard medieval account can be seen by a comparison with Anselm's *Cur Deus Homo?*, 1.24, in which Anselm also uses the example of a lord who sends a servant out on a task, whereupon the servant falls into a pit and cannot arise. However in Anselm's version the servant had been warned about the pit and thus is without excuse before the lord. For a comparison of Julian and Anselm, see Joan

Nuth, "Two Medieval Soteriologies: Anselm of Canterbury and Julian of Norwich," *Theological Studies* 53 (1992), pp. 611–645.

40   Augustine, *Confessions* 8.8.19, Henry Chadwick, trans. (Oxford: Oxford University Press, 1991), p. 147.

41   She writes, "I believe it hath no manner of substance nor no part of being" (XXVII. 56).

42   Colledge and Walsh note that Julian uses the word "forthspreading" as a translation of the Latin term *circumsessio*, which is the technical term describing the mutual indwelling of the persons of the Trinity. See *A Book of Showings*, pp. 157–158.

43   See Julian's discussion of "means" in Chapter VI.

44   Warrack reads, "in general I am, I hope ..."

45   The Paris manuscript presents an even stronger claim. Where Sloane 2499 reads "it is his Holy Church," Paris reads "he it is, holy chyrch" (*A Book of Showings*, p. 431). Also, following Paris, Warrack reads "He is the end," whereas Glasscoe's edition of 2499 reads "he is the leryd" (34.47), which I have rendered as "he is the one taught." This text is a point of controversy between advocates for the two different textual traditions. For Glasscoe's defense of "leryd" see "Visions and Revisions: A Further Look at the Manuscripts of Julian of Norwich," *Studies in Bibliography* 42 (1989), p. 117.

46   For a discussion of Julian's "universalism", see Barbara Newman, *From Virile Woman to WomanChrist: Studies in Medieval Religion and Literature* (Philadelphia: University of Pennsylvania Press, 1995), pp. 130–133.

47   Warrack, following Paris, reads "together" for "to God".

48   My thanks to William Cavanaugh and Angela Russell Christman for their comments on an earlier draft of this essay.

"A CHRISTIAN, HOLY PEOPLE" MARTIN LUTHER ON SALVATION AND THE CHURCH

DAVID S. YEAGO

Introduction

Until fairly recently, most Protestants had little doubt about the central significance of Martin Luther for the relationship of spirituality and politics, faith and community: his great achievement, it was agreed, was to have *separated* them, to have *liberated* spirituality and faith from dependence on community in the form of the Roman Church and the pretensions of its priesthood. As Karl Heim put it, in a work written in 1929 but translated into English as recently as 1963, it is the first principle of Protestantism that we can find God "only in a spiritual act that occurs in deep solitude and with full mental clarity."[1] Thus no mystic raptures and no mediating priesthood, only the sober inwardness of the Protestant conscience, "entirely alone with Christ."[2]

In this, Heim was simply restating the universally shared consensus of Protestant modernity, formulated inimitably by Hegel: for the Reformation, each person "has to accomplish the work of reconciliation in his own soul. Subjective Spirit has to receive the Spirit of Truth into itself, and give it a dwelling-place there. Thus that absolute inwardness of soul which pertains to religion itself, and Freedom in the Church are both secured."[3] Likewise, Protestant modernism's other great founder, Friedrich Schleiermacher, wrote that

> the antithesis between Protestantism and Catholicism may provisionally
> be conceived thus: the former makes the individual's relation to the

Dr. David S. Yeago
Lutheran Theological Southern Seminary, Columbia, SC 29203, USA.

Church dependent on his relation to Christ, while the latter makes his relation to Christ dependent on his relation to the Church.[4]

This view continues to be both widely shared and ecumenically powerful; for example, in a controversial interview given during the Luther-anniversary of 1983, published under the title "Luther and the Unity of the Churches," Cardinal Ratzinger summed up Luther's fundamental divergence from Catholicism thus:

> ... in Luther's view faith is no longer, as it is for Catholics, of its essence a sharing of faith with the entire Church; for him at least the Church can neither assume the guarantee of certainty for one's personal salvation nor decide in a definitively binding manner about the content of faith. For Catholics on the contrary the Church itself is contained in the inmost principle of the act of faith; it is only by sharing in faith with the Church that I have a part in that certainty on which I can base my life.[5]

Thus interpreted, Luther seems an obvious spiritual ancestor of *Habits of the Heart*'s "Nan Pfautz", who says: "I believe I have a commitment to God which is beyond church. I felt my relationship to God was O.K. when I wasn't with the church."[6] Communal involvement is thus not constitutive of faith, but subsequent to it; faith is *expressed* by commitment to "an association of loving individuals."[7] Compare Wilhelm Pauck's defensive insistence that Luther: "did not speak as an individualist when he emphasized the personal character of the Christian life. What he taught was that, *though one becomes a Christian only in the secrecy of his own personal encounter with God in Christ*, the Christian life is never a life of self-secluded isolation but always one of fellowship and mutual self-giving love: to be a Christian and to be in the church, the community of believers, is one and the same."[8] In some such way, one supposes, "Nan Pfautz" might respond to her classification as a religious individualist by Bellah and his colleagues: by confusing the description with an accusation of selfishness and moving rather rapidly past the fundamental point, that relationship with God is constituted strictly apart from relationship to any particular community.

It is just from this point, of course, that a good many contemporary second thoughts take wing. We are uncomfortably aware today of the degree to which the doughty Protestant individualists of days gone by were formed by strong ecclesial communities which the ideology of Protestant individualism does little to sustain. More than that, however, we have been afflicted with doubts about the whole "Protestant" sensibility described so uncompromisingly by Stephen Ozment:

> Now, as then, Protestants are society's most spiritually defiant and venturesome citizens. When it comes to making their spiritual and moral lives whole, they have not hesitated to sacrifice institutions to conscience, unity to efficiency, and obedience to results ... In the quest for a

religious life that works, they unhesitatingly change churches and denominations, shedding the spiritual truths of yesterday as if they were just another bad investment or failed love affair. No other modern religious communion is marked by such variety and mobility.[9]

Unsettled by communitarian sentiment, we ask: do we really want to be like that? Or, granted that we Protestants generally *are* a lot like that, should we be? Is it really desirable to be the sort of person who will *unhesitatingly* sacrifice to private conscience the institutions which order and sustain life for thousands of one's fellows? The sort of person for whom unity, and therefore the labor of living in communion with others, is strictly secondary to "efficiency", that is, to "what works for me"? Is it not perhaps just a little sinister when Ozment describes Protestant spiritual "variety and mobility" by evoking in one breath the fluidity of the capitalist marketplace and the inconstancy of Don Juan? In contrast to the robust individualism of our forebears, "we brighten," as Jean Bethke Elshtain has said in another context, "to tales of community, especially if the talk is soothing and doesn't demand very much from us." But the old paradigms retain their power in the absence of concrete alternatives, and so "when discussion turns to institutions and the need to sustain authoritative institutions of all kinds ... attention withers and a certain sourness sets in."[10]

Ozment's *Protestants* describes what came of the Reformation as a social movement, the style and temper of spirit formed above all by the overwhelming *disillusionment* experienced by those who came to believe that they had been bamboozled by the most venerable institution in their world. On his reading, it is as though the *theology* of the Reformers was efficacious among their constituents only as it was configured around this powerful experience of rejection, of "principled flight from people they believed had deceived and deluded them."[11] It may indeed be the case that nothing Luther *said* about the church and its role in the ways of God had any hope of achieving anything like the cultural potency of the sheer *fact* of his repudiation of the Roman Church, for all practical purposes the only "church" the western European population had ever known. But it may nonetheless be worthwhile to recall that the "Protestant" temperament as Ozment describes it is by no means what Luther (or for that matter, Calvin) set out to create. As we struggle with the long-term effects of the "revolution" he may have initiated, we may find more to aid us in Luther's theological legacy than in his historical achievement, in what he said as distinguished from what he helped to bring about.

Indeed, we need badly to learn to read all the Reformers, and especially Luther, as creative theologians of the later middle ages, theologians who in important ways had more in common with the tradition they so bitterly criticized than they do with us, the inheritors of the world they inadvertently made. It is the coexistence in their thought of what seems typically

Protestant or modern or "reforming" with elements that bind them to a
tradition from which we have become estranged that promises to show us
ways forward, possibilities other than those represented by Cardinal Ratzinger (in his more austere recent pronouncements) and "Nan Pfautz". This
means, paradoxically, that Luther—like other witnesses of the tradition—
says most to us when we allow him to be a theologian of his day, not ours,
one who is not out to found our culture or solve our problems but to speak
out of late medieval assumptions to late medieval issues.

The rest of this paper will reconsider Luther's theology of the church, and
particularly the relationship of the church to justification and faith. It is
written in the light of recent ecumenical conversation on this theme, especially the remarkable convergence achieved in the recent report of the International Lutheran-Roman Catholic Joint Commission, *Church and Justification*.
In chapter 4 of that report, the church is presented as both "recipient and
mediator of salvation":

> A comparison of Lutheran and Catholic views of the church cannot dis-
> regard the fact that there are two fundamentally inseparable aspects of
> being church: on the one hand the church is the place of God's saving
> activity (the church as an assembly, as the recipient of salvation) and on
> the other hand it is God's instrument (the church as ambassador, as
> mediator of salvation). But it is one and the same church which we speak
> of as the recipient and mediator of salvation.[12]

In light of the consensus just evoked, the Joint Commission's use of the
language of "mediating salvation" in a *common* Lutheran-Roman Catholic
statement about the church is extraordinarily provocative, however hesit-
antly it is worked out in the document as a whole. Is this simply more evidence of a Protestant failure of nerve, of the cultural exhaustion of Protestant
individualism, or is there a coherent way to say this, perhaps even a *necessity*
to say this, in light of the core theological concerns of the Reformation?

To explore these questions, I shall look first at the very idea of "the
church" in Luther's thought: to what, most basically, does he take the word
to refer? Then we will consider briefly the vexed question of the relation
between ordained ministry and the so-called "universal priesthood"; this is
important for our present purposes because it forces us to consider Luther's
account of the church as a concrete, ordered, "political" community. Finally,
we will address directly the relationship between church and justification.

The "Spiritual Church" in the Early Luther

How does the church figure in Luther's theology? To begin with, I believe,
we must reckon with a genuine development in the clarity, if not the substance, of his ecclesiological thinking. In two early polemical writings
(1520/1521), *On the Papacy at Rome* and *Against Ambrosius Catharinus*, Luther

speaks of the church as essentially a "gathering of souls in one faith," as a "spiritual, inward unity" which is, as such, *invisible*. In the treatise *On the Papacy*, he goes so far as to speak of *two churches*: the first, which is "natural, basic, essential, and true" is a "spiritual, inward Christian people"; the latter, which is "artificial and external" (*gemacht und eusserlich*) is a bodily, external Christian people.[13]

This apparent ecclesiological dualism, which seems to deny concrete presence in history to the true church, has been an ecclesiological and ecumenical stone of stumbling from that day to this. Some Lutherans, especially in the 19th century, have seized on it as the basic principle of a true Protestant ecclesiology, while to others it has been a source of acute embarrassment. Ecumenically-minded scholars have pointed out how Luther goes on to make more complex this apparently simple dualistic picture: he insists that the "two churches" should not be separated from one another, and he goes on to talk about the "signs" of the true, inward church, which are unmistakably *external* and *public*: the word, baptism, the bread of the supper. It has likewise often been pointed out that after 1521, Luther seldom if ever talks in quite this way again.

All this is important, but there may be something more to be said. In these early works, I would suggest, Luther has let his opponents set the terms of the debate; this is why he finds himself pressed into an initial dualistic posture which he must then somewhat laboriously complicate and qualify in order to say what is important to him. In later writings, when he is free to develop ecclesiological themes on his own terms, we hear no more of the invisible church or the two churches. Furthermore, I want to argue that the definition of the church as a "spiritual, inward unity" is unsatisfactory *on Luther's own terms*; his own theological principles give him good reasons to proceed differently.

The great Roman Catholic ecumenist and ecclesiologist Yves Congar has argued, in a number of works, that the late middle ages typically thought of the church as the worldwide society of the faithful, united in a sacred institutional structure under the governance of the Pope.[14] This was the ecclesiology Luther encountered in his opponents; thus the first of them, Sylvester Prieras, who played a fateful role in fixing Luther's image of Roman theology:

> Essentially the universal church is the gathering of all believers in Christ for God's worship. But virtually the universal church is the Roman church, the head of all churches, and the supreme pontiff. Representatively the Roman church is the college of cardinals, but virtually it is the supreme pontiff, who is the head of the church, although in a different way than Christ.[15]

In the polemical writings of 1520/1521, I would suggest, Luther has accepted this framework from his opponents and then struggles to say what is important to him within it. He wants first to reject the identification of the church with its institutional regimen; in his view, this secularizes the church, diminishes its mystery, reducing it to the level of one worldly polity among others. And of course he wants particularly to deny the implication that for all practical purposes the Roman church *is* the universal church, with the Pope being, for all practical purposes, the Roman church. But within this late medieval pattern of thought, if the papacy is removed from the picture, what is left is Prieras's "essential" universal church (notice that Luther uses the same terms), the universal company of the faithful; and since the faith of the faithful is inward, spiritual, and invisible, that leaves Luther with a spiritual, invisible church.

But this is a bad theological situation for Luther to find himself in, on his own theological terms. In Luther's theology, that which is inward and spiritual can never stand on its own, and can never be approached theologically on its own. Inward and spiritual gifts and graces come to us *only through God's bodily, sacramental word* and can only be understood in their union with the outward word. As Luther was to write five years later:

> Now that God has let his holy gospel go forth, he deals with us in two ways: on the one hand, outwardly, on the other hand, inwardly. Outwardly he deals with us through the oral word of the gospel and through bodily signs, such as baptism and the sacrament. Inwardly he deals with us through the Holy Spirit and faith along with other gifts. But all this in such measure and in such order that the outward elements should and must come first. And the inward things come afterwards and by means of the outward, for he has decided to give the inward element to no one except by means of the outward element. For he will give no one the Spirit or faith without the outward word and sign which he has instituted ...[16]

The ecclesiology of the early polemical writings does not exactly *deny* this, but it goes at the matter backwards: it begins with an inward, spiritual church and then complicates the picture by reference to the external word and sign. What Luther needs, though, is an ecclesiology that *begins* with outward, sacramental practice ("the outward elements should and must come first") and apprehends the inward, spiritual reality of the church in its living unity with, and dependence on, the public epiphany of God's grace in the oral word and bodily sign.

We can get some sense of what this might mean by thinking a bit further about the views of Luther's opponents. When we encounter an ecclesiology like that of Sylvester Prieras, what probably strikes even Roman Catholics is its pronounced juridicism and papalism. But there is another point which is perhaps even more important: such ecclesiologies simply leave out the *local* church, the concrete worshipping assembly which gathers to celebrate the Eucharist. The church is seen as a worldwide collection of believing individuals within an overarching legal structure; despite, for example, Prieras's mention of worship, the fact that these believers belong to particular *local* worshipping communities presided over by bishops and pastors plays no role at all in the definition of the church. This is in sharp contrast, as Congar has pointed out, to the ecclesiological thinking of the Fathers, for whom the eucharistic assembly is nearly always the focal point for reflection on the church.

Luther's own theological priorities might be expected to press him in the direction of this more ancient, patristic ecclesiology, which is, of course, also dominant in recent ecumenical ecclesiology. Luther's theological axiom, that *the inward follows the outward*, that spiritual grace is inseparable from and dependent for its presence on the bodily and sacramental, seems by its own logic to call for a primary identification of the church as *the concrete worshipping community*, whose inward unity in faith and the Spirit is constituted precisely *in and through* its public sacramental practice.

The Gathered People in the Mature Luther

A look at Luther's most extensive later treatment of ecclesiology, in the third part of his 1539 treatise *On the Councils and the Church*, will show that his thought did in fact develop in just that direction. As he almost invariably does, Luther appeals first to the Apostles Creed for a definition of the church: "We want to stick simply with the children's creed, which says: *I believe one holy Christian church, the communion of saints.* Here the creed explains clearly what the church is, a communion of saints, that is, a multitude or gathering of people who are Christians and holy ..."[17] But on this occasion, Luther further unpacks this standard short definition, appealing to the meaning of *ekklesia* in secular Greek:

> For in Acts 19, the town clerk uses the word *ekklesia* to mean the assembly or people which had gathered in the marketplace, and says: 'It must be settled in the regular assembly.' And again: 'When he had said this, he dismissed the assembly.' In this and other passages, *ekklesia* or church means nothing else than a gathered people (*ein versamlet Volck*), although they were of course heathen and not Christians, just as town councilmen summon their assembly at the town hall. Now there are in the world many different peoples, but the Christians are a specially called people (*ein besonder beruffen Volck*) and so are called not sim-ply *ekklesia*, church, or people, but rather *sancta Catholica Christiana*, a Christian holy people, which believes in Christ. Therefore it is called a Christian people, and has the Holy Spirit, which sanctifies them daily, not only through the forgiveness of sins which Christ has won for them (as the Antinomians stupidly believe) but also through the putting-off, purging, and putting-to-death of sins, from which they are called a holy people.[18]

One can see clearly here how the logic of Luther's view of the right ordering of the inward and the outward has reshaped the structure of his ecclesiology. Here the starting-point is not the inward and spiritual, but the outward and public: the church is *ekklesia*, an assembly, "a gathered people," an essentially *public* phenomenon, therefore, just as public and bodily as a town meeting. The uniqueness of the church is not secured by making the "real" church something invisible and disembodied; rather, the church is distinctive on account of the particular *character* of its public gathering. The church is a "specially called people," a people summoned together not by a town council but by the holy gospel of Christ. It is this special calling, this unique summons, that constitutes *this* public assembly, this gathered people, as something singular and unprecedented among all the peoples of the world; it is the assembly or people which believes in Christ and has the Holy Spirit. The inward is given through the outward: it is by virtue of its distinctive character *as* a bodily, public assembly that this community is endowed with these inward, spiritual blessings.

According to Luther, the Creed teaches us that a "Christian holy people" in this precise sense "must exist and abide on earth until the world's end …"[19] The church actually exists; it is not a Platonic republic or an utopia, but a concretely and continuously existing human community, which will always be present on this earth until the last day. This is an article of faith, for Christ has promised the church, "I am with you always until the end of the world" (Matthew 28:20). But as Luther has pointed out, there are a great many different peoples in the world, and more than one of them claims to be the Christian holy people, the church. How then do we *identify* the church amongst all the peoples of the world? Or as Luther puts it, "How can a poor confused person tell where this Christian holy people is in the world?"[20]

Luther's answer is that we identify the church by its *public practices*, the distinctive practices that make it a distinctive public phenomenon. Where you see a people, an assembly, whose life as a people is constituted by these distinctive practices, there you see the Christian holy people, the church. Luther lists seven such practices:

—First and foremost, the Christian people is the people which has *the holy Word of God*. Luther means by this the public proclamation of the gospel of Christ: "We are talking about the outward word, orally preached by human beings like you and me. Christ has left this behind as an outward sign by which one is to recognize his church or his Christian holy people in the world."[21] Interestingly, Luther explicitly recognizes that the word of God is preached with more or less purity among different groups of Christians.[22] Of course, it is better to have pure doctrine, but here Luther is saying simply that we know the church by the public proclamation of something *recognizable* as the gospel of Christ.

—The second and third distinctive practices are *baptism and the sacrament of the altar*. Where these rites are taught, believed, and celebrated according to Christ's institution, there is the Christian holy people, the church of Christ.

—The fourth distinctive practice is *the public exercise of the Keys*, as Christ teaches in Matthew 18. Luther is not simply talking about private absolution as a means of pastoral care, but very explicitly about *church discipline*, the exclusion of unrepentant public sinners from the assembly and their readmission upon confession and amendment of life. Thus understood, the exercise of the keys is a means which the Holy Spirit uses to "sanctify fallen sinners once again" but also a practice by which "Christians confess that they are a holy people under the rule of Christ in this world: those who refuse to be converted and let themselves be sanctified again are cast out from this holy people and excluded through the keys ..."[23]

—The fifth practice which constitutes the church is *the consecration or calling of ministers*. Luther speaks rather more plainly about this than we may expect: "For there must be bishops, pastors, or preachers who publicly and privately give, offer, and exercise the four elements or holy things just mentioned, for the sake of and in the name of the church, but much more on account of Christ's institution ..."[24] Luther gets sidetracked into a long discussion of clerical celibacy, but then concludes: "Where you see such offices or officeholders, know that the holy Christian people must be there, for the church cannot exist without such bishops, pastors, preachers, and priests, and in turn they cannot exist without the church: they must be together with one another."[25]

—The sixth practice is *liturgical prayer*, "praising and thanking God publicly."[26] The church is the assembly that invokes God publicly in prayer and song and hymn, with the Lord's Prayer and the psalms. Interestingly, Luther includes the public proclamation of the creed and the ten commandments in this practice of public praise, doubtless because his central thought is that the holy Christian people *confesses and honors God* in its public worship.

—The seventh practice is that of *bearing the holy cross*: the church as a people is characterized by suffering and persecution in the world. What Luther is talking about here is the public commitment of the church *as a community* to the *sole lordship* of Christ; the sufferings of Christians come upon them, he says, "not because they are adulterers, murderers, thieves, or scoundrels, but because they want to have Christ alone and no other God."[27] Thus here too Luther is talking about public, communal practice: the church is that people among all the peoples of the earth which worships and obeys no other God besides the one proclaimed in the gospel of Christ, and this brings the holy Christian people into conflict with the nations and their gods.

These seven public practices are what distinguish the church, according to Luther, from every other people on earth; we believe, as an article of our faith, that this community, this assembly, whose public common life is shaped in this distinctive way, will exist continuously in the world until the last day.

But for Luther, these practices not only *identify* the church, they *constitute* it *as* church, as the holy Christian people. Luther speaks of these seven practices as *Heilthümer*, perhaps best translated as "holy things." But there is an untranslatable play on words here: *Heilthum* is the usual word for one of the miracle-working relics which played such a large role in medieval piety. Luther is saying, in effect, that these seven practices are the true "miracle-working holy things" through which the Holy Spirit fashions a holy people in the world. The holiness of the church is not merely a matter of a purely forensic imputation to Christians of the holiness of Christ (in this treatise, Luther explicitly ascribes that view to the Antinomian heretics); the church is sanctified by the holy practices which make up its common life, through which practices the inward gifts of faith and the Holy Spirit are bestowed on the gathered people.

Furthermore, these holy practices which constitute and sanctify, and *therefore* identify, the church, are all in one way or another related to public worship, to the liturgy. The proclamation of the word of God, the celebration of baptism and the eucharist, and the public praise of God are all themselves liturgical acts; the office of ministry is essentially an office of liturgical presidency; the public exercise of the keys excludes hard-hearted sinners from the eucharist and readmits the penitent; the cross is imposed on the church precisely because of the exclusive loyalty to Christ confessed and enacted in its practices of worship.

In conceiving of the church in this way, I would suggest, Luther has recovered, in his own time and in his own idiom, essential elements of the ecclesiological vision of the Fathers as described by Yves Congar: "It is the local ecclesial community, it is rather, more precisely, its cultic, eucharistic life, which is the immediate given of Christian experience."[28] Luther's theology of the church, like the ecclesiology of the Fathers, has this primary datum of Christian ecclesial experience as its focal point and living heart. As the Roman Catholic liturgical scholar Reinhard Messner has written, for Luther, the gathering for worship "*is* the essence of the church" and the church can be defined as "*the assembly which celebrates the liturgy.*"[29]

Common Priesthood and Ordained Ministry

I want now to take a look at Luther's account of the relationship between ordained ministry and the common priesthood of the faithful, a much-debated topic in ecumenical theology and Luther studies. I want to suggest that Luther's views can only be understood in light of his understanding of the church as liturgical assembly, the holy Christian people sanctified by the outward, bodily signs and practices through which faith and the Holy Spirit are bestowed. This will prove, I believe, a valuable bridge to a closing discussion of justification and church. I will draw chiefly from his 1523 essay

On the Appointment of Ministers in the Church, addressed to the Hussites in Bohemia.[30]

It has sometimes been claimed that Luther *derived* the ordained ministry from what is usually called the *universal priesthood of all believers* as a matter of merely pragmatic necessity. Every baptized person is already, in principle, "ordained" and has a right to do all that a pastor does, but since it would cause confusion for everyone to perform these tasks at once, congregations of believers delegate some of their prerogatives to one of their number, and this delegation, rather than any divine institution, is what founds the ministry.

This is a gross distortion of Luther's actual view; it proceeds from two basic misunderstandings. In the first place, it misinterprets Luther's doctrine of the common priesthood in an individualistic fashion. It is not Luther's teaching that each Christian *individually* is a priest and holds priestly authority *as his or her private property*. Rather, he teaches that *the holy Christian people*, the worshipping assembly, shares in the priesthood and therefore the authority of Christ because it is united with Christ.

Thus the notion of the common priesthood is based, for Luther, on the doctrine that the church, the holy Christian people, is the body of Christ. Thus Luther writes:

> Therefore we are priests, just as he is, sons just as he is; kings just as he is. For he has made us to sit with him in the heavenly places, that we may be companions and co-heirs with him, in whom and with whom all things are given us. And there are many such statements by which we are said to be one with Christ, one bread, one cup, one body, members of his body, one flesh, bone of his bone, and to have all things in common with him.[31]

This corporate unity of the church with Christ is the ground for what Luther calls the *sacerdotium commune* or *gemeine Priestertum*, which might be best be translated *the communal priesthood*. The "offices of priesthood," which are substantially identical with the "holy things" in *On the Councils and the Church*, the holy practices which sanctify the church, are entrusted to the church *as a community*, as a corporate body gathered in Christ. The holy practices which we have discussed are, so to speak, the "community property" of the holy Christian people, not the property of any individual or group. We must remember that medieval property law, on which Luther often draws conceptually to explain this point, was not dominated, as our thinking is, by the norm of private ownership; communal property, for example common lands which belonged to no one individually but rather to a village corporately, was a well-known phenomenon.[32]

Thus when Luther writes that Christians generally have a *communio iuris*, a communion or community of right, with respect to the holy things which sanctify the church, the conclusion he draws from this is precisely that therefore *no one* possesses them individually. "For since all these things are the communal property of all Christians ... therefore it is illicit for any one to stand forth on his or her own authority and seize for him- or herself alone what belongs to all."[33] It should be clear that when Luther says that the priestly offices, the holy practices which sanctify the church, are the property "of all Christians," this means *of all Christians corporately* not *of each Christian individually*. This *communio iuris* of the whole church is, according to Luther, what makes sense of the special ministry: this makes it necessary "that one person, or however many are pleasing to the community, be chosen and received, who are to exercise these offices publicly in the stead and name of all who have the same *jus* ..."[34]

Does this mean that Luther bases the ordained ministry exclusively on the practical necessities of communal life and not on divine institution? The misunderstanding here lies in the peculiar assumption that communal necessity and divine institution are mutually exclusive; for Luther, the ordained ministry is a divine institution, a gift of Christ to the church, whose *rationale* can be clearly seen in the obvious necessities of common life. One can see how the two go together from his discussion of ministry in *On the Councils and the Church*:

> In the fifth place, one recognizes the church outwardly from the fact that it consecrates or calls ministers of the church, or has offices to which it must appoint people. For there must be bishops, pastors, or preachers who publicly and privately give, offer, and exercise the four elements or holy things already mentioned, for the sake of and in the name of the church, but much more because of the institution of Christ, as St. Paul says in Ephesians 4: "He gave gifts to human beings." He has given some as apostles, prophets, evangelists, teachers, rulers, etc. For the multitude cannot do this, but must commission one person or let one person be commissioned. For what would happen if each one wanted to speak or offer the sacraments and no one would yield to anyone else? One alone must be commissioned, and this one alone be allowed to preach, baptize, absolve, and offer the sacrament, and the rest must be satisfied and give their consent.[35]

Ordained ministry is thus established by Christ's institution, but the rationale for this institution is no mystery: it serves the peace and order of the public, communal life of the people of God.[36]

The ordained minister, according to Luther, acts "in the stead and name of all." There is not the slightest reason to take this in the sense of modern delegation-theories; on the contrary, there are compelling reasons not to do so. To begin with, when Luther says that ordained ministers act "in the stead and name of all who have the same *jus*," he is not talking about a group of individuals with "equal rights" in the modern sense of private entitlements, but about a corporate body which holds a property in common. The point is not that individuals yield up their private rights for pragmatic reasons to form an ecclesiastical polity—it seems doubtful that anyone would have conceived of such a notion before the contractarian political theories of Hobbes and Locke—but that the minister is consecrated to the stewardship of those holy things which Christ has bestowed on his body, the holy Christian people, as a corporate unity.

In a slightly earlier work, the address *To the Christian Nobility*, Luther says that the bishop who ordains acts "in the stead and person of the whole assembly."[37] "In the stead and name of all" thus means the same thing as the thoroughly traditional notion that the ordained minister acts *gerens personam ecclesiae*, in the person of the church, which is familiar, for example, to Thomas Aquinas.[38] The contemporary Roman Catholic theologian Gisbert Greshake has defined the notion of *in persona ecclesiae* in terms which seem quite congenial to Luther: the minister acting in the person of the church, he writes, "is not acting in the place of the Church as if he were someone delegated by it—we are not in the juridical sphere!—but *as that organ through which and in which the Church is speaking and acting.*"[39] Luther's concurrence with this view is clarified by a remark which he makes when discussing the office of the keys: the question, he says, is whether the *potestas*, the power and authority, exercised by the clergy in excommunication and absolution is "something other than the communal *potestas* of the church."[40] According to Luther, therefore, in the exercise of the Keys by the ordained, we encounter the corporate *potestas* which Christ has conferred on the church which is his body; it is in the ministry of the ordained that this *potestas* is publicly actualized and most fully exercised, "in the stead and name of all."

It is from this perspective that we can better understand the view of ministry and ordination to which Luther was so vigorously opposed. Luther's polemics have nothing whatever to do with the spirit of democracy, with suspicion of the very ideas of office and institution, or latent spiritualism. He believed himself to be faced with an understanding of the ordained ministry as a self-contained cadre of power-holders which ruled the church but did not really need the church, which was *over* the church but not *in* it. In other words, the holy things that constitute the church were being claimed as the private property of the priesthood rather than the communal property of the Christian people. That the papacy believed its priesthood to be autonomous over against the Christian people he thought was clear, given the widespread practice of absolute ordination, ordination to priestly status with no particular pastoral charge in view. This practice, though forbidden by the canons of the Council of Chalcedon, had become common in the Middle Ages with the rise of the private mass and the ordination of priests for the sole function of performing such masses.

Luther understood the doctrine of the indelible character as the *ideology* by which this cadre justified its domination of the church; as Luther understood it, this doctrine claimed that the clergy were endowed with a spiritual *potestas* inhering *in their own persons*, apart from the communion of the body of Christ, which was transmitted from one to another in an autonomous, self-contained succession through the humanly invented ritual of anointing. Certainly this is not what the doctrine of the indelible character meant in its origins, or in the theology of someone like Thomas Aquinas, and it would certainly be unjust to attribute such an account of ministry to the Roman Catholic Church today. But it is important to be precise about what Luther was *against*, if only in order to be equally precise about what he was *for*.

The relationship between communal priesthood and ordained ministry in Luther's thought is well summed up in some lines which we have already quoted from *On the Councils*: "... the church cannot exist without such bishops, pastors, preachers, and priests, and in turn they cannot exist without the church: *they must be together with one another*."[41] Luther's position here is very close, I believe, to that represented in our own day by the Greek Orthodox theologian John Zizioulas (now Metropolitan John of Pergamon), for whom ministry is *a specific mode of relationship to the eucharistic community*, not an authority which could inhere in ordained persons apart from such relationship.[42]

Communal priesthood and ordained ministry are coinherent with one another and, so to speak, *constitutive of one another*. Ordained ministry is service to the church and has its whole reality in relationship to the gathered assembly, in whose person and name it administers the holy things which are the gifts of Christ to his holy people. But the Christian people is likewise dependent on the ministry, for only through the ministry of the ordained can the church exercise its full authority as the body of Christ. Although Luther, like nearly all medieval theologians, believed that in case of necessity a layperson could baptize or absolve, one line remained absolute: Luther *never* allowed that any but an ordained servant of the church could rightly preside at the eucharist, the communal feast which Christ has bestowed on his church. Precisely *because* the eucharist belongs to the *whole* church, only one who by virtue of ordination and calling can act *in persona ecclesiae* may preside at the eucharist.[43] Therefore *the church can only realize to the full the gifts which Christ has given it through the service of the ordained ministry*. Thus communal priesthood and ordained pastor, the holy people and the holy ministry, depend on one another and constitute one another; as Luther says, *sie müssen bey einander sein*, "they must be together with one another."

Church and Salvation

On the basis of what has been said so far, I want to conclude by calling Luther to witness on behalf of the Joint Commission's provocative claim that Lutherans and Roman Catholics should agree that the church "mediates salvation." For Luther, I want to argue, the church, the holy Christian people with its office of ministry, is indeed not only *recipient* of salvation, but likewise, precisely—and only—*as* recipient of salvation, also *mediator* of salvation as the body of Christ. Or to put it another way, which avoids the not entirely helpful term "mediation," Luther holds, Schleiermacher to the contrary notwithstanding, that individuals relate to Christ only by way of a relationship to Christ's holy people.

Here it is impossible to resist quoting in full a text which is cited in the dialogue report. It is from a Christmas sermon published in 1522; Luther is interpreting Luke 2:16: "And so they went with haste, and found Mary, and Joseph, and the child, lying in the manger." Luther gives this verse an allegorical reading:

> Mary is the Christian church, while Joseph is the minister of the church … The Christian church keeps all God's words in her heart, and mulls them over, clarifying them in relation to one another and to the Scriptures. Therefore anyone who is to find Christ must find the church first. How would one know where Christ and his faith are, if one did not know where his faithful are? And one who wants to know something about Christ must not trust self and build a bridge of one's own into heaven through one's own reason, but rather go to the church, visit and question her. Now the church is not wood and stone, but rather the multitude of Christ's faithful people; they certainly have Christ present with them, for outside the Christian church there is no truth, no Christ, no salvation.[44]

This is an early sermon, but Luther presents the same view, with a more careful theological rationale, in the *Large Catechism*. In his exposition of the third article of the creed in the *Catechism*, Luther maintains that we are not saved by the work of Christ except by way of the complementary work of the Holy Spirit. Our salvation is just as dependent on what we may call the "economy of the Spirit" as it is on the "economy of the Son." Without the economy of the Spirit, who brings us to Christ, the treasure which Christ won for us would lie buried and idle, doing us no good. Christ has *won* our salvation through his incarnation, death, and resurrection, but the Spirit must *distribute* this salvation *through the Christian church* and through the forgiveness of sins imparted *in* the church.

Thus in his exposition of the saving work of the Spirit, Luther begins immediately with what the Joint Commission calls the church's "mediation" of salvation:

> In the first place, he has a singular assembly (*gemeine*) in the world, which is the mother which begets and bears every Christian through the word, which he reveals and urges, so that hearts are illumined and kindled, so that they grasp it, accept it, hang on it, and abide with it.[45]

But of course, the church is the mother of believers only as *recipient* of salvation, the communion of saints, the company of believers on which God has poured out the Spirit and all spiritual gifts.

> I believe that there is on the earth a holy little gathering and assembly of holy people only, called together by the Holy Spirit, in one faith, mind, and understanding, with many different gifts, yet unanimous in love, without sects and schisms.[46]

It is precisely *as* the people which has *received* salvation that the church *communicates* salvation: for each person, salvation means sharing in the blessings which God has showered on his beloved little flock.

> Of this assembly I too am a part and member, a sharer and partner in all the goods which it has, brought in and incorporated through the same Holy Spirit, through the fact that I have heard God's word and still hear it, which is the beginning of entering into it.[47]

Two points seem especially important about this. First, Luther's use of the language of joint-ownership—"a sharer and partner in all the goods which it has"—should remind us of the way he talks about the communal priesthood. The church is a priestly people because it is one body with Christ the high-priest; as a community, as a gathered, unified people, it shares by grace in all that is his. This communal priesthood is not, moreover, something other than or subsequent to justification; it is precisely the *content* of the righteousness which Christ bestows on his people. Thus, for example, in the treatise *On Christian Liberty*, Luther introduces the theme of the royal priesthood of believers as a description of "this grace which we have in Christ"; in context, the adjective "this" refers back to the preceding discussion of the threefold *virtus fidei*, which culminates in Luther's famous account of the marriage of Christ with the believer by faith and their sharing of all possessions in common.[48]

Thus when Luther says that the Holy Spirit brings us to Christ to receive *salvation*, and when he says that the Holy Spirit incorporates us into the *church*, he is saying exactly the same thing. Justification by faith is not, for Luther, the establishment of a private, individual relationship to God which may subsequently find *expression* in adherence to the church. Justification *is* incorporation into the communal priesthood of the church, into the unity of the Body of Christ with its Head. By faith the Spirit brings us into a *corporate* union and communion with Christ, and so with one another. Moreover, the inward is not given except through the outward: sharing in the hidden mystery of the church's union with Christ takes place in, with, and through participation in the church's common life and its holy practices.[49]

Second, this ecclesial character of Luther's theology of justification has implications for his doctrine of *faith*. Luther says that I am incorporated into the church "through the fact that I have heard God's word and still hear it, which is the beginning of entering into it." Hearing the word of God, which is faith, has, so to speak, a public side to it, for the "word of God" to which faith hearkens is nothing other than *the gospel taught and preached in the*

Christian assembly. Hearing and believing the word of God is thus always the beginning of *adherence* to that assembly: it involves *assenting to what is taught by the church*, to the faith which the church confesses and proclaims. There is, to be sure, *more* to faith for Luther than simply assenting to the church's teaching and confession; but faith is never *less* than such assent. Here too the inward and spiritual comes only through the outward and ecclesial.

Moreover, for Luther, this does not mean assenting to some ideally pure *kerygma* which only Paul, perhaps, has ever really succeeded in uttering, and that only on good days. According to Luther, faith assents to the teaching and confession of the holy Christian people *as it actually exists in space and time*. In an open letter of 1532 to the Margrave of Brandenburg, Luther encouraged him to resist Zwinglian eucharistic teaching in terms which may surprise us:

> This witness of the entire holy Christian church (even if we had nothing more) should be sufficient to convince us all by itself to abide by this article and to neither hear nor put up with any sectarian spirit concerning it. For it is dangerous and fearful to hear or believe something contrary to the unanimous witness, faith, and doctrine of the entire holy Christian church, as it has been held unanimously from the beginning through fifteen hundred years in all the world. If it were a new article and not from the beginning of the holy Christian church, or were it not so unanimously held in all churches and in the whole Christian community in all the world, then it would not be so dangerous and fearful to doubt it or to dispute whether it is correct. But since it has been held unanimously from the beginning, and through the whole extent of the Christian community, anyone who doubts it acts as though he believed that there was no Christian church, and therewith condemns not only the entire holy Christian church as a damned heretic, but also Christ himself with all the prophets and apostles, who have founded and powerfully attested this article which we confess: 'I believe one holy Christian Church.' For Christ says in the last chapter of Matthew: 'Lo, I am with you always till the end of the world.' And St. Paul in 2 Timothy 2: 'God's church is a pillar and foundation of the truth' ... I would rather let not only all the sectarian spirits, but the wisdom and law of all emperors, kings, and princes testify against me, than hear or see one jot or title of [the faith of] the entire Christian church against me.[50]

Thus Luther believed, as Harry McSorley has pointed out, that the authentic teaching of the church, of the *actual historic church*, is *infallible*: it cannot be wrong.[51] Cardinal Ratzinger, and with him many, many Protestants, is therefore simply mistaken when he says that for Luther the faith of the church neither grounds nor binds the faith of the individual; moreover, the catholic position, as he states it, that it is "only by sharing in faith with the Church that I have a part in that certainty on which I can base my life," is precisely what Luther very intensely believed.

It is true, to be sure, that for Luther the *authentic* teaching of the church is that teaching which is *received* as authentic by the holy Christian people; the assembly has the obligation to test and judge the doctrine presented to it by its ministers. But this should not be confused with an individualistic doctrine of "private judgment," as though I by myself with my Bible were the final arbiter of what I am to believe. Once again, the context of Luther's thought is the corporate priesthood of the whole church as the body of Christ. Sharing in all that is Christ's, the holy Christian people has received the anointing of the Spirit and knows all things (cf. 1 John 2:20).[52] That charism, bestowed on the church corporately, comes to public exercise in the preaching and teaching of the called and ordained servants of the church, but the church's preachers and teachers are authenticated in their turn by the *Amen* of the Spirit-anointed assembly.

Luther's doctrine thus has nothing to do with democracy or opposition to hierarchy; here again, his call was for interdependence and mutual accountability within an ordered community with a clear structure of roles, which he thought had been laid down in 1 Corinthians 14:29: let the (called and ordained) prophets speak and let the others weigh what is said.[53] Luther's thought has a great deal more in common with contemporary ecumenical reflection on reception and the *sensus fidelium* than with any democratic theory of private judgment.[54]

Thus for Luther the church, the little flock which has received the salvation of God, is at the same time the mother-mediator of salvation to every believer; we can come to Christ and be saved *only by adhering bodily to the church*, sharing in the visible common life of the church, and believing the public teaching of the church. It is in and through this outward, bodily involvement with the holy Christian people that we are joined to Christ as members of his ecclesial body and thus share in his righteousness and, indeed, all that is his. Notice how Luther's theologically basic understanding of the right order of the inward and the outward seems irresistibly to invite us to speak of the church in terms which some Lutherans (as well as other Protestants), oddly find problematic: the outward, visible church, the bodily people in the world, is like a *sacrament* of salvation, in, with, and under which we become one body together with the Lord.

NOTES

1   Karl Heim, *The Nature of Protestantism*, trans. by John Schmidt (Philadelphia: Fortress Press, 1963), p. 79.
2   *Ibid.*, p. 104.
3   G. W. F. Hegel, *The Philosophy of History*, trans. by J. Sibree (New York: Dover, 1956), p. 416.
4   F. D. E. Schleiermacher, *The Christian Faith*, trans. by Mackintosh and Stewart (Edinburgh: T & T Clark, 1928), p. 103.
5   Ratzinger, *Church, Ecumenism, and Politics* (New York: Crossroad, 1988), p. 113. For a matching view from the Protestant side, cf. André Birmilé, *Le Salut en Jésus Christ dans les dialogues oecuméniques* (Paris: Cerf, 1986).

6 Robert N. Bellah, et al, *Habits of the Heart: Individualism and Commitment in American Life* (Berkeley: University of California Press, 1985), p. 228.

7 *Ibid.*

8 Wilhelm Pauck, "Luther's Conception of the Church," *The Heritage of the Reformation*, revised and enlarged edition (London: Oxford, 1968), p. 33. Emphasis added.

9 Stephen Ozment, *Protestants: The Birth of a Revolution* (New York: Doubleday, 1992), p. xiii.

10 Jean Bethke Elshtain, *Augustine and the Limits of Politics* (Notre Dame: University of Notre Dame Press, 1995), p. 2.

11 Ozment, *Protestants*, p. 6.

12 International Lutheran-Roman Catholic Joint Commission, *Church and Justification: Understanding the Church in the Light of the Doctrine of Justification* (Geneva: Lutheran World Federation, 1994), p. 60.

13 *WA* 6:296–297.

14 Cf. for example, "De la communion des Églises à une ecclésiologie de l'Église universelle" in Y. Congar and B.-D. Dupuy, ed., *L'épiscopate et l'Église universelle* (Paris: Cerf, 1964), pp. 227–260.

15 My trans. from Latin text in Benjamin Kidd, ed., *Documents of the Continental Reformation* (Oxford: Oxford University Press, 1911), p. 31.

16 *WA* 18:136.

17 *WA* 50:624.

18 *WA* 50:624.

19 *WA* 50:628.

20 *WA* 50:628.

21 *WA* 50:628.

22 *WA* 50:628.

23 *WA* 50:631–632.

24 *WA* 50:632–633.

25 *WA* 50:641.

26 *WA* 50:641.

27 *WA* 50:642.

28 Congar, p. 228.

29 Messner, *Die Messreform Martin Luthers und die Eucharistie der alten Kirche* (Innsbruck: Tyrolia, 1989), p. 147: "Die Kirche ist die Gottesdienst feiernde Versammlung." My emphasis.

30 The English translation of this treatise in *LW* 40 (under the title *On the Ministry*) needs watching; it gratuitously slips in the code words of the delegation theory whenever possible.

31 *WA* 12:179.

32 I have a hunch that one would find the individualistic reading of Luther's doctrine of the common priesthood arising along with capitalism in the seventeenth century.

33 *WA* 12:189.

34 *WA* 12:189.

35 *WA* 50:632–633.

36 Cf. Vatican II, *Decree on the Ministry and Life of Priests*, chapter 1, par. 2, for an account of the origin of the ordained ministry which seems framed in similar, if not identical, terms.

37 *WA* 6:407.

38 *Summa Theologiae, Suppl* q. 37,a. 4, ad 2.

39 Gisbert Greshake, *The Meaning of Christian Priesthood* (Westminster, Maryland: Christian Classics, 1989), pp. 83–84. My emphasis. For another Roman Catholic theology of ordained ministry which seems materially quite close to Luther, cf. Susan Wood, "Priestly Identity: Sacrament of the Ecclesial Community," *Worship*, March 1995, pp. 109–127.

40 *WA* 12:184.

41 *WA* 50:641. My emphasis.

42 Cf. John D. Zizioulas, "Ministry and Communion", *Being and Communion: Studies in Personhood and the Church* (Crestwood: St. Vladimir's, 1985), pp. 209–246.

43 This point has been exhaustively verified by Peter Manns in "Amt und Eucharistie in der Theologie Martin Luthers," in Manns, *Vater im Glauben: Studien zur Theologie Martin Luthers* (Stuttgart: Steiner, 1988), pp. 111–216.

44   *WA* 10/I/1:140.
45   My translation from *Die Bekenntnisschriften der Evangelisch-Lutherischen Kirche, Kirche* (Göttingen: Vandenhoeck & Ruprecht, 1992), p. 655.
46   *Ibid., p. 657.*
47   *Ibid.*, p. 657.
48   *WA* 7:56.
49   For more on this point cf. "Holy Spirit—Church—Sanctification: Insights from Luther's Instructions on the Faith," in Jared Wicks, *Luther's Reform: Studies on Conversion and the Church* (Mainz: Philipp von Zabern, 1992), pp. 197–220.
50   *WA* 30/III: 552–553.
51   Harry McSorley, "Luther: Model or Teacher for Church Reform?" in George Yule, (ed.) *Luther—Theologian for Protestants and Catholics* (Edinburgh: T & T Clark, 1985), pp. 23–45, here 32–35.
52   Cf. *WA* 12:187–189.
53   Cf. "Against Infiltrating and Clandestine Preachers" in *WA* 30/III:518–527.
54   Here too a comparison with Orthodox theology is interesting, for example the following from Paul Evdokimov: "All episcopal power *is* always exercised *in* the church and *with* the church and never *from above* or *on* the church, if the organism of love is not to transform itself into a juridical and clerical society, and create a division between a teaching church and a church that is taught. 'The guardian of piety and of faith is the whole people of the church,' affirms the encyclical of the eastern patriarchs of 1848. There is only one single church taught by Christ himself. The people is not opposed to the hierarchy, for the latter is a proper organic part of it—all are above all members of the 'people of God'; and this is why the Orthodox teaching authority does not come to completion except in the *consensus* of the body in its totality, expression of the spiritual law of unity, where there is realized its *conformity to the truth*. The decisions of the councils are never either imposed by a monarchical power or reached by democratic suffrage, but always *ex consensu ecclesiae*, conformed to the faith of the whole church." *L'Orthodoxi* (Paris, Delachaux & Nestlé, 1965), pp. 158–159. Despite Evdokimov's polemical reference to the *non ex consensu ecclesiae* of Vatican I, I would suggest that the role of the reception of teaching by the people of God is simply unclear, rather than decided wrongly, in official Roman Catholic ecclesiology.

THE CHURCH IN THE STATE WE'RE IN[1]

NICHOLAS LASH

1. What state are we in?

1.1 Quite a state

'The numbers living in poverty have grown to awesome proportions, and the signs of social stress ... mount almost daily. As the economy weakens the country's international prestige is waning ... British institutions ... are cracking under the pressure as pretension meets reality ... the state is regressing to a system of patronage and privatised carelessness with public money' such as we have not witnessed since the middle of the nineteenth century. 'One in three of the nation's children grows up in poverty. In 1991 one twenty-one-year old in five was innumerate; one in seven was illiterate. The prison population is the highest in Europe. The British are failing.'[2] That was Will Hutton. And Andrew Marr, who says that he 'yields to no one (except Will Hutton) in fashionable gloom,' noting that 'Serious voices from the right suggest that we are condemned to increasing economic insecurity and deeper social division, a harsh era in which the international economic élite thrive behind the barriers their money builds for them, while the losers fester hopelessly and violently in the ghetto' (suggesting, in other words, that European cities are doomed increasingly to resemble American ones) nevertheless asks: 'Has there ever been a time when societies so rich, so relatively secure and so peaceful were so close to losing their collective nerve?'[3]

To these voices of two of the most intelligent and respected contemporary commentators on British political economy, we could add a third: that of the Chief Rabbi, Jonathan Sacks. While insisting on the necessity for what he calls 'a principled rejection of despair,' Dr Sacks takes very seriously the dark tones sounded in the famous final paragraph of Alasdair MacIntyre's *After Virtue*, argues that 'the greatest danger facing humanity after the

Dr. Nicholas Lash
The Divinity School, St. John's Street, Cambridge, CB2 1TW, UK

collapse of secular ideologies [is] religiously-fuelled nationalism,' and adds: 'The mood in world politics is dark, darker than I have known it in my lifetime.'[4] We are not, it would seem, in a very good state.

Christianity inherited from Judaism the habit of viewing social existence under three aspects—represented by the institutions of kingship, prophecy and priesthood[5]—aspects interpreted, in Christian thought, as categories of christology. Later in this essay, I shall use this framework as the basis for some remarks on piety, and nationalism, and the dangerous absence of theology from public understanding. Before setting out in that direction, however, there are some preliminary observations to be made concerning the ambiguity of three words in my title: 'church' and 'state' and 'we'.

1.2 What state?

The most straightforward of these words is 'state'. The state has, since the sixteenth century, been understood to be that form of public power which constitutes 'the supreme political authority within a certain defined territory.'[6] And, of course, the point of Hutton's title is to suggest that the British state is in a most unhealthy state.

1.3 Church and state?

'Church' is much more tricky. We have been so well indoctrinated by the metaphysics of the modern state that even Christians talk quite happily about 'relations between church and state'. There are, however, two good reasons why all such talk should be avoided.

In the first place, there is a matter of Christian doctrine. The church, God's gathered people, gives visible expression, sacramental utterance, to God's promised healing of the human race. This particular people finds its identity in the exercise of its vocation to narrate, announce and dramatise the origin, identity and destiny of humankind as common life, *koinonia*, communion in God.[7]

There is, to my mind, no better symbol of the *doctrinal* achievement of Vatican II than that found in the ordering of the chapters of its two Dogmatic Constitutions—on revelation and the church. Thus *Lumen Gentium*, the Constitution on the Church, devotes a chapter to the 'mystery' of the church before it treats, in Chapter 2, of the church as God's people; and only then does it proceed, in Chapter 3, to discuss the church's structure. It is only as the fruit of God's self-gift, God's outpoured Spirit, that the church is the people breathed by that Spirit into life; and it is only as this grace-borne people that it has the structure which it needs to order its affairs.[8]

To speak of 'church and state', as if these were the names of commensurable entities or institutions, is to speak as if the church consisted of its governing structures. But the British people is not the British state; nor is the church in Britain the General Synod of the Church of England or the General Assembly of the Church of Scotland. It is really quite bizarre, that, when people speak of 'entering the church', they invariably refer not to baptism but to ordination! (The structures of British Catholicism or of other non-conformist bodies, such as the United Reformed Church or the Episcopal Church of Scotland, need not, at this point, concern us because, constitutionally, they do not exist.)

The second reason for refusing to talk about relations 'between church and state' is that such language was born of that victory of secular over ecclesiastical authority, the birth of the modern state in sixteenth-century Europe, which led to the 'eventual elimination of the Church from the public sphere.'[9] In countries such as Britain, still burdened by the anachronism of 'establishment', the ritual semblance of authority enjoyed by bishops as 'lords spiritual' is in stark contrast to the ineffectiveness of their pronouncements. This is not surprising for, with the emergence of the state as the sole agency of governance and public power, ecclesiastical authority no longer has any business in this realm: its remit is confined to what is now deemed 'spiritual' territory: namely, to the 'inside' of Cartesian man, the opinions, dreams and preferences of the private self (the exception being those occasions on which the state calls on the church to enjoin obedience and loyalty to the powers that be).

'The Church needs to reclaim the political nature of its faith if it is to resist the violence of the State.'[10] But this reclamation is *not* a matter (as a number of recent studies have suggested) of trying to escape the confines of the private, into which it was banished by modernity, and to discover once again a 'public' role. It is the very distinction between public and private realms which, since it was first invented for this purpose, has been an instrument by which the state controls the church. When ecclesiastical authorities agree that they must 'keep out of politics', it is only the powerful who smile.

To play the game according to these rules is, in other words, wittingly or unwittingly to accept 'the myth of the State as [public] peacemaker, as that which takes up and reconciles the contradictions in civil society.' Instead of wondering what place the church might occupy in the public realm, we would do better to ask: how might the kind of 'people' that Christians (like Jews) confess themselves to be, acquire the discipline, sustain the culture, that would render us capable of 'speaking truth to power'?[11]

As an example of the proper exercise of ecclesiastical authority, Cavanaugh instances the sermon preached by Archbishop Oscar Romero the day before his assassination, in which he ordered 'the National Guard, the police and the military' to refuse to obey those who ordered them to kill 'our own people ... your own fellow peasants.'[12]

1.4 Who are we?
'All identity', one sociologist has said, 'constitutes itself through negations.'[13] 'We' are those who are not 'them', 'the others', those who are (potentially, at

least) the enemy. Christianity, I think, could almost be defined as a project for the subversion of the truth of this assertion. I have often suggested that, if there is one phrase which indicates the heart and centre of the Gospel it is that 'we have been made capable of friendship'—where the passive voice acknowledges the ground of this capacity, and duty, in God's grace, and where the range of reference of 'we' is, in principle, entirely unrestricted.

This is a most disturbing thought. As a British Catholic theologian, invited by an Anglican institution to address an audience in a British university, the most immediate reference of the pronoun in the title of my lecture is to the group of people whom 'we', this evening, are: mostly, I imagine, well-educated middle-class white British Christians. If so, then 'we' are a people sustained in well-being, in no small measure, in consequence of past and present exploitation of societies and individuals less powerful than our own. With what integrity could *we* then say that 'we have been made capable of friendship' while, in so doing, giving to that pronoun an unrestricted range of reference, encompassing (therefore) both our victims and ourselves?

Whichever way we turn, the picture darkens. Whether we broaden the background to take in centuries of inhumanity and devastation, or focus more narrowly upon the ingenious devices, in immigration law and social policy, by means of which the rich, today, in Britain, express their distaste for and terror of the poor, it seems that we could only say that *we* had been made capable of friendship as the outcome of some miracle of generosity wrought by other people—by those whom we deemed 'them'.

This might sound mere utopian fantasy were it not that just this miracle of forgiveness does, in principle, occur—whenever the Lord's Prayer is uttered. Such things are, I know, only too easily said. Words come cheap, and fuel our appetite for abstract piety evasive of the darkness and the contradiction of the facts. Nevertheless, it is of paramount importance that we remind ourselves how interesting, strange, and dangerous, how exhilarating and subversive, the politics of the Gospel are.

As the power and autonomy of nation-states decline, the forces of 'globalisation' and 'localisation'—one operating at a level 'above', the other 'below', that of the state—gather strength. Thus, on the one hand, Andrew Marr speaks of the 'diminution of national relevance and diversity implied by the new globalism,' as popular culture, information and the money markets all spin 'beyond the control of any government.'[14] On the other hand, as the diminishing power of the nation-state renders it increasingly incapable of answering 'the most basic questions of personal identity, so we see larger societies disintegrate into religiously, culturally, or ethnically defined entities.'[15]

From Bosnia or Rwanda to the destruction of the rain forests and the devastation of fragile third-world economies through the structural rapacity of transnational capitalism, the destructive potential of these two forces is all too evident. It is therefore not surprising that people who receive their fundamental sense of who they are, as human beings, through being citizens of *this* state, and not some other, should find their own identity and dignity and freedom threatened by the forces that contribute to the nation-state's decline.

But those whose fundamental sense of 'peoplehood', of who 'we' are, is grounded elsewhere than in the nation-state—people, for example, such as Christians and Jews—may be better placed to understand that these same forces are, like all forms of energy, ambivalent: notwithstanding their undoubted danger, they are also rich in possibility for the freedom and the flourishing of humankind.

'Jews do not form a single ethnic group but a great many.' This multi-national, multi-ethnic composition posed no threat to Judaism just as long as being a Jew was a matter of being born not only 'into a people with a shared history of suffering and hope,' but also 'into a way of life, a religious destiny,' a narrative tradition interpreting that history. Dr. Sacks' fear, however, is that, with emergence of what he calls the 'curious phenomenon' of 'Jewishness without Judaism', 'Jewish peoplehood' might, in the absence of tradition, dissolve 'into a variety of subcultures, brought together only at moments of crisis.' He does not, of course, surrender hope: 'The ever-dying people at least knows this: that in contemplating its future pessimism has always prevailed, and that it has never once come true.'[16]

We, too, call ourselves 'God's people', and the phrase trips lightly off the tongue. But the resonances set up by that passage, for our consideration of who 'we' are, as Christians; of how we might understand that 'peoplehood' which furnishes us—more fundamentally than does our colour, race, or citizenship—with our identity, are very powerful. And the standpoint from which Jews and Christians might hope to make a contribution to the politics of peoplehood in a world in which global and local factors are likely to play at least as large a part as national ones may perhaps be illustrated, autobiographically, by the confession that, as I once put it, 'I have been taught by that particular people which identifies me more deeply than does my British nationality: namely, by Catholic Christianity, that I must try to learn to place my fundamental loyalty with no people, no possibility of friendship, more restricted than the human race.'[17]

2. The role of religion

'Grand narratives' are out of fashion. Nevertheless, most people work with or take for granted some general account of what is going on. Thus, for example, the story of the modern world was told, by Marx, as a tale of things going through the awful to the delightful (like all revolutionaries, Marx was an optimist); by Durkheim, as a matter of more or less successfully managing the awfulness of things; and, by Weber, as the story of a world going downhill all the way. My Cambridge colleague Tim Jenkins (to whom I am indebted for that splendid sketch) believes it to be largely a matter of accident that most British sociology of religion is sung to a Weberian tune.

Thus, for example, one recent study of *Religion in Modern Britain* tells a straightforward story of decline from the splendour of an established 'church' to competition between a variety of 'sects' (both terms being understood in broadly Troeltschian terms) to today's pluralism of mutually tolerant and politically irrelevant 'denominations'.[18] Those who find this story plausible may not be surprised to learn that neither Will Hutton's book nor Andrew Marr's contains any entry in its index either for 'religion' or for 'church'. The Chief Rabbi is surely going with the grain of what is generally agreed when he declares that 'We have become less religious.'[19]

In August 1995, nearly three hundred theologians from some twenty-seven European countries assembled in Freising, in Bavaria, for the second Congress of the European Society for Catholic Theology. At a lavish reception in Munich, our host, the Deputy Minister-President of Bavaria, spoke of his fear that, throughout Europe, both 'church and faith' were 'evaporating'. The prospect alarmed him as a politician convinced that 'a decisive role for European unity accrues to the Christian churches' because these churches are 'top-class integration factors of our society and our state [which] stabilise the political culture.'

In short, the story of religion in modern Europe, in its most widespread and influential versions, is a story of the apparently irreversible evaporation of what was once a most effective instrument of social control. But is this story true and, in the measure that it is, should Christians regard it as bad news? The first is a question about 'secularisation' and the second about the relationship between Christianity and modern concepts of 'religion'.

2.1 Is religion evaporating?

Troeltsch's distinction between 'church' and 'sect', to which I alluded earlier, continues to be influential, but those who have recourse to it often overlook the fact that his typology was not two- but threefold. As well as 'church' and 'sect' he spoke of 'mysticism', which has 'an affinity with the autonomy of science' and 'forms a refuge for the religious life of the cultured classes', which 'in sections of the population untouched by science it leads to extravagant and emotional forms of piety.'[20] Whatever the fate of 'church' and 'sect' in Britain today, a glance at any bookshop shows that—from astrology to witchcraft, from yoga to the enneagram—thick mists of something very much like 'mysticism' in Troeltsch's sense, far from 'evaporating', flourish with positively tropical luxuriance. And, almost without exception, it seems to be taken for granted in these circles that 'religion', in *their* sense, has nothing to do with politics. Which should give Christians pause for thought.

It is nearly twenty years since David Martin defined 'secularization' as 'the process whereby religious institutions become less powerful in a society and religious beliefs less easily accepted.'[21] And there seems little doubt but that, in Britain today, those institutions and beliefs which most people think of as 'religious' are less powerful and persuasive than they were even a few decades ago.

In his Foreword to Grace Davie's recent study of *Religion in Britain since 1945*, however, Martin acknowledges the possibility that 'the "grand narratives" of the enlightenment are themselves collapsing.'[22] In other words, instead of asking: Is the evaporation of religion irreversible? We should be asking awkward questions about the origins of that understanding of 'religion' which the grand narratives of secularization simply presuppose.

'Religion' once named the virtue of appropriate behaviour in relation to the mystery of God. In other words, it functioned not unlike 'piety' or 'reverence'. And, of course, *everything* that human beings, as God's creatures, think and do and undergo—in political or domestic life, in art and agriculture, in law and medicine and economics—should be tempered, disciplined, by the requirements of due reverence or 'religion'.

During the seventeenth and eighteenth centuries, however, this view of the matter was supplanted by another: by the invention of a particular district of existence which people may inhabit if they feel so inclined; a district quite distinct from politics and science, though subject to their evaluation and control; a district called 'religion'.

This dramatic transformation did not come about by accident. The so-called 'Wars of Religion' are, in fact, anachronistically described, because 'what was at issue in these wars was the very creation of religion as a set of privately held beliefs without direct political relevance. The creation of religion was necessitated by the new State's need to secure absolute sovereignty over its subjects.'[23]

That modern State is now, as we have seen, in crisis. And perhaps the evaporation or, at least, the weakening, of those forms of 'religion' invented for this State's convenience is not merely evidence of the completeness of the victory which the (secularized) 'throne' won over the (domesticated) 'altar', but is also itself a function of the State's decline. Be that as it may, no account of the condition of 'religion' in contemporary Britain will be remotely adequate unless it takes into consideration (as the grand narratives of evaporation generally fail to do) that burgeoning of Troeltschian 'mysticism' which I mentioned earlier. Far from being simply 'secularized', British society seems dangerously polarised between the bleak utilitarian rationalism of the public realm and an increasingly exotic private paganism. But where does this leave Christianity?

2.2 Back to school

It leaves Christianity free to stop being 'a religion'. By the same token, it leaves everyone free to stop trying to fit such varied traditions as Judaism, Buddhism, Hinduism and Islam into the procrustean bed invented, for political purposes, by the theorists of the early modern State.

Dr. Sacks emphasises the centrality, in Judaism, of a 'particular concept of education, one sharply at odds with prevailing moral fashion ... it is a matter of inducting successive generations into the society in which they will become participants ... Education is an apprenticeship in being a citizen.'[24] But of what city? The remarks I have just quoted need to be taken in conjunction with a later passage in which he insists that 'There is no more potent symbol of Jewish history than the *sukkah*, the temporary dwelling ... The very name *ivri*, or Hebrew, means one who wanders from place to place.'[25] And not only Jews, but Christians also, are required to educate each other into citizenship of a promised city that has not yet been reached.

Christianity, and Judaism, and the other great traditions, are perhaps best understood as *schools*. The pedagogy of these schools has the twofold purpose (variously conceived and executed in the different traditions) of weaning us from our idolatry—from the setting of our heart upon some feature of the world: some fact or thing or nation, some institution, system or ideal—and of purifying our desire.[26]

'There is such a thing as an ecology of hope. There are environments in which it flourishes and others in which it dies. Hope is born and has its being in the context of family, community and religious faith.'[27] This image of an 'ecology of hope' indicates quite admirably the kind of environment which the schools that we call Judaism and Christianity are—each of them on their own terms—required to be and to provide.

'Community', which Andrew Marr says is 'the watchword of the nineties,' has become 'the intellectually respectable form of nostalgia' and 'the propaganda of optimists everywhere.' The note of irritated scepticism in his voice seems justified by the banality of much contemporary discussion of community and of what is now known as 'communitarianism'.[28] Meanwhile, the wealth of Christian and Jewish wisdom and experience in the making and sustaining of ecosystems of the common life is, on the whole, ignored.[29] Thus, for example, Marr's discussion of the 'growing and irrefutable evidence of the rise of a new kind of community politics in Britain' contains no mention of the contribution made to these developments by Jewish, Christian and Muslim groups, institutions and associations.[30]

2.3 People of peace

The hope sustaining and sustained by the people-constituting schools of Judaism and Christianity is a hope for peace, true peace, a peace with generosity and justice at its heart. Central to both traditions is the conviction that, notwithstanding the violence and oppression which characterise human history so pervasively that they sometimes seem to constitute the fundamental structure of the world, it is, in the last analysis, from peace, and not from violence, that all things come—for creation 'out of nothing' is pure gift—and in peace that all things find their promised consummation. To be a Christian is to inhabit and enact a politics, a social narrative, of humankind called out of nothing towards the *polis* that we call the new Jerusalem. And, though thus set between memory and hope, this narrative is neither optimistic nor nostalgic, because the route it follows is the *via dolorosa*, the road taken by him in whose shed blood all things, whether in heaven or on earth, are reconciled.[31]

Neither mainstream Judaism nor mainstream Christianity have interpreted their recognition that peace has both the first word and the last as a requirement that their politics be, in all circumstances, pacifist. Moreover, in the history of Christianity, peace and violence, kingdom and 'counter-kingdom', [32] wheat and tares, are inextricably intertwined. Nevertheless, the recognition of the primacy of peace has not been wholly ineffective in enabling Christians to restrain and moderate the violence both of public power and of its revolutionary subversion. The politics of the Gospel demands, at least in principle, that oppression be resisted, not by counter-vailing violence but by the strength of its refusal.

'Christianity', said Michel de Certeau, 'was founded upon *the loss of a body*—the loss of the body of Jesus Christ, compounded with the loss of the "body" of Israel, of a "nation" and its genealogy.'[33] The politics of the Gospel are complicated by this twofold loss which, in some respects, differentiates the politics of Christianity from that of Judaism. Thus, for example, whereas the latter allows the Jewish people—though they live in many places and belong to many nations, many cultures, many races—to find in Israel 'again a Jewish home,'[34] to recognize (we might say) Jerusalem in Jerusalem, Christianity has never been quite comfortable with such realisation of its eschatology.[35] The body of the risen Christ, the city illuminated by the Lamb,[36] is what the church both is and seeks to find.

This is, of course, in no way to deny that Jews know, at least as well as Christians do, that peace remains a hope, a duty, and a promise, rather than a fact. Jonathan Sacks quotes one rabbi who said that 'with the birth of the State of Israel there ended the "hiding of the face" of God ... It was the beginning of the end of exile.' One promise remained to be fulfilled, the promise of God's peace: 'The Jewish people always knew that this would be the last of the promises to come true ... Peace is always our last prayer, never our first, because we know how hard peace is to achieve ... Today our final prayer is no longer a dream. It has become a hope.'[37] Those words come from an address delivered in September 1993. I found a terrible poignancy in reading them, two years later, a few days after Yitzhak Rabin's assassination —by a Jew. Peace remains our common duty, and our prayer.

3. Devotion, polity, thought

3.1 Humankind's 'three principal conditions'
How, I asked earlier, might the kind of people that Christians, like Jews, confess themselves to be, acquire the discipline, sustain the culture, that

would render us capable of speaking truth to power? I know no better framework for reflection on this issue than that traditionally provided by the representation of 'three different aspects of the life of society' in terms of the threefold offices of priesthood, kingship and prophecy.[38]

This 'division of leadership into three domains ... seems to have been a consistent feature of Jewish political organisation at most times. It does not correspond to a division between secular and spiritual authority'—as if, for instance, kingship were deemed purely secular and priesthood merely the business of religion—'since each domain drew its ultimate mandate from God and was bound by the Divine Law.'[39]

In its Christian versions, this differentiation of what Newman called the 'three principal conditions of mankind'[40] was understood as the social refraction of Christ's threefold messianic 'anointing' as prophet, priest and king. This is how Calvin, dissatisfied with existing treatments—the three offices 'are spoken of in the Papacy, but frigidly, and with no great benefit'[41]— handled the matter, and Calvin's greatest twentieth-century disciple took the three offices as the framework for his discussion of the doctrine of reconciliation in the massive fourth volume of the *Church Dogmatics*.[42]

The interpretation of the theme that I shall take as a guide, however, is neither Barth's, nor Calvin's, but that provided by Newman, especially in his 1877 Preface to the third edition of *The Via Media of the Anglican Church.*[43] 'I have long wished to write an Essay', he wrote in 1874, 'on the conflicting interests, and therefore difficulties of the Catholic Church, because she is at once, first a devotion, secondly a philosophy, thirdly a polity.'[44] In the measure that the three offices do, indeed, reflect 'the principal conditions of mankind,' they will find expression, in some form, in all societies. Moreover, the endless variety of ways in which 'such contrary modes of life, and their contrary excellence' correct, distort, restrain each other's operations gives to the history of each society its particular dramatic texture.[45] Where Christianity is concerned, the distinctiveness of what I have called the politics of the Gospel arises from the requirement that, in the life of Christian people, not only is the exercise of each office dialectically transformed by its inter-action with the other two, but also that each office be paradoxically refigured in conformity to the pattern set by one in whose existence kingship took the form of servitude, priesthood of obedience and prophetic witness the testimony of the Crucified.

Thus, on Newman's account, Christianity is 'at once a philosophy, a polit-ical power, and a religious rite ... As a religion, its special centre of action is pastor and flock; as a philosophy, the [theological] Schools; as a rule, the Papacy and its curia.' The language invites us to put narrative flesh upon what might, in other hands, be mere abstractions: to think, for example, of a village church or 'base community', a department of theology, a centre of ecclesiastical administration. And no sooner has he told us that 'Truth is the guiding principle of theology ... devotion and edification, of worship; and of government, expedience', than, twisting the knife, he adds: 'In man as he is, reasoning tends to rationalism; devotion to superstition and enthusiasm; and power to ambition and tyranny.' Thus it is that the outcome of the 'chronic collisions and contrasts' between Christianity's 'three several departments of duty,—her government, her devotions, and her schools' is, humanly speaking, quite uncertain; and such health, stability and harmony as is, from time to time, achieved, is the fruit, not of human virtue, strength or ingenuity, but of God's sustaining and transforming grace.[46]

3.2 Devotion

The brevity of my remarks on the 'devotion' that is the exercise of priestly office is by no means an indication that this dimension of the church's life is unimportant. Quite the contrary: it is the 'priestly' life of particular, small-scale communities of men and women—especially, in Newman's words, 'the oppressed, the poor, the sick, the bereaved, the troubled in mind',[47]— the prophetic witness which such devotion and 'endurance' bears and the political influence that it exerts, which the *other* two offices—the organisational and scholarly dimensions of the church—exist to serve. Moreover, I suspect that, at this fundamental level, British Christianity is a good deal healthier than one might suppose if one only listened to the chattering classes as they lament or celebrate the 'evaporation' of 'religion'.

There is, however, one aspect of the church's priestly task which is of overwhelming urgency, and that is education in something like the virtue of 'religion' in its older sense. 'Priesthood', says Dr. Sacks, 'is about constructing communities where the life of faith is given tangible expression.'[48] But, if these communities are to foster the 'ecology of hope', it is of paramount importance that they be schools of stillness, of attentiveness; of courtesy, respect and reverence; academies of contemplativity.

Again and again, Will Hutton laments the 'short-termism' of British political and economic planning, and 'the real challenge', according to Andrew Marr, 'is to evolve a society which replicates, generation after generation, well-educated, adaptable and secure people who can think long and plan carefully.'[49] What might be the *ground* of their security? Charles Elliott has defined the church as 'a contrite and forgiven community that is seeking to live out its forgiveness.'[50] In the measure that we were, in fact, a people thus schooled in forgiveness, able to relate, without resentment, to 'a past both revered and unsatisfactory,'[51] we might be better able to contribute to the disciplining of short-term ambition by acknowledgement of common duty to 'a people yet unborn.'[52]

3.3 Polity

Christianity is, in the second place, 'a political power,' that is to say: a public, social fact, an institution or set of institutions; an organisation with arrangements for its governance. As such, its relationship with those other aspects of social governance which find focus in the state will vary from outright resistance through many different kinds of tension and cooperation to subservience—known in Britain as 'establishment'. Having already indicated my belief that this particular arrangement is anachronistic, I will say no more on the subject beyond pointing out how odd it is, to Catholic ears, to hear defenders of the status quo argue that the consequence of *dis*establishment would be the reduction of the Church of England to a 'sect'. Odd because, to my knowledge, Scottish Episcopalians do not see themselves as 'sectaries', nor do the several million members of the other provinces of the Anglican Communion.

Seven, as any student of the Scriptures knows, signifies completeness. In early medieval thought, 'royal anointing was reckoned amongst the sacraments proper' but, by 1274, when the second Council of Lyons endorsed Peter Lombard's list of seven sacraments, 'the great majority of theological writers had adhered to the fixed number of sacraments which excluded royal unction.'[53] In other words, what the church in due time came to understand was that no particular political community, no earthly kingdom, is itself a sacrament and, were the church to designate as sacrament any such community—any nation-state or empire, any tribe or ethnic group—it would thereby renege on its responsibility to serve as sacrament of the community of *all* of humankind in that communion which is the reign of God.[54] It follows, I suggest, that there is no better context in which to explore the relationships between the politics of the Gospel and the politics of the nation-state than consideration of the question of nationalism.

It is sometimes said that 'patriotism is a good thing and nationalism a bad thing,'[55] but such slogans need handling with care. The virtue of 'piety' (close cousin, as I mentioned earlier, to an older sense of what 'religion' might mean) was, for Aquinas as for the tradition in which he stood, the virtue of duty to and reverence for one's *patria*: one's family and fellow-citizens; the place which one calls 'home'.[56] And the virtue of piety may be corrupted by vices both of excess and defect. In other words, the absolutisation of patriotism into idolatrous forms of nationalism is as much a corruption of patriotism, or civic piety, as is its evanescence.

'There was', says the Luxembourg historian Victor Conzemius, 'no such thing as nationalism in the real sense before the eighteenth century.' The decisive break came, not with the Reformation, but with the enlightenment 'stylizing of nationalism as religion.' At the end of the eighteenth century, the nation became, for the first time, 'the supreme and ultimate point of reference both for the individual and for the state as a whole.'[57] In consequence, 'Christian universalism, which had also always stood under God's judgement, was displaced by the sacred egotism of the nation state.'[58]

There is, admittedly, another side to the story: thus, for example, there is no denying the constructive part played by modern nationalism in 'the origin and liberation of the new nations of the Third World.'[59] Nevertheless, at the point at which patriotism corrupts into idolatry, the resistance offered by those traditions (such as Christianity) whose very raison d'être it is to recognise and to withstand the worship of false gods—the worship of some feature of the world as God—has all too often proved, at best, half-hearted.

Finally, over and above the duty to withstand nationalism's idolatrous propensities, religious traditions may have more constructive functions to perform. In every country, suggests the Hungarian sociologist Miklos Tomka, 'they can further the recognition of the concerns of other countries and nations.' Moreover, in the measure that they succeed in displaying due independence from state control, they may, he suggests, serve in an increasingly complex and fractured world as 'institutions for dialogue' in international affairs.[60]

3.4 Thought

'Endurance, active life, thought':[61] if the privatization of religion in modern Western cultures has seriously hindered the appropriate exercise and interpretation of the 'priestly' and 'royal' offices in the church—of Christianity as 'devotion' and as 'polity'—it is perhaps to the prophetic office that the greatest damage has been done.

There is no doubting the failure of Christian theologians effectively to contribute to the public conversation through which we seek to clarify the crises of contemporary culture. In Britain today, to describe an argument as 'theological' is to say nothing whatsoever concerning its bearing on our understanding of the holy mystery of God, but merely to indicate that it freewheels in speculative unconcern for evidence and context. Unfashionably, however, I would contend that responsibility for this absence of theology from the conversations of the culture does not, for the most part, lie at the theologians' door. The combined impact of the dedicated anti-intellectualism of the devout, and the stultifyingly complacent and patronising ignorance of the irreligious, has been devastating. Not that it is surprising: built into that very definition of 'religion' which the cultured despisers of our day have been cultured to despise is the conviction that religion—whether as the culture's superseded infancy or as its first-aid posts for private solace—has nothing to contribute to the common quest for truth.

In the short term, the situation will continue to deteriorate as the idolatry implicit in the unacknowledged worship of the primacy of violence—a worship disguised as the 'rational' calculus of secularity—continues to do untold damage to the fabric of our common life.[62] In the longer term, the hope must be that, in renewed acknowledgement of the difference it is called upon to make through exercise of the priestly and political offices, the church will, even in the state we're in, and in collaboration with such other similar traditions as Judaism and Islam, be stimulated into rediscovery of its identity as a kind of school, within the wider culture, in which idolatry can be recognized and subjected to critique, and in which the Word of life that is the wisdom of God's peace may once again be heard, enfleshed, considered, and prophetically displayed.

4. Postscript

In an article published to coincide with the appearance of a second edition of *The State We're In*, Will Hutton saw little reason to revise his judgments of the previous year. 'In some respects', he said, 'the book understated its case—and its main arguments have been borne out by events,' whether political, with 'gathering privatisation of the state,' economic, in the languishing of investment, or social: 'A number of chief police officers privately tell me that the social conditions in the inner city are on the edge; the incidents of arson and riot ... foretell much worse to come.' All the more surprising, therefore was his comparatively upbeat concluding appeal to 'an old anchor in British politics—the progressive Whig tradition ... The past sixteen years may prove to have been a necessary but temporary interlude before British liberalism in its best sense reasserts itself.'[63]

When a commentator as intelligent, humane and well-informed as Hutton fails to recognise the extent to which the predicament of contemporary Western culture springs from contradictions at the heart of modern liberalism, we are in a serious state indeed. In an article published a few days before his death in November 1995, Ernest Gellner—'one of the unpolished ornaments of modern Britain'[64]—put his finger on the issue with characteristic trenchancy.

Commenting on John Gray's exposition of the thought of Isaiah Berlin, [65] Gellner was scornful of the incoherence of the 'camouflaged relativism' of the liberal tradition. His observation that 'relativism deprives us of the means—indeed of the right, to express deep revulsion,'[66] stands very close to the texture of pre-modern appeals to natural law (although it would probably have surprised him to have this pointed out). What is missing in Berlin's work, according to Gellner, 'is a concrete sense of the social context of liberal practices ... It is sensible to try to look at what happens to liberty in the real world ... If, at one end, this philosophy is insufficiently preoccupied with transcendence and objectivity, then, at the other end, it is far too ethereal.'[67]

The church, and the synagogue, embody rich and ancient traditions of experience of piety and polity and thought, the strength of which consists in the extent to which each strand is disciplined and shaped by interaction with the other two and by their common recognition of overriding duty owed only to the life-giving and saving mystery of God. If these traditions are to contribute to the clarification and the healing of the state we're in, then they will best do so on their own terms. They will, of course, be most unpopular.

NOTES

1 A lecture given in the University of Essex, on 5 March 1996, in my capacity as 1995–1996 Visiting Professor to the Centre for the Study of Theology.
2 Will Hutton, *The State We're In* (London: Jonathan Cape, 1995), pp. 1, 2, 5, 2.
3 Andrew Marr, *Ruling Britannia. The Failure and Future of British Democracy* (London: Michael Joseph, 1995), pp. 9, 316–7.
4 Jonathan Sacks, *Faith in the Future* (London: Darton, Longman & Todd, 1995), pp. 65, 83; cf. p. 63.
5 Sacks, *Faith in the Future*, p. 111.
6 Quentin Skinner, *The Foundations of Modern Political Thought* (Cambridge: Cambridge University Press, 1978), II, p. 353.
7 See Nicholas Lash, *Believing Three Ways in One God* (London: SCM Press, 1992), p. 86; *Lumen Gentium*, art. 1.
8 The correlative achievement, in the case of divine revelation, is the placing of Chapter 1 of *Dei Verbum*, on revelation as God's Word, God's self-disclosure, before the chapter on the 'transmission' of that Word in Scripture and tradition.
   In 1985, a special Synod was convened in Rome, to consider the extent to which the constitutions and decrees of the Council, which had ended in 1965, had borne fruit in the life of the Church. One of the English bishops attending the Synod asked me what my criteria would be for testing how well the message of the Council had sunk in. I suggested that he should ask his colleagues how important they thought the sequence of chapters in those two documents to be. For a detailed and lively account of what transpired, see Peter Hebblethwaite, *Synod Extraordinary. The Inside Story of the Roman Synod, November–December 1985* (London: Darton, Longman and Todd, 1986).
9 William T. Cavanaugh, '"A fire strong enough to consume the house": the wars of religion and the rise of the state,' *Modern Theology* 11/4 (1995), p. 400.
10 Cavanaugh, '"A fire"', p. 409.
11 See Cavanaugh, '"A fire"', pp. 414–5.
12 Oscar Romero, 'The Church: defender of human dignity,' *A Martyr's Message of Hope* (Kansas City: Celebration Books), p. 161, quoted from Cavanaugh, '"A fire"', p. 415.
13 Niklas Luhmann, 'Sinn als Grundbegriff der Soziologie,' in J. Habermas and N. Luhmann, *Theorie der Gesellschaft oder Sozialtechnologie* (Frankfurt, 1971), p. 60: quoted from Heinrich Schneider, 'Patriotism and nationalism,' in John Coleman and Miklos Tomka (eds) *Religion and Nationalism, Concilium* (1995/6), p. 41.
14 Marr, *Ruling Britannia*, p. 205.
15 Sacks, *Faith in the Future*, p. 114.
16 *Ibid.*, pp. 235–6.
17 Nicholas Lash, 'Hoping against hope, or Abraham's dilemma,' *Modern Theology* 10/3 (1994), p. 243.
18 See Steve Bruce, *Religion in Modern Britain* (Oxford: Oxford University Press, 1995). I am grateful to Mr. Jenkins for drawing my attention to Bruce's book, and also to Grace Davie's only slightly less gloomy account of *Religion in Britain since 1945* (Oxford: Blackwell, 1994), according to which ecclesiastical decline is accompanied by an increase in 'believing without belonging'.
19 Sacks, *Faith in the Future*, p. 17.
20 Ernst Troeltsch, *The Social Teaching of the Christian Churches*, trans. Olive Wyon (London: George Allen and Unwin, 1931), Vol.II, p. 994.
21 David Martin, *A General Theory of Secularization* (Oxford: Basil Blackwell, 1978), p. 12.
22 Davie, *Religion in Britain*, p. ix.
23 Cavanaugh, '"A Fire"', p. 398. There have been many excellent studies of this transformation, from Wilfred Cantwell Smith's *The Meaning and End of Religion* (New York: Macmillan, 1962), to Peter Harrison, '*Religion' and the Religions in the English Enlightenment* (Cambridge: Cambridge University Press, 1990). I hope that some essays of mine entitled *The Beginning and the End of 'Religion'* (Cambridge: Cambridge University Press, 1996), will make a small contribution to the discussion.
24 Sacks, *Faith in the Future*, p. 49.
25 *Ibid.*, p. 150.

26 In my 1994 Teape Lectures, I tried to develop this suggestion in conversation between Christianity and Hinduism. See the first three chapters of *The Beginning and the end of 'Religion'*.

27 Sacks, *Faith in the Future*, p. 5.

28 Marr, *Ruling Britannia*, pp. 75, 321; on 'communitarianism', see pp. 100–2, 321–2. Marr seems to me correct in saying that 'the word community is in danger of becoming so overused that it is subsiding into bland nothingness.'

29 One small exception being the recognition, at the theoretical level, that 'the tradition of social solidarity and "subsidiarity"' is inherited 'from Catholicism' (Hutton, *The State We're In*, p. 267).

30 Marr, *Ruling Britannia*, p. 100. To which, in fairness, I should add that, in a more recent essay on 'The rise of do-it-yourself democracy' (*Independent*, 18 January, 1996, p. 15), Marr emphasises the importance of such phenomena as the 'Citizen Organising Foundation', a network of local, 'overwhelmingly working class' political organisations 'partly made up of what they call "faith communities"—local churches, mosques, synagogues and Hindu temples—alongside community groups, tenants' associations and so on.' Such burgeoning community politics matters, he insists, 'because as globalisation starts to bite, almost every serious political thinker appears to be investigating the web of social relationships below the level of the state'.

31 See Colossians 1:20.

32 See John Milbank, *Theology and Social Theory. Beyond Secular Reason* (Oxford: Basil Blackwell, 1990), pp. 432f.

33 Michel de Certeau, *The Mystic Fable*, trans. Michael B. Smith, (Chicago: University of Chicago Press, 1992), p. 81, his stress.

34 Sacks, *Faith in the Future*, p. 181.

35 Perhaps the papal states might be most benignly viewed as a secularized caricature of the new Jerusalem! Whatever the guidebooks say, Rome is not 'the eternal city' if, by that, one means the city of God.

36 See Revelation 21:23.

37 Sacks, *Faith in the Future*, p. 95.

38 *Ibid.*, p. 111.

39 *Ibid.*, p. 111.

40 John Henry Newman, 'The three offices of Christ', *Sermons Bearing on Subjects of the Day* (London, 1869), pp. 53–4.

41 John Calvin, *Institutes of the Christian Religion*, trans. Henry Beveridge (Grand Rapids, Michigan: W. B. Eerdmans, 1983), Book II, Ch. xv, p. 426.

42 In Karl Barth's treatment, the exercise of Christ's priestly office—'the Lord as servant'—finds ecclesial expression in the 'gathering' of the Christian community; that of the royal office—'the servant as Lord'—in the community's 'upbuilding'; and that of the prophetic office—'the true witness'—in the community's 'sending'. See the titles of chapters XIV, XV and XVI, and of paragraphs 62, 67 and 72, of the *Church Dogmatics*.

43 J. H. Newman, *The Via Media of the Anglican Church*, I, ³(London, 1877), pp. xv–xcv. I have discussed this text on a number of occasions: see, for example, Nicholas Lash, 'Life, language and organization: aspects of the theological ministry, ' *Theology on Dover Beach* (London: Darton, Longman and Todd, 1979), pp. 89–108; *Easter in Ordinary. Reflections on Human Experience and Knowledge of God* (Charlottesville, Virginia: University of Virginia Press, 1988), pp. 136–140.

44 C. S. Dessain (ed.) *The Letters and Diaries of John Henry Newman*, Vol. xxvii (Oxford: Clarendon Press, 1975), p. 70.

45 Newman, 'The three offices', p. 55; see *Via Media*, p. xlvii.

46 See *Via Media*, pp. xl–xliii, lxxxii.

47 Newman, 'The three offices', p. 54.

48 Sacks, *Faith in the Future*, p. 113.

49 Marr, *Ruling Britannia*, p.12.

50 Charles Elliott, *Memory and Salvation* (London: Darton, Longman and Todd, 1995), p. 274.

51 See P. J. FitzPatrick, *In Breaking of Bread. The Eucharist and Ritual* (Cambridge University Press, 1993), p. 194.

52 Psalm 22.31. It was, after all, this psalm which was on the lips of our high priest at the consummation of his sacrifice.

53 Walter Ullmann, *The Carolingian Renaissance and the Idea of Kingship* (London: Methuen, 1969), p. 74.

54 See *Lumen Gentium*, art. 1, which describes the church as, 'by her relationship with Christ ... a kind of sacrament or sign of intimate union with God, and of the unity of all mankind.' The extent to which the church has, in different times and different places, in fact succumbed to what we might call 'Constantinian captivity' is for the historian, rather than the theologian, to decide.

   Moreover, what is true of particular communities is also true of particular *kinds* of community. As Jonathan Sacks puts it: 'Systems of government do not form a proper subject of revelation' (*Faith in the Future*, p. 107).

55 Schneider, 'Patriotism and nationalism', p. 33.

56 See Schneider, pp. 34–35. For Aquinas, both 'religion' and 'piety 'are 'parts of justice' (see *Summa Theologiae*, IIa. IIae, qq. 81–100, 101). However, for reasons given in IIa. IIae., q. 121, art. 1, ad. 2, that 'gift of the Spirit' which corresponds to the ('natural') virtue of justice is named not as religion, but as piety—the gift enabling us to live in relation to God as not merely creator and lord but as father.

57 Victor Conzemius, 'Universal Christian faith and nationalism. *'Religion and Nationalism'*, pp. 16, 19.

58 Conzemius, 'Universal Christian faith', p. 19. Hence Schneider's description of 'the modern idea of the nation which derives from Rousseau' as 'the political appropriation of a theological concept' ('Patriotism and nationalism', p. 39).

59 Miklos Tomka, 'Secularization and nationalism,' *Religion and Nationalism*, p. 28.

60 *Ibid.*, p. 30.

61 Newman, 'The three offices', p. 54.

62 That the narratives of secularity are but the masks of Nietzschean paganism is a central contention of John Milbank's *Theology and Social Theory*: cf. e.g., pp. 2-6.

63 Will Hutton, 'New hope for the good society', *Guardian* (3 January 1996), p. 13.

64 Marr, *Ruling Britannia*, p. 57.

65 John Gray, *Isaiah Berlin* (London: HarperCollins , 1995).

66 Ernest Gellner, 'A case of the Liberal's new clothes,' *Guardian* (4 November 1995), p. 29. He went on: 'Given those incommensurates, how do you cope with societies which contain slavery, gulags, female circumcision, or gas chambers, and whose apologists might well invoke that deep pluralism?'

67 *Ibid.*

WRESTLING WITH A WOUNDING WORD: READING THE DISJOINTED LINES OF AFRICAN AMERICAN SPIRITUALITY

WILLIE JAMES JENNINGS

> Jacob was left alone; and a man wrestled with him until daybreak. When the man saw that he did not prevail against Jacob, he struck him on the hip socket; and Jacob's hip was put out of joint as he wrestled with him.
>
> Genesis 32: 24–25

> When black people gather together for worship and praise to the Lord, it is not because they have made a decision about the theological merits of Luther's ninety-five theses or of Calvin's *Institutes*. These are not our traditions. At most, they are secondary structures in which God has placed us so that we might 'work out our salvation in fear and trembling.' Since we did not create the various Catholic and Protestant structures we cannot use these labels as the primary definition of our religious experience.
>
> James Cone[1]

African American spirituality defies a simple and straightforward definition. This is due both to its complex history within the formation of western (Christian) spirituality, and also its connection to the multiple locations and functions of African identity within western modernity. Given the complexities involved in delineating the character of African American spirituality, any descriptive account will carry with it multi-valenced polemics in the contemporary currents of African American intellectual and cultural life. My intention in this essay is twofold. First, I outline the nature of African American spirituality by means of its most often articulated arguments,

Dr. Willie James Jennings
The Divinity School, Duke University, Durham, NC 27708, USA

hoping in the process to offer a different (somewhat tentative) vision of this spirituality. Second, in doing this, I also challenge the appropriateness of the prevailing conceptual framework within which African American spirituality continues to be articulated. The opening quotation by theologian James Cone is one version of this, but we find another more powerful articulation of this framework in the work of Theophus H. Smith.

> Black Spirituality in North America seems at once a type of Western spirituality and yet also strikingly non-Western. In its Christian forms it appears simultaneously conventional—an imitation of, or a gloss on, the major Protestant and evangelical traditions—and also something alien, intransigently different. What accounts for both aspects[?] ... the intersection of black America's two master stories—its mundane story and its sacred story. The mundane story ... is the cultural narrative of disparate African communities forcibly removed from their homelands and enslaved in the Americas, then emancipated and segregated, and now struggling for parity in the New World. The other story is composed of biblical texts that are shared within Western culture ... the sacred narrative of ancient Israel's divine election and deliverance from bondage ... [the] narrative correlations [of these two stories] provides an incomparable opportunity to disclose and to display the spirituality itself.[2]

The acceptance of this formulation of Afro-spirituality is almost uniform and certainly not without its merits. As Smith's definition illumines, there is an important recognition both of a history of struggle that characterizes African American existence and the importance of the biblical narrative for that same way of life. Smith's somewhat unique focus upon the correlation of these two realities will merit our consideration.[3] However, what I find problematic is the hypostatization of spirituality as a reality outside (or inside) the "forms" within which it appears. Smith's "spirituality itself" signifies an intellectual habit born in modernity that posits a spirituality for Africans (and their descendants) specific only to racial identity, only to their blackness. The multiple purposes of this formation of Afro-spirituality are beyond complete capture, but they could be fruitfully organized around a desire to thwart a racially derogatory description of the African—one rooted in a distorted Christian colonialist vision. This desire gives birth to an intellectual resistance to locating the origins of African spirituality in Christianity itself, a Christian spirituality without remainder. Instead, a majority of Afro-intellectuals posit a fundamental transparency to Christianity. That is, "the African" can be *and* must be seen through all theological formulations, religious communities, and liturgical forms.[4] This desire, in large measure, drives the articulation of Afro-American spirituality and is constitutive of the formation of a long-standing polemic. The articulation of Afro-American spirituality reveals a drama of struggle with Christianity itself. Christianity has been and continues to be the life giving yet wounding word of

Afro-Spirituality. Struggling with, i.e. "wrestling" with, this word has been the preoccupation of generations of Afro-scholars. In a real sense, African American spirituality cannot be recognized by itself, but instead involves acknowledgment of at least three arguments that are constitutive of its articulation and thus its very being. With each form of argument we are gathering together the characteristics of this struggle with the word of Christian existence.

I. The Spirituality Itself: An Argument Against the Theological

In 1975, The Reverend Dr. Henry Mitchell, then Director of the Ecumenical Center for Black Church Studies in Los Angeles, published his seminal work, *Black Belief: Folk Beliefs of Blacks in America and West Africa*. This text followed the already suggestive work of Mitchell's *Black Preaching*. In both these texts, Mitchell sought to establish the African origins of African American belief. Mitchell's work is significant as one of the first clear markers of an intellectual trajectory within which Afro-scholars sought to join western theological reflection to authentic African existence. Mitchell had as his goal the articulation of an essentially African character in the worship, faith-life, and belief-structure of African Americans. As Gayraud Wilmore stated in the foreword of the 1975 edition of *Black Belief*, expressing the sentiments behind this text, finally with the advent and examination of African belief-systems, there was now "the possibility of an African theology that is something more than a blackenization of the canons of Rome, Geneva, and Canterbury."[5]

Mitchell sought to draw an organic line from African religions to biblical Christianity. In this regard, Mitchell wanted to reveal the Christian character of these belief-structures, the "Christian" presence in African religious thought and life prior to the advent of European slavery and colonialism. This proto-Christianity did not mean Christian faith as such; rather Mitchell, in part reflecting on the work of historians of Afro-American slavery, posited a religious bent in these displaced Africans that made them great religious adapters. In effect, they were ready for Christianity, ready to take it and transform it.

> In their estrangement from powers over their own community they embraced the new nearness of their once too-transcendent deity; and they focused their earlier trust in intermediaries in a new and near and likewise-rebuked-and-scorned Jesus, the Mediator in the White-style Trinity. They baptized their highly healing and expressive possession tradition into a sound manifestation of the presence of the now-only-one Holy Ghost or Spirit, third person in the Trinity ... *the African slave was the author of the adaptations*, under the guidance of God, as expressed in and through the spiritual and practical instincts with which [God]

endowed Black humanity. The resulting faith has become so deeply imbedded in the unconscious life of Blackamericans that it still will not give way to the onslaughts of modern disbelief and materialistic inhumanity, even among the most antireligious and/or intellectually cynical sons of the Black culture.[6]

In Mitchell's view, Christian faith was amenable to African belief at a deep and abiding level. This faith was no real cultural leap for the African slaves or their descendants. At all points Mitchell focuses on those he terms the common "folk". Here with the black people *on the ground* we find the place of connection, between the "faith" brought across the Atlantic and the "form" given in the new world. The Christianity that Mitchell wishes to detect and elaborate is folk Christianity, black folk Christianity. This Christianity is not simply Christian form and African faith; rather, according to Mitchell, in the body of the African, Christian faith is reborn, baptized in the sea of blackness and emerging as a signature of Afro-American religious existence, an essentially Christian existence.

In order to press forward this thesis, Mitchell works with and through conceptual dissonance at two levels. The first is already suggested in the central thesis itself: While the slaves were literally chained to white slaveholding society, black folk Christianity existed both before the face and behind the back of white (elite) Christianity, without being *chained* to such Christianity. For Mitchell, these African slaves were agents in the formation of Christian belief. These Africans were, in the words of Talal Asad, "not the passive objects of their own history."[7] Mitchell must press cultural adaptation without passivity in order to banish any culturally derogatory mimesis. Yet as we shall soon see, this is a very dangerous and difficult concept to control.

The other conceptual dissonance is part and parcel of the first. Mitchell draws a crucial distinction between low and high African religion. Low religion is the social and political economy of conjuring, witchcraft, and culturally decreed superstitions, executed through the complex machinations of hoodoo or voodoo. High religion refers to a structuring set of core beliefs that in the context of the new world gain articulation through Christian faith as that faith is turned toward an "unrelenting resistance to slavery."[8] This distinction is meant to address what Mitchell keenly senses as a white ethnographic propensity to fix the literary gaze on that which appears to be most African, *most* black, which in effect is that which presents the greatest instances of nonwestern and thus nonChristian alterity.[9] In this regard, Mitchell perceives an attempt by some anthropologists to conceal the Christian in the African, a concealment only illumined by recognizing the distinction between low and high religion itself.

Emphasizing this distinction also serves another purpose. Mitchell, as do many others, draws strong historical lines of continuity between the lives of the slaves (and their theological struggle) and our own. In a real sense, the struggle of those in the midst of the divide between low religion and high religion is a present reality.

> Most Blacks, in or out of slavery, resisted 'conjure' or magic both because it so seldom seemed to be effective, and because it was contrary to the belief system and ethical rules of the higher tradition. There was and still is, a tension between the low and high religious traditions in the psyche of most Blacks, but the higher prevails. There are superstitious habits buried in my own unconscious that resist all high insight. I live *with* these habits but not *by* them. The experience of the descendants of North Europeans is no different. They feel strange when a black cat crosses their path, but such feelings do not order their lives. The preponderance of superstition in the literature by Whites about Blacks is the product of the writers' selectivity.[10]

Indeed Christianity in some sense helped create the struggle, pressing the need to establish this distinction. Yet in the end, the struggle is in black flesh. While a similar struggle may be a part of the racial histories of any people, according to Mitchell, the point here is that the struggle finds life in the currents of black blood, sustaining intensity with each generation. The significance of this distinction will occupy our attention later; however, what needs to be recognized at this point is that Mitchell discerns along with this distinction recognizable religious (i.e. theological) motifs that he finds permeating the street culture of the *everyday black* (man or woman).

Following a Dubosian-like racial vision of the essential character of black folk mediated through a Tillichian theological lens, Mitchell then offers what he believes to be fundamental theological motifs deeply embedded in black culture that illumine the nature of black belief.[11]

There is belief in the one high God who is the creator and who is sovereign. This African belief becomes, in the new world context, belief in the goodness and providence of God coupled with the goodness of creation. Second, there is belief in the righteousness and justice of God especially as they are brought to focus in addressing the plight of Africans in the new world. Third is the interpenetration of the material and the spiritual that informs a comprehensive and dynamic pneumatology. Ironically, for Mitchell these motifs, while fully theological, resist theological systematization. They are core beliefs rooted in "culture", as opposed to idea or system. This black cultural theological speech demands proper consideration and reflection. What stands in the background here is the constant denigration of this speech at the hands of white theologians both by their benign neglect (to borrow a term from C. Eric Lincoln) and their active disrespect. In this regard, Mitchell himself embodies the central form in which this black cultural theological speech is performed and where the demand for proper consideration and reflection is proclaimed: the black preacher.

Mitchell finds the black preacher to be the central embodiment of black (African) spirituality as it signifies a vibrant black folk culture. Of course, crucial to this embodiment is the recognition for Mitchell of the black preacher at her or his *best*—in the textual performance both in and out of the pulpit. Following the same cultural processes by which Africans actively created a Christian witness in the new world, Mitchell understands the black preaching tradition to be a uniquely African appropriation of a Christian practice that is also an art-form. Mitchell posits an essential moment of blackness, black preaching. And here (with black preaching) is all the dissonance of his central thesis:[12] At one instance what Mitchell sees is Christian but discerned as African through an ethnographic perspective. At another instance what he sees is aggressively Christian turned toward the banishment of a polytheistic economy found in the continuing struggle against low (African) religion but also discerned as an African aesthetic that promotes a black sameness that binds together all African (religious) form. At yet another instance he sees in the discussion of black religion the constructing hand of a white hegemonic and derogatory vision of black life, a vision that directly implicates Christianity. But this vision in some sense gives rise to a process of selectivity and a form of critique by which Mitchell discerns the positive "uplift" that Christianity brings to the African.

This dissonance is not born in the thought of Mitchell. Mitchell is a powerful example of the conflicting lines of thought that confront any attempt to delimit the nature of an Afro-American spiritual presence. To the credit of Mitchell and those who have been in some measure at home in his synthesis of Afro-Christian spirituality (if not with my construal of his synthesis), we find here a theoretical sophistication born of the necessity of what Houston Baker Jr. calls "crafting a voice out of tight places." Baker refers to the "manipulations of [conceptual] form that ... *are* rhetorical possibilities ..."[13] The tight place that Mitchell must work in is the very small space between the derogatory and false image of the African created by white (Christian) society and the African Christian he perceives as the authentically African. Mitchell wants to make the African Christian (while remaining essentially African). But he wishes to perform this literary reading without making Christianity imply simply an imitating reflex of an "African" formed in the colonialist imagination. This is a tricky endeavour, in which Mitchell is compelled to form the image of both African and Christian in a very tight conceptual space. We can discern two opposing starting points which themselves move us much closer to the origins of the conceptual dissonance found in Mitchell's work.

While Mitchell's *Black Belief* and his other texts were foundational in a theological reading of African religion and its impact on Afro-spirituality, his work stands on the shoulders of the African theologian and philosopher, John Mbiti. Mbiti represents an African-Christian reading of African religion. With Mbiti we have, more significantly, the formation of a Christian vision of the African that also seeks to reconstitute the African outside a European image. In this regard, Mbiti's work is a thorough-going ethnography that is at the same time profoundly theological. He unrelentingly pursues a theological agenda. However, this agenda itself illumines the difficulties of employing an ethnographic vision to launch a theological project.

Mbiti must negotiate a proscribed image of Africa and the African in such a way as to overcome both the history of the colonialist's "blessed imposition"—we brought the gospel to the heathen—while at the same time grasping for an essential African that will not dissolve into a Christianity mediated through white western culture. Mbiti's strategy for presenting this African involves recasting a European vision of a racially unified Africa (i.e. black Africa) into an anthropologically framed characterization of an African way, an African spirit present in traditional African religion and culture. This allows Mbiti to offer a kind of quasi-[trans]national identity that is itself the primordial material upon which the gospel works. Thus African traditional religion(s) and culture(s) become the necessary *preparatio evangelica*. The effect of Mbiti's reframing is to forge a weapon of theological warfare for the African from the very tools used by European Christianity to create an essential African *as* essentially heathen and ontologically Other.

> Africans are notoriously religious, and each people has its own religious system with a set of beliefs and practices. Religion permeates into all the departments of life so fully that it is not easy or possible always to isolate it. A study of these religious systems is, therefore ultimately a study of the peoples themselves in all the complexities of both traditional and modern life.[14]

For Mbiti, the African is essentially a spiritual being. Those endowed with this African spirituality are (by nature) open to the gospel of Jesus Christ. This re-inscription of African spiritual essence transfers the privileges and power of agency away from the European subject and returns them to the African. With Mbiti, the African receives what V. Y. Mudimbe calls the "rights of subjectivity".[15] This means that the African must be understood on her own terms, in light of her authentic being. With this African spiritual subject at the center, Mbiti can narrate the history of the African Christian from the very origins of Christianity itself to its distorted forms presented by the Europeans.

> Christianity in Africa is so old that it can rightly be described as an indigenous, traditional and African religion. Long before the start of Islam in the seventh century, Christianity was well established all over north Africa, Egypt, parts of the Sudan and Ethiopia. It was a dynamic form of Christianity, producing great scholars and theologians like Tertullian, Origen, Clement of Alexandria and Augustine.[16]

This narration presents a powerful and complex critique of white western culture which allows Mbiti to separate what he considers to be the essential reality of the gospel of Jesus Christ and its important and affirmative connection to African culture from the damaging and damnable imposition of white Euro-American culture upon African soil. As Kwame Bediako notes, for Mbiti the gospel is "the eternal gift of God" for the African while Christianity (especially as presented by the European) is "always a beggar seeking food and drink, cover and shelter from the cultures it encounters in its never-ending journeys and wanderings."[17] Thus Mbiti resists an African Christian identity clothed with European culture which includes both European theology and spirituality. In its place he constructs an African Christian identity that has as its core reality an African spirituality capable of discerning the operations of white western hegemony. In Mbiti's work this African spirituality carries, in a sense, the African religious genius.

Mbiti's reading of African identity is intensely theological, but in a way different from and foundational for Mitchell's reading. Mbiti locates the African (theologically speaking) prior to the theological construction of Europeans; in this way, he thwarts a vision of African Christian spirituality that has as its origin the derogatory gaze of the European. Thus both form and content, posture and practice, how the African prays and what the African prays, how the African believes and what the African believes in a very real sense are inherent in the African and are not imposed on the African from the outside. Of course, this does not mean that theological (and cultural) imposition has not occurred, but this is exactly the problem that must be addressed by African Christians. Mbiti's reading of African identity facilitates a cultural confidence in the results of the outworking of African spirituality. One result has been Mbiti's commitment to the position that Christian existence in its historic formation, in large measure, is essentially African, born in the African soil, shaped in the African air and established in the African mood and sound, though forgotten over time and concealed over the geographic space between Africa and Europe.

More importantly, another result for Mbiti of the outworking of this spirituality is the theological articulation of an essentially African faith that may make use at a formal level of some western theological structure and discourse. But that use is not mandatory or binding, because such discourse is not essential to the spirituality itself. So in a manner similar to Mitchell after him, Mbiti employs doctrinal themes and configurations in his elaboration of African religious consciousness and spirituality.[18] Yet, for Mbiti, these doctrinal themes and configurations are not the controlling center of that elaboration; the controlling center is the (spiritual) reality of the African. To establish the contours of this spiritual reality, Mbiti must draw heavily upon the work of anthropologists and ethnographers as well as engage in ethnographic work himself. In effect, Mbiti borrows the gaze (the forms of perception) of the colonialist *as* anthropologist and ethnographer to establish this "reality of the African."[19] The benefit he gains by doing this is to invoke the power of objectivity as established in the social sciences. With such scientific objectivity Mbiti can offer powerful resistance to one particular genre of theological reading of the reality of the African—those ways of conceiving the African-Christian born and formed on the shores of Europe, those ecclesial, denominational, doctrinal, liturgical ways of seeing that in truth have concealed the authentically spiritual African. Therefore Mbiti commends those ways of truly perceiving the African which would reject the discourse of alterity and otherness embedded in Euro-missiological and theological discussions of the African. However, Mbiti has only rejected one form of alterity and otherness, one formed in European theological discourse.

Like Mitchell, Mbiti wishes to circumvent the theological imagination of the European as it forms an image of the African. Unlike Mitchell, Mbiti is seemingly less aware of the power of that imagination. Mitchell is well aware that the discourse of alterity and otherness is not simply a function of theology but is also at home in the foundations of modern anthropology and ethnography. The African constructed by the anthropologist is no safe conceptual space either, and Mitchell's vigilance against the anthropologist's gaze is not much more secure than Mbiti. Thus, like Mbiti, he has incorporated a problematic reading that presses against his Christian construction of African and Afro-American existence. If on the one hand Mitchell's work stands on the shoulders of theologian/philosopher Mbiti who is concerned with the nature of the African, then on the other hand Mitchell's (and to a lesser extent, Mbiti's) work stands in the shadow of anthropologist Melville Herskovits' concern with the essentially African.

Herskovits is the person whose name is most often associated with the argument for the continuing presence of an African signature in the architecture of Afro-western culture. While Herskovits is not the first to assert the "African present" in black American life, he is significant in locating his argument in the "science of anthropology and ethnography."[20] He places the African fully in this discourse of modernity, a discourse that itself polices theology. If Mbiti finds an African identity for *Christian* spirituality, Herskovits finds an *African* identity for Christian spirituality that dissolves that spirituality without remainder into an African image. Christian identity (as well as every other form of theological identity) becomes a non sequitur.

What Herskovits helps to achieve is the defeat of a derogatory image of the African in the west, one which in his day carried the ideological power of black assimilation.

> Here [in a quotation he listed above] we again meet the familiar theme—the Negro as a naked savage, whose exposure to European patterns destroyed what little endownment of culture he brought with him; the Negro as a culture-less man, with his entire traditional baggage limited to the fragments he has been able to pick up from his white masters and, because of innate temperamental qualities, to 'exaggerate' them into exuberant and exotic counterparts.[21]

Herskovits challenges the reach of an assimilation thesis, whether it is descriptive or prescriptive. In this regard he has gained a critical place in the formation of studies on black religion and black religious consciousness. The power of Herskovits' writing on the African is found in the ways the ethnographic takes the form of a tentative posture; that is, he can discern "fragments of the African" leading to the unassailable conclusion of African survivals of Africanisms. The literary and theoretical power of his work can be grasped in the very notions of "survivals" and "Africanisms". Both notions connote something that is living and breathing, even though threatened with death and destruction. Indeed, this is exactly the case with these displaced Africans. They themselves are survivors and their bodies mark the oft-concealed desire of a black nationalism. Thus Herskovits theorizes on top of a history known and compelling to all African Americans: Although who we really are (as black folk) is concealed, we are actually present though hidden in the distorted pictures of us.

Fundamentally, where Herskovits locates the African (of us) is in the ritualized black body. Herskovits grasps a "deep religious bent" in the American black that has no other informative source than in the behavior of black bodies.[22] It would be a tremendous understatement to say that for Herskovits the black body speaks, instead all black speech is of that body. Thus for this rigorous anthropologist, all Christian dogma and ritual with the Negro mean *Negro* versions of all Christian dogma and ritual. Of course, Herskovits considers his perspective to be shaped by "the *outer forms* of religious expression rather than on inner values and beliefs,"[23] yet these outer forms (because they are black forms) offer much of those inner values and beliefs. Hence for him the African body seen in the new world must entail the continuation of a *black(body)* theology, understood as the continuation of black form which is a quintessentially religious form.

> [W]hile Christian doctrine by no means escaped change as it passed into Negro hands, the most striking and recognizable survivals of African religion are in those behavioristic aspects that, given overt expression, are susceptible of reinterpretation in terms of a new theology while retaining their older established forms.[24]

Given the interpretive power of the black body, Herskovits can draw lines of connection between black behavior across space and time, locating in each instance a uniform African presence. In the worship practices of black people, whether voodoo in Brazil, or cult worship in Africa, or worship in a sanctified church in North America, Herskovits "hears" behind whatever music or words are being sung or spoken, the sound of the black body.

> The *motor behavior* depicted in these reproductions, furthermore, links West Africa, on the one hand, and spirit possession in North American Negro churches, on the other, in *unmistakable* fashion.[25]

In this way, Herskovits gives life to the African and that life is a religious consciousness, a spirituality that denies slavery and social death its final victory. The appeal of such a vision of Afro-spirituality would be obvious to many, because here you have not only a source of historic black triumph but also possibly a resource for black emancipation: the conceptualization of black existence from the starting point of an insurgent and resilient black spiritual form rooted in the black body itself. In this way, Herskovits has forged a weapon even more powerful than Mbiti's rhetorical weapon. Herskovits has created an African in the very conceptual space provided to show the death of the African. However, the effect of this creation for the African as Christian is devastating. As he notes in his favourable use of a conclusion drawn by the famous folklorist, Newbell Puckett, African has never really been fully Christian.

> The mere fact that a people *profess* to be Christians does not necessarily mean that their Christianity is of the same type as our own. The way in which a people interpret Christian doctrines depends largely upon their secular customs and their traditions of the past. There is an infinite difference between the Christianity … of whites and colored … Most of the time the Negro outwardly accepts the doctrines of Christianity and goes on living according to his own conflicting secular mores, but sometimes he enlarges upon the activities of God to explain certain phenomena not specifically dealt with in the Holy Scriptures.[26]

For Herskovits, if not for Puckett as well, more is implied by this difference in Christianity than a different *type* of Christian. Indeed in the black body, Christian belief (dis-)appears and African belief (re-)appears. Herskovits finds African belief where Christian belief is supposed to be, so that, for example, good and evil do not exist as they do for (white) Christians. Instead, in the black body, good and evil become personified in the drama of black sacred existence.[27] Herskovits then concludes that black people are comfortable with their own moral evil in the same manner that they are comfortable with the good, because both are a part of their blackness. Herskovits, in this way, establishes a theological vision that is also a hermeneutic. Here now is a way always to see the African in a way stunningly sophisticated and strikingly similar to the way the colonialist-Christians looked upon the African: These Africans can only be inauthentic Christians, because they are always black. That blackness brings with it a theological vision that is mythological and culturally binding—a theological alterity. Thus professed Christian beliefs cannot really signify their identity, because that has already been determined by their culture and their culture is determined by their race.[28]

Here then with Herskovits is a Afro-spirituality constituted within the intellectual currents of modernity and having the power of modernity to silence the theological. However it should now be clear that this substitutes one form of theology for another: theology (as the product of an anthropological construction) that stands against the theological (i.e., *articulated* Christian beliefs held by Africans and their descendants). As Talal Asad notes concerning anthropologists at work,

> Anthropologists have, I would suggest, incorporated a theological preoccupation into an avowedly secular intellectual task—that is, the preoccupation with establishing as authoritatively as possible the meanings of representations where the explanations offered by indigenous discourses are considered ethnographically inadequate or incomplete.[29]

In this case Christian theology is superseded by a secular theology—a black aesthetic which is also a culturally formed mosaic of African existence. All [Christian] theological description of the African must give way to this real truth. However it would be a mistake to find in Herskovits the origins or even the strongest articulation of this black aesthetic. Indeed Herskovits acknowledges the importance of [literally] the black body of his research assistant, Zora Neale Hurston for helping to illuminate [the aesthetic-theology of] the black body. As Walter Jackson notes concerning Herskovits' observations of Hurston's body, here was proof of the black aesthetic.

> Although she was 'more White than Negro in her ancestry,' her 'manner of speech, her expressions, in short her motor behavior'—were 'what would be termed typically Negro.'[30]

Houston Baker Jr. surmises the origins of the formation of this aesthetic in the Harlem Renaissance and thus in the foundations of Afro-American Modernism. For Baker this aesthetic is an arena of desired freedom. It is the desire to birth a new self in which "the birth of such a self is never simply a coming into being but always, also, a release from a being possessed."[31] Indeed the black aesthetic is not merely an essential concept of blackness built within and around a vision of African spirituality as the ruling symbol of blackness. This aesthetic is a vision of emancipation which is also a way of organizing a multiplicity of readings of the lives of black folk. Thus black political, social, cultural, or artistic practices are all constituted in *and* as primarily an aesthetic. With this aesthetic, we have before us a powerful construal of religion as a central source of the creation of cultural meanings. However with this place of honor comes a necessary discernment—the articulations of Christian theology by Africans is a site of cultural concealment that must be decoded. This means that in order to understand what black folk do at their places of Christian worship, just as in their politics, or in their jobs, one needs *to recognize* the black aesthetic at work, an aesthetic that cannot be reduced to any one of those socially constituted sites. Thus Zora Neale Hurston can move from one site to the next both in her ethnofiction and her ethnography without attending to any of the theological contradictions, conflicts, or differences in the recorded experiences of black folk. Such dissonances do not, in the end, matter. Thus sermons, chants, spells, and spirituals are all part of the one African body.[32] As Hazel Carby notes, commenting on the rhetorical strategy of Hurston's *Mules and Men*,

> The folk as community remain the 'other,' and exist principally as an aesthetic device, a means for creating an essential concept of blackness. The framing of that novel is the process of working out, or mapping, a way of writing and discovering the subject position of the intellectual, in relation to what she represents.[33]

In a sense, what Carby says of Hurston's mapping of that novel is more central to much of the current mapping of Afro-spirituality. Such mapping is the process of the Afro-intellectual attempting to discover herself in relationship to the thing represented—in this case "black folk". In such an endeavor Christian theology (understood as European dogma, doctrine, and polity) must be cleared away or overlooked in order to begin with a grasp of the real thing, the real African, This "real African" therefore now serves as a literary and theoretical prolegomenon for many of the projects in Afro-spirituality and theology. Although in many cases these mappings of Afro-spirituality will employ a theological reading and intend a theological project, they all assume the power of this black aesthetic.[34]

What, therefore, we found at work in Mitchell and Mbiti as attempts to negotiate a derogatory vision of the African (as heathen become Christian, yet still heathen), we now find fully ensconced as the necessary first word of Afro-religious existence. However the problem here is that once the black aesthetic is launched it cannot be controlled; indeed, it is a controlling gaze. And as a controlling gaze it is at once modern and colonializing; that is, it is universalizing and totalizing without ever claiming to be such. As Homi K. Bhabha notes, colonialist discourse demands difference and that this difference be *determinative*.

> The construction of the colonial subject in discourse, and the exercise of colonial power through discourse, demands an articulation of forms of difference—racial and sexual. Such an articulation becomes crucial if it is held that the body is always simultaneously (if conflictually) inscribed in both the economy of pleasure and desire and the economy of discourse, domination and power.[35]

The irony of the black aesthetic is that it is fundamentally a form of black resistance, a "weapon of the weak" (if you will) to overcome the domination and power of colonialist discourse, especially the theologies of the colonialists. It effectively frees the black body from all conceptualizations not "naturally" inscribed therein. What constitutes the natural is not simply a matter of political and social commitments, but also has a scientific base that is discerned ethnographically. The science of anthropology, it is alleged, shows us that the African body is the natural body. Thus the effect of this aesthetic is to banish all theology that is not of the black body, and in this banishment Christian theology is the first to go.

While someone like Henry Mitchell would argue that theology's disappearance is not a necessary predicate of ethnography's appearance, when we arrive at the articulation of an *Afro*-spirituality this disappearance is exactly intended and conceptually complete. Take, for example, the recent work of Theophus Smith, *Conjuring Culture: Biblical Formations of Black America*. Rightly held as a significant achievement in Afro-America religious thought, it exemplifies the silencing power of the ethnographic gaze. Yet what is most significant in Smith's text is the site upon which he theorizes, the Bible. The scriptures become the quintessential (ethnic) text. Indeed, Smith recognizes that the Bible has played a central role in the formation of Western and North American consciousness, as well as in a large number of religious communities, Christian and nonChristian. But he also discerns a scriptural form in Afro-American culture, a foundational placement of the scriptures in the cultural imagination of the Afro-American. However, with Smith this form gives sight of the African imagination. In the very place where Christian reflection begins and the theological imagination takes flight in and toward Christian identity with the reading of scripture, Smith finds an African.

> [T]he Bible comes to view as a magical formulary for African Americans; a book of ritual prescriptions for reenvisioning and therein, transforming history and culture … Folk practices like conjure … are as old as magic everywhere. What is innovative is a remarkably efficacious use of biblical figures, with a historically transformative and therapeutic intent, in the social imagination and political performance of black North Americans. The term 'conjuring culture' expresses that magical intent as explicitly as possible.[36]

Smith engages in an ethnography of Afro-American spirituality that stands in concert with and draws deeply from the modernist impulses of the Harlem Renaissance. In that light, he also wishes to map a way forward between the often conflicting agendas of a history of religions' approach to black religion and the concerns of black theologies of liberation. (Both of these could also be shown to have their methodological origins in the Harlem Renaissance.) The result of his efforts is a vision of Afro-spirituality that enacts the power of a social science—that of the cultural anthropologist extended over the reading of biblical texts. Much like Mitchell and Herskovits before him, Smith brings together two ways of reading black life, but now focused on the scriptures: One which constructs an African who reads the Bible, that is, an African reading the Bible, and another which finds an African reading of the Bible, a form of interpretation of the biblical text that receives the designation African. With this twofold reading in place, Smith not only decodes African-American experience in black folks' renderings of the biblical narrative, he simultaneously discerns the African spirit behind or beneath that Afro-biblical reading and interpretation. Thus he decodes the "conjurational employment of biblical figures" and indeed, as he notes, such conjuring becomes both "transparent" and "compelling" "once one knows what to look for."[37]

Much like Hurston, Smith has discovered African identity "right outside" the Bible in such a way as always to see exactly what is African in the ways black folks read the Bible. He discerns this is to be at the heart of Afro-spirituality. So for Smith this discernment requires a bicultural perspective.

> Maintaining a bicultural perspective ensures that the complexity of a culture and the density of its formations are displayed, rather than reducing black religion either to imputed African (ritual) elements alone or to conventionally Christian (theological) influences alone.[38]

In this sense, both the Bible and the African are necessary for the discernment of Afro-spirituality. But Smith understands both as primarily socially constituted influences that can be charted ethnographically. The Bible as a theological text is transformed in Smith's reading into the Bible as a necessary (and essentially) ethnographic phenomenon. Reading this Bible properly requires, in his words, an "extra-Christian" and a "pre-theological" grasp of African American biblical reading/interpretive practice. In this admonition, Smith displays the power of the black aesthetic—he locates a site for the creation of black cultural meaning without being confined to that site. He actually presents the Bible as crucial to black spirituality, yet he presents the Bible as fully confined by the control of the ethnographic gaze.

Even more problematic, he renders the African as a subject whose reading of scripture only *confirms* what is already known about these beings, that they are black/Africans. In ethnographic fashion, as Smith watches *them* read, he writes their identity and completes their entrapment in his image of blackness. While an African reading of Scripture is meant to be transformative of the world, in a sense, the African is never transformed, but is always the African, an identity always just outside the Bible. Smith employs James McClendon's suggestive treatment of theology as biography as a way of articulating the lived theology of African Americans. To accomplish this very difficult task, Smith treats African Americans as a "collective rather than individual character."[39] While collective characterization continues to be a standard though contested procedure for social scientific study of subjects, its use in this context exposes a tragic fiction—black folk inscribed as a literary device, devoid of Christian theological specificity and texture. Thus what is suggestive and (in my opinion) compelling about McClendon's use of biography, someone who embodies a *Christian* theological vision, someone whose life gives witness to doctrinal and liturgical realities, is denied these Christians.

Smith's treatment is not simply a problem of what Anthony Appiah terms racialism—the rendering of subjects based solely on their race. In that regard, he engages in the same kind of folkloric construction that characterizes the work of someone like Zora Neale Hurston. The more significant problem is that Smith posits an African spiritual reality devoid of Christian theological content yet rooted in the Bible. While Smith resists a theological reading of Afro-spirituality, he offers a version filled with confused and confusing Africanisms, ones similar to those elaborated by Herskovits (and Puckett) fifty years earlier. Building on the work of Sollors, Bercovitch, and others, he posits "Afro-American modes of spiritual perception" that exist in a manner similar to Puritan modes of spiritual perception.[40] What becomes significant is what the notion of "Afro-American modes of spiritual perception" signifies. Here Smith re-introduces the colonialist vision of Africans as morally ambiguous but now refracted through the complex traditional attempts of black scholars to rework this vision.

Once again the black modernist desire to create conceptual space in tight places is at work. In outlining Afro-spirituality, Smith builds on the work of scholars like James Cone's *The Spirituals and the Blues* (1972), Lerone Bennett's *The Negro Mood and Other Essays* (1964), and Sheila Walker's *Ceremonial Spirit Possession in Africa and Afro-America* (1972). In their work, the moral ambiguity of the African understood in colonialist discourse as a derogatory theological flaw now becomes an ethnographic and enlightenment virtue—blacks operate with no dualisms: no good-evil, no body-mind, no sacred-secular dichotomies. Of course, in the work of these scholars and others this nondualist theme is treated differently and signifies different agendas, agendas which we cannot adequately deal with in this space. Nevertheless Smith identifies in this now generally accepted thesis a flattening of the spiritual contours of Afro-life. Conjure and Christianity (to borrow the terms employed by Bennett) are not two complex-conflictual theological agendas (as, in a sense, with Mitchell); rather, with Smith, they are aesthetic forms of the one black body. Thus Smith discerns a covert transformation, a cultural shift in which conjurational strategies go underground (as it were) and are then expressed through "a more transparent mode of spirituality."[41]

Following Herskovits' rhetorical strategy (noted above), Smith ties his ethnography to that history known and compelling to all African Americans —that common narrative of concealment and subversion within which who we really are (as African Americans) is hidden from the view of white society. Like Herskovits, once this history is presented, Smith can place on top of this narrative his construal of an African whose actions are (with the right key) transparent—they immediately reveal conjurational strategies. Therefore, for Smith, black church communities that have condemned conjure as an unacceptable theological posture are not reading these activities correctly, that is, as black/African activities to which they are inseparably joined. In this way, Smith continues the long (colonialist) tradition of speaking for the black body, because that body indeed sends messages.

By the time Smith considers the place of the black preacher in black culture, he has in large measure intensified lines of thought found in Mitchell and others. The black preacher, in Smith's schema, embodies the black cultural tradition of conjurational practices and impulses and in this regard embodies the reality of a shaman. Following the foundational work of M. Eliade mediated (and modified) through A. Porterfield's socio-historical vision of shamanism, Smith notes the therapeutic, empowering, emancipatory functions of the preacher as shaman. Unfortunately, much of the conceptual dissonance present in Mitchell's treatment of the black preacher disappears, and Smith strips the preacher of her theological speci-ficity, ecclesial context, and thus her spiritual complexity. The black preacher becomes a black body working magic.[42]

This ethnographic treatment of Afro-spirituality is most stark when Smith attempts an elaboration of what he rightly perceives as an *imitatio Christi* at work in Afro-Christian communities. He interprets this imitation of Christ embodied in African American Christian communities as a form of (defi-cient) cultural mimesis projected toward white society in an unrealistic hope of a reciprocal mimetic transformation. That is, the black body of the slave (as suffering servant) contains "magical or conjurational intent" prepared to be offered up either by the slave herself or by an advocate who releases this magic in literary and/or oratorical witness.[43] In the end, Smith offers an Afro-spirituality tied to the scriptures with a loose fitting (Christian) form. However what fits tightly is the constructed image of the African, an image that is the organizing center of this first line of argument.

Smith, however, provides us with an important and provocative insight: Articulating Afro-American spirituality requires in some measure acknow-ledging the permutations, problems, and possibilities established by Chris-tianity for African existence. Like Mitchell, Smith will now allow us to articulate that spirituality without confronting this Christian dimension. However, as we have seen, controlling the reach of that Christian (i.e., theo-logical) dimension has both directly and indirectly occupied a considerable portion of the theoretical agenda in many articulations of Afro-spirituality. Rather than growing out of an inherently anti-Christian stance, this intellect-ual strategy at heart grows out of a time-honored resistance to the historic and derogatory vision born of the colonialist who landed upon the shores of West Africa and rendered a theological judgment upon those peoples, a judgment which followed them throughout the history of slavery and beyond: They may become Christian but they are inauthentic Christians. The African (as heathen) always remains with them, because it is in them and we can see it as we see their black bodies.

In a real sense, visions of Afro-spirituality that emphasize "the African" are valiant though mis-guided attempts to theorize in a very tight conceptual space, between a racially-distorted theological discourse and the race-constructing tendencies of cultural anthropology and ethnography. Yet, in a sense, with this line of argument we are in the midst of what is itself a spiritual exercise, an *intention toward spirituality*, that being the desire to claim oneself before and in relationship with God, without the need of a (in this case, white Christian) mediator. Therefore to bind the *authenticity* of a spirituality to the idealized vision of "Africa, the motherland" has been the dominant way in which Afro-western scholars have sought to envision the needed freedom of the black body. This rhetorical strategy has spiritual content and intent. In this way, such scholars have been drawn to what they have perceived as the most powerful and true connection between all black people, and thus between themselves as intellectuals and the black community, an African body with an inherent spirituality that resists any foreign (conceptual) covering.

And ... [they] ... were naked and not ashamed. (Gen. 2:25)

In this (spiritual) endeavor, Christian theology is most often rendered transparent—that which must be looked past in order to arrive at the spiritual essence of the African. However transparency is a visual characteristic that may also connote vision-rendering capabilities. This means that something rendered transparent may also in effect allow one to see something not seen before, and thus something transparent may be in character opaque. In this case, something newly seen may not be clearly understood. Indeed, the relation of Christian theological vision to African existence in the new worlds of colonialism constitutes a seen but not clearly understood reality. Therefore even in the midst of theology's being rendered transparent in this first argument, a second argument is exposed.

II. The Spirituality Itself: An Argument Within the Theological

This second argument moves below the surface (as it were) always present, yet hardly acknowledged for fear it would be used to affirm a derogatory image of these displaced Africans. The comments by Henry Mitchell noted earlier partially illumine this second line of argument.

> Most Blacks, in or out of slavery, resisted 'conjure' or magic both because it so seldom seemed to be effective, and because it was contrary to the belief system and ethical rules of the higher tradition. There was and still is, of course, a tension between the low and high religious traditions in the psyche of most Blacks, but the higher prevails. There are superstitious habits buried in my own unconscious that resist all high insight. I live *with* these habits but not *by* them.[44]

What Mitchell alludes to is an arena of argument within the theological—the African questioning the African. With this questioning, Christian existence creates a struggle of belief within and among the Africans, in which old ways (i.e. old theological practices) confront new and the new conflict with the old ways. The primary way this struggle has been treated by Afro-western scholars is to dismiss this as a real struggle. The early work of Albert J. Raboteau, *Slave Religion*, is characteristic.

> The conflict between Christianity and conjure was more *theoretical* than *actual*. Even those slaves who condemned conjure as evil did not deny its reality. Moreover, among black folk there was refusal to dichotomize power into good and evil—a refusal which Herskovits and others see as African.[45]

Raboteau's assertions here are guided by two stunning refusals. He resists the presence among these displaced Africans of a new configuration, a Christian vision of good and evil constructed *over* familiar practices. While he admits that slaves condemned conjurational practices *as evil*, he must posit a transparency—through the words of the slave he yet sees the African essence. This means, for him, that the real conflict displayed by their words manifests a theoretical posture as opposed to their actual African being. Whether that theory implied a white influence, a white voice speaking through the African or latter interpreters attempting to render a Christian judgment upon these slaves' discourse, makes little difference. A hermeneutic is in place in Raboteau's reading that renders no new possibilities for the African. Raboteau's reading of the relation of Christianity and conjure resists the presence of a fundamental theological distinction now embodied in practices (possibly) even among the early slaves.

> The practice of conjure was, at least in theory, in conflict with Christian beliefs about the providence of God, and indeed one way of relating conjure to Christianity was to make the former the realm of the devil, in effect creating a balance of good and evil. Willis Easter *recited a song his mother had taught him* 'to keep from being' conjure ... *Keep 'way from me, hoodoo and witch, Lead my path from de porehouse gate; I pines for golden harps and sich, Lawd, I'll jer' set down and wait. Old Satan am a liar and con-jurer, too—If you don't watch out, he'll conjure you.* Another former slave put it this way: *I'm a believer, an' dishere voodoo an' hoodoo an sper'ts ain't nothin' but a lot of folks outten Christ.* And yet conjure was not always employed for evil. Puckett noted that conjurers in the twentieth century were all very religious.[46]

At all points Raboteau surrounds the words of the slaves with ethnographic discourse; thus what he knows of the slaves by the insightful reasoning of cultural anthropology makes the advent of their theological innovations[?] a non sequitur. Because an African worldview means a nondichotomous vision of divine power, slaves who mark realities as evil could not *really* mean them as evil [as within a Christian vision of evil], but as readjusted markers in the larger cultural economy of voodoo. Moreover, the fact that the child of a slave has been taught something genuinely new—a song that questions—by his mother is wholly missed by Raboteau. Ironically, the child's slave name foreshadows that newness (Willis Easter). Of course, it is a slave name and this may in part account for Raboteau's literary unease. In fact this now famous account rendered by Raboteau implies that a so-called undeniable cultural marker (voodoo as *the* symbol of a unified worldview) is being questioned, even challenged.

Raboteau's seminal text, however, is not alone in looking past this questioning, this challenge being raised by slaves. For many black western scholars, such questioning has been interpreted along racial lines. For many scholars, when the slaves take upon their lips the theological language of the church, they have in fact taken up the world of the slaveholders and thereby have taken up a "worldview" foreign to their (African) being. The authenticity of such language (in the slaves) must be in the first instance questioned. Note Theophus Smith once again:

> Indeed, here I must acknowledge that such flawed perspectives also characterize black theological and scholarly interpretations. Many traditional black religionists also insist on treating black Christianity and conjure as thoroughly dichotomous. In this regard black church communities have conventionally condemned conjurational practice as uniformly 'the devil's work.' [O]ther commentators ... have observed a moral ambivalence in the practice of conjure ... Because of this conjunctive feature in folk cognitive patterns, conjure intentions can readily modulate from harming or toxic modes of operation to healing or curative modes, *without thereby ceasing to be conjurational.*[47]

Again we see the ironic move: Smith must resist a black ecclesial practice (i.e., *condemning* conjurational practices) that reaches back to the slaves themselves in order to protect his idealized version of black folk as essentially *conjuring* Africans. For Smith, there is an inherent "folk cognitive pattern" in black people that makes black church discourse inauthentic (and disingenuous) in so far as it condemns what is authentically African.[48] This implies that to the extent that conjure is condemned Africans cease to be Africans, and this would leave only one other option, nonbeing (i.e., white). In effect, what we find in many of the foundational texts that treat slave religion and the religion of their children is an inability to conceive (at least in their characterization of the African slave past or folk present) of a new being for this displaced African, one which is a *becoming* in the face of a derogatory vision of the African as heathen.

Historically speaking, this African questioning the African does not mean that a new being has fully arrived. Indeed this is a questioning, a *becoming* Christian. However it in fact displaces the implicit notion of "an African" without remainder at work in the majority of treatments concerning

Afro-American religious history. With Christian faith an African is being created in a new cultural space, one which is being formed by a new theological vision. The comments of Mitchell again illumine this: "I live *with* these habits and not *by* them." Of course, Mitchell's use of an anthropological framework for this insight is not helpful. If we place his insight into a different frame, his comments become not merely insightful but descriptive for this second argument. Afro-spirituality has also involved a theological struggle over which frame of reference is most appropriate to read the spiritual life of the African. In this section, we have been in the midst of one aspect of that struggle that now needs more straightforward elaboration—many scholars have made a conscious decision to posit a generalized religious frame of reference in which an African religious consciousness is at work in every theological decision, impression, thought, word and deed of the slaves and their descendants.

This generalized religious frame of reference requires a kind of reification (and even romanticization) to be present in the characterization of African American spirituality. This frame of reference renders black life as religiously symbolic and therefore the theological statements, visions, and theological impressions of black people *always* demand a hermeneutic that primarily reaches for meaning in their blackness (African). If such meaning cannot be found then it may be "found" (i.e., posited) in a derogatory cultural mimesis (European), or worst of all, one could posit a fictional syncretist, a third thing, neither just African nor only European, but both in spirituality. For example, in an otherwise extremely interesting text, Mechal Sobel constantly employs a hermeneutic that reaches for meaning in the constructed image of an African in order to make sense of a liturgical practice engaged in by these African slaves.

> The African symbolism of spirit as water was carried to America and may have been brought into the Baptist cosmos. The death and rebirth in the watery grave may have incorporated African memories of spirit as water. Later Baptists would sing:
> *I've just come from the fountain, Lord,*
> *I've just come from the fountain, His name's so sweet.*
> *O brothers I love Jesus, His name's so sweet.*
> *O sister I love Jesus, His name's so sweet.*
> *Been drinking from the fountain,*
> *His name's so sweet.*

Sobel's text, which closely follows the rhetorical strategies of Zora Neale Hurston (with her idealized black folk), depends heavily upon a particular methodological decision growing out of cultural anthropology: the theological frameworks of different African tribes may be seen as continuous with different ecclesial frameworks over space and time, because the object of analysis is uniform—a black African. In Sobel's analysis, differences in theological articulations are organized racially which means they are organized along an African/Christian axis. Once such an axis is in place, statements of slaves and their children are interpreted in such a way that only reaffirms a kind of racial Nestorianism. That is, the African grasps a Christian vision by means of an already established African theological vision.

> The white and black visions of death and rebirth share some elements but are nevertheless significantly different ...In each case, these differences between white and black visions can be attributed to an African ethos which was an integral part of the black's Christian cosmos. This is not simply to say that elements of the black ethos were incorporated into a Euro-Christian one ... However, black Baptists reached another level of integration ... in which *a new cosmos was forged uniting African and Baptist elements in a new whole.* Aspects of African soul and spirit found an intrinsic role in the black Baptist rebirth experience, infusing the Christian Sacred Cosmos with an African one.[50]

With this frame of reference, even where slave statements might indicate radical transformation and change, a new becoming in midst of struggle, it can only be the re-configuration of an African-Christian theological vision. The point here is that with this framework one can only see a stable racialized identity that then manifests (racial) theological elements.

This frame of reference resists another possibility: the coming to life of a Christian consciousness within which the African will question "received" wisdom in light of a Christian message overflowing with theological content. In this alternative frame, the positing of a stable cosmos, African or synthetic (i.e., Afro-Euro) falls away. Instead the cosmos is now the chaos out of which God creates—the African is changing, becoming something else. Because of this changing, these Africans are now entering the world created by the God of Jesus Christ. With this other possibility no attempt should be made to freeze the "spiritual life" of African slaves in some romanticized past African state. Instead a *struggle* is being articulated here: The struggle of these displaced and oppressed human beings, these Africans to grasp the world (anew) in the light of a revelation—the fountain Jesus. The genuine conflict with an alternative theological worldview (signified by conjure/voodoo) then is the second line of argument that constitutes Afro-spirituality. It is the conflict *with* a worldview, not *within* a stable worldview. For the African positioned at a Christian *becoming*, an old worldview is not only passing away, but is being challenged.

Ironically, though, the preoccupation of modern black scholars with positing a general religious frame of reference for the African indicates a struggle is still being engaged—the resistance to a Christian theological *specificity* for understanding the clearly theological comments of these African slaves and their descendants. In a sense, Christian agency as authentically tied to these Africans is being resisted. While many scholars of African

American history accept what Albert Raboteau insightfully calls "the death of the [African] gods," the passing away for the slaves of the gods of Africa, this death is interpreted along the lines of an historical discontinuity and/or the weakening of African social and cultural influence. While both are indeed still compelling factors, what is not generally accepted is the agency of the African actively becoming Christian. In this process, these Africans were not simply emptying what was left of an African religious essence to a Christian mold, or worse, weaving together Christian and African cloth to form a "distinctively African" garment. This history gives witness to a theological struggle, the effects of which are still with us. Receiving this witness would entail that theological statements in the mouths of slaves and their children may demand a new paradigm for historical research in which their statements indicate something new and are not the mask of an African world(view), painted with a Christian color. However, this is a possibility not without controversy in the current intellectual climate.

Here I am in fact suggesting both an historical continuity and an analogical relationship. Africans in their coming to be Christian argued over two competing theological visions of existence: one in which the appropriateness of conjure/voodoo was still seen as theologically consistent with a former way of life, and one which found such practices and the spiritual economy they represented to be no longer viable as an expression of faith. The letter involved not merely shifting a theological center in a *continuing* theological worldview, but an utter *transformation* of worldview, a real theological death and rebirth. These competing theological visions established a struggle for Africans in the new world, a struggle within the community over its identity and destiny. And this struggle continues. We too as African Americans argue over which theological frame of reference is best to judge "our spirituality" (both past and present) and thus which vision of the theological is best. Quite often appeals are made to forms of spirituality (and thus theology) which are supposed to reflect a more authentically African reality and therefore ought to be commended as the best way to interpret our past as well as to envision an appropriate theological posture for all descendants of enslaved and colonized Africans.

One final example of this strategy is found in the work of the late Robert E. Hood in *Must God Remain Greek?: Afro Cultures and God-Talk.*[51] This text shows the continuing struggle over an African past and its theological import. In that text, Hood attempts to reconstruct Christian theology freed from the derogatory and colonialist gaze of white Christianity and theology. Hood seeks to sever the connection of theology to Europeanized Greek-Roman philosophical categories and rethink theology in the light of Afro-cultures. Hood takes as the fundamental resource for theology indigenous cultures and what he perceives as their inherent theological visions. They are the ground upon which to build different Christian theologies, theologies that would be truly at home in their respective cultures. To offer an authentically indigenous vision of Afro-theology, Hood builds on the work of Herskovits, Mbiti, and a host of others. Seldom can one find a project so convinced of a racial vision of African religious existence. Clearly, for Hood the central reality that connects West Africa, South Africa, the Caribbean, the Americas, and North American Afro religious communities is our race.

From start to finish, his text is an eloquent if not tragic witness to the utter transparency of all theology in relation to the constructed image of the African. This is because what he perceives throughout all the disparate ecclesial and nonecclesial religious communities in the places where displaced and colonized Africans live is a speaking black body that offers up its own religious consciousness over against all its forms. Nothing (whether Catholic, Protestant, Eastern/Oriental orthodox, Christian heterodox, non-Christian) really matters other than the ways in which an indigenous theology is being worked out by this black body. The great significance of Hood's text is his profound commitment to a vision of a sacred cosmos that joins all Afro-people(s). Thus fundamental theological decisions can be made based on his reconstruction of the African past along rigid racial lines. Based on this racial vision, Hood then reads the entire history of Christian thought through a racial lens. He imports his vision of a racial Africa, i.e. black Africa, right back to the very origins of Christianity and then discerns a racial dynamic at work from the very beginning of the church. One implication of this reading is that, following Mbiti (but without Mbiti's sophistication), Hood seeks to connect a modern black Africa to early African theologians by showing a connection in their theologies. They are connected culturally, which means for Hood they are connected racially. Hood binds a particular theological vision to particular cultures, in this case, European and African understood respectively as white and black. Consider his conclusion concerning the way "the African" understands salvation.

> [S]alvation for the African, as for the early Graeco-Romans Fathers, means deliverance and redemption. For the African it is not so much deliverance from the power of death or even original sin; rather salvation means deliverance from the evil and mysterious powers and forces that destabilize the community and the person and injure the relationship between God, the divinities, the ancestors, and the community or person. Death is therefore not seen as an evil or as the consequence of sin or disobedience to God or the supreme deity. Death is a welcomed passage for joining the ancestors, provided one dies a 'good death.' This is a very different mind-set from the understanding of death and sin in the Christian dogmatic tradition as embodied in the Nicene Creed and in the church's classical liturgical tradition.[52]

The great irony of his treatment is that Hood completely ignores those churches populated with African descendants (located in all the "indigenous" places) that are not what he considers indigenous. So the various black mainline and Pentecostal churches, churches which have condemned much of the religious practice(s) and theological posture that he conceives as authentically African, receive no real consideration. Indeed, Hood is so committed to offering a black unity in religious vision that he ignores every possible line of conflict between churches, finding conflict only in terms of white and black cultures. Though Hood views cultures as theological prisms, they in fact become theological prisons. He indeed takes the position of one who has the power of surveillance from which to map strategies of escape or further containment.

Hood's work, however, needs to be placed in this larger struggle over a worldview. His is an attempt to argue for a particular theological vision that carries with it an authentic African spirituality (and theology). Whereas the first line of argument presents the desire to have an African freed from the constructing power of white hegemony, this second line of argument proposes a unified and unifying worldview, a place within which an African spiritual presence finds its proper home. Once again a hoped for freedom is being posited—the freedom to construct a world of one's own choosing. Such a world is adaptable, open to new elements, yet remains constant. In this way, the African, though in the (white) world, is certainly not of that world. In this sense, we could understand this second line of argument with its need to posit a general theological frame of reference like the first line of argument as also a kind of spiritual exercise. However that characterization would be less than adequate. Instead this second context in which to understand Afro-spirituality presents one side of the spiritual drama within which people of African descent live. As spiritual drama, this struggle within the theological presents the radical decision often placed before African descendants: to imagine, to (re)construct, to engage life by means of and through a theological vision authentic to our own lives. Of course, there is the important related question of Christianity's relation to cultures, and what makes for multicultural Christian existence. However, in this case, the question at heart is not the relation of Christianity to culture(s), but what should constitute a unifying theological vision for African descendants. This second line of argument is, however, only one side of the spiritual drama within which African Americans live. There is yet another side that in fact constitutes the third line of argument.

III. *The Spirituality Itself: An Argument against White Christianity*

Throughout our exposition on African American spirituality, the effects and presence of a White Christianity have been a constant though unexamined factor in the articulations of that spirituality. Indeed, without ignoring African American agency, it must be said that White Christian existence is a decisive factor in the formation of African American spirituality. In fact, life before a white racist Christianity forms the other side of the spiritual drama within which Africans and their descendants live. This presents us with a third line of argument that helps to define African American spirituality. It is the attempt of Africans and their children to argue for an authentic Christianity in the face of a grotesque distortion: slaveholding, colonializing, white supremacist Christianity. While the argument itself may in a sense seem quite obvious, that it exists at all is quite remarkable and remains one of the great realities (i.e. mysteries) of western Christianity (and western Christian spirituality)—in the face of a profoundly distorted Christian witness, people of African descent became authentically Christian, an authenticity they called forth.

This calling forth of authentic Christianity in the face of its opposite is a profound theological marker of African American spirituality. Yet there is indeed a tragic element present in this argument, namely, that it must be made in the first place. Thus this argument exposes pathos as well as great suffering. This argument witnesses self-inflicted wounds in the body of Christ, wounds seen and acutely felt by African American Christians. However this argument seen in the witness of Afro-Christians reveals theological protest at its best. Take for a marvelous example a speech delivered by that great orator, Frederick Douglass, on September 1847 at Market Hall in Syracuse, New York. In this speech entitled *On the Union, Religion and the Constitution*, Douglass, while neither theologian or black preacher, wages theological war against the church's active participation in institutional slavery.[53] The ideas presented in that speech, while by no means original, do reveal many of the unique features of this argument and thus expose features of this aspect of Afro-spirituality.

Douglass engages in an unrelenting critique of the posture of the church in relation to the African slave. According to Douglass, slavery could be defeated if not for the support of the church, especially the ministers. As he notes, there is a diabolical reciprocity between what is preached in the pulpit and what is believed in society. In this case, Douglass discerns a joint justification for slavery.

> Say what we may of politicians and political parties, the power that holds the keys of the dungeon in which the bondman is confined, is the pulpit. It is that power which is dropping ... constantly dropping on the ear of this people, creating and moulding the moral sentiment of the land. This they have sufficiently under their control that they can change it from the spirit of hatred to that of love of mankind. That they do it not, is evident from the results of their teaching. The men who wield the blood-clotted cow-skin come from our Sabbath Schools in the Southern States. Who act as slave-drivers? The men who go forth from our own congregations here.[54]

While it was certainly not unusual for someone of Douglass' time to hold the church up as a crucial institution in the life of a society, that does not diminish Douglass' overwhelming esteem for the importance of Christian practice for shaping lives.

In fact, Douglass in this speech criticizes the sermon of one Bishop Meade of Virginia, a sermon (portions of the manuscript) he read to his audience. That he would find it important to criticize the sermon of a southern bishop is quite remarkable, but not as amazing as Douglass' questioning of the bishop's interpretation and application of biblical texts. Douglass, in his review of the sermon, questions the bishop's correlation of the master/slave relation in the Bible to the American master/slave situation as the theological justification for evangelical flogging, the beating of the slaves in order to make them more properly Christian slaves. Douglass has made the hermeneutical decision that slavery and Christianity are fundamentally at odds. Thus according to Douglass this sermon represents the same sort of distorted reading of the Bible as the one that finds a justification for slavery in the supposed race-creation story of Shem, Ham, and Japhet in Genesis.

All are willing to acknowledge my right to be free; but after this acknowledgement, the good man goes to the Bible and says 'after all I see some difficulty about this thing. You know, after the deluge, there was Shem, Ham, and Japhet; and you know that Ham was black and had a curse put on him; and I know not but it would be an attempt to thwart the purposes of Jehovah, if these men were set at liberty.' It is this kind of religion I wish to have you laugh at—it breaks the charm there is about it. If I could have the men at this meeting who hold such sentiments and could hold up the mirror to let them see themselves as others see them, we should soon make head against this pro-slavery religion.[55]

As Douglass engages in a critique of slaveholding society, he registers his estrangement from Christian America which for him is inherently racist and committed to enslaving Africans. Yet this is to be distinguished for him from his love for Christianity. This love of Christian faith consists in a quite stunning reclamation of certain key elements of proper Christian vision.

Do not misunderstand my railing—do not class me with those who despise religion—do not identify me with the infidel. I love the religion of Christianity—which cometh from above ... which ... is full of good fruits and without hypocrisy. I love that religion which sends its votaries to bind up the wounds of those who have fallen among thieves. By all the love I bear to such a Christianity as this, I hate that of the Priest and Levite ... that ... leaves the bruised and wounded to die.[56]

Here then is a vision of Christian witness against slavery and thus has grasped the heart of Christian faith, reaching to the weakest and most humbled among us.

It spreads its table to the lame, the halt, and the blind. It goes down after a long neglected race. It passes, link by link till it finds the lowest link in humanity's chain—humanity's most degraded form in the most abject condition. It reaches down its arm and tells them to stand up. This is Anti-Slavery—this is Christianity.[57]

With Douglass (as with other representatives of this argument) there is a clear minimalism to his Christian vision; little is found here or elsewhere of high-level doctrinal considerations of orthodoxy. However the lack of such considerations are not signs of a preferred Christian utilitarianism, an alleged orthopraxis that shuns doctrinal orthodoxy (as so much ideology). Instead the struggle of Christian faith is being waged on its other front: the Afro-Christian confronting racist Christian faith by means of a growing awareness of its contradictions. Indeed this is the nature of theological protest. It has discovered theological contradiction as it has grown in consciousness of its own theologically Christian identity. Of course, Christian identity is a tentative project for these displaced Africans; however, even with Frederick Douglass, the markers of formation in progress are present.

Since the light of God's truth beamed upon my mind, I have become a friend of that religion which teaches us to pray for our enemies—which, instead of shooting balls into their hearts, loves them. I would not hurt a hair of a slaveholder's head. I will tell you what else I would not do. I would not stand around the slave with my bayonet pointed at his breast, in order to keep him in the power of the slaveholder.[58]

We need not romanticize Douglass (or those who present this form of argument) as model Christians. Rather, if this argument shows the attempt to create rhetorical space for reclaiming Christian vision and envisioning Christian identity, then ironically, the presence of such an argument points to the power over against which the African must theologize, a power constituted by the ecclesial mechanisms of control and prohibition that deny these Africans full and free access to the mysteries of the Christian faith—the full range of its stories, lessons, language, life, and indeed love. Thus in effect this Christian witness is as a mustard seed demanding that the resources for cultivation and nurture be released on their behalf. While there is triumph in this witness, there is also great tragedy.

Douglass' Christian witness is characteristic of a line of argument the effects of which remain with us. In Douglass we find an articulation of Christian faith that holds its social and political import as constants. Along with this demand for continuous display of faith's social relevance, there is also the presence of an abiding critical distance from white Christianity. This argument against white (slaveholding) Christianity then illumines a practice constitutive of Afro-spirituality—the constant demand that articulation of Christian faith display social and political relevance aimed particularly at the plight of those marginalized in society, which in this case begins with the displaced and oppressed African. This argument also illumines a posture inherent in that spirituality—a critical eye cast on white Christian existence, in full awareness of its history of hypocrisy and allegiance to the forces of racial oppression. However the demand to love one's enemies—in this case, white racists—is also a part of this posture.

This argument against white Christianity not only characterizes Afro-spirituality, it also profoundly shapes the contours of the articulation of Afro-spirituality. Indeed, any articulation of Afro-spirituality that does not display in that characterization some form of this argument becomes suspect. Unfortunately the continuing display of this argument gives witness to the continuing tragic realities of a Christian community deeply divided along racial lines with a continuing legacy of white Christian compliance in the oppression and marginalization of Afro-people. Ironically, this display also means that Afro-Christians are still being pressed toward a kind of theological (and doctrinal) minimalism with a view toward the centrality of social-critique. One finds among Afro-intellectuals (even those who are Christian) a very critical posture toward Christianity and a resistance to theological reflection that does not establish its immediate justification as an effective form of social and political engagement. Certainly in this regard, the freedom of Christian identity as a project of those displaced slave-Africans and their first children remains to be fulfilled.

Gathering together the three lines of argument that constitute Afro-spirituality does not render a simple definition of that spirituality. Indeed if anything my task has been to offer a more complex and certainly more troubling definition of that spirituality. Centrally, I have taken Christianity to be at the heart of a definition of Afro-spirituality, but also at its heart is resistance to a totalizing comprehensive Christian definition to that spirituality. Christianity, then, in a real sense, presents "the wrestlin," the struggle, that is Afro-spirituality. As with the story of Jacob alluded to at the beginning of this essay, Christianity has been a wounding word, a wounding revelation for the African in the new world. This revelation has meant and means struggle but it has also meant and means promise. We have indeed been marked by the struggle as children of the promise.

NOTES

1 "Black Worship," in *The Study of Spirituality*, eds. C. Jones, G. Wainwright, and E. Yarnold (New York: Oxford University Press, 1986), pp. 481–482.
2 "The Spirituality of Afro-American Traditions," in *Christian Spirituality* III (New York, Crossroad, 1985), pp. 372–414.
3 See Theophus H. Smith, *Conjuring Culture: Biblical Formations of Black America* (New York: Oxford University Press, 1994). Cf. also his "Ethnography-as-Theology: Inscribing the African American Sacred Story," in *Theology Without Foundations: Religious Practice & the Future of Theological Truth*, eds. Stanley Hauerwas, Nancey Murphy, & Mark Nation (Nashville: Abingdon Press, 1994), pp. 117–139.

4   Part of the difficulty in addressing this transparency is the use of the terms "African,"
    "Afro-American," "black," etc. Here I challenge what D. T. Goldberg (following Foucault)
    calls a [racial] episteme, "characterized by a 'regime of rationality.' While employing these
    and related notions, I do so in an effort to overcome their 'general politics of truth.' That is
    I will reject *the African* as a set of discursive rules [which] emerge from an economy of
    epistemological production in virtue of which 'truth' may be differentiated from 'falsity'."
    As Goldberg also notes (and I in agreement), "At issue in any such economy are competing
    interpretations of the language of truth, assertion, and representation—in short of 'know-
    ledge' and its relation to power." Thus while I will employ the notion of *the African* to refer
    to a kind of historic agency, I question that very use as an epistemic regime. Cf. David Theo
    Goldberg, *Racist Culture: Philosophy and the Politics of Meaning* (Oxford: Blackwell, 1993), p. 52.
5   *Black Belief: Folk Beliefs of Blacks in America and West Africa* (New York: Harper & Row, 1975),
    p. xii; *Black Preaching* (New York: Harper & Row, 1970); also see his *The Recovery of Preaching*
    (New York: Harper & Row, 1977).
6   Mitchell, *Black Belief*, p. 11.
7   *Genealogies of Religion: Discipline and Reasons of Power in Christianity and Islam* (Baltimore:
    The Johns Hopkins University Press, 1993), p. 4. He is quoting here the important work by
    Sahlins.
8   Mitchell, *Black Belief*, p. 33.
9   Mitchell, *Black Belief*, pp. 31–34; 50–57.
10 Mitchell, *Black Belief*, p. 32.
11 W. E. B. DuBois, *Dusk of Dawn: An Essay Toward an Autobiography of a Race Concept* (New
    York: Schocken Books, [reprinted] 1968); Cf. Paul Tillich, *A Theology of Culture* (London:
    Oxford University Press, 1959); also see Mitchell, *Black Belief*, pp. 125ff.
12 Mitchell, *The Recovery of Preaching*, pp. 11ff; Also see his *Black Preaching*, pp. 32ff.
13 *Modernism and the Harlem Renaissance* (Chicago: University of Chicago Press, 1987), p. 33.
14 John S. Mbiti, *African Religions and Philosophy* (New Hampshire: Heinemann Educational
    Books, Inc., 1969), p. 1.
15 V.Y. Mudimbe (ed.) *The Surreptitious Speech: Présence Africaine and the Politics of Otherness
    1947–1987* (Chicago: Chicago University Press, 1992), p. xvii.
16 Mbiti, *African Religions and Philosophy*, p. 223.
17 Cited in Kwame Bediako, "John Mbiti's Contribution to African Theology," in *Religious
    Plurality in Africa: Essays in Honor of John S. Mbiti*, eds Jacob K. Olupona & S. S. Nyang
    (Berlin: Mouton De Gruyter, 1993), p. 369.
18 One could argue that the entire corpus of Mbiti's work is set up like a systematic theology.
    Indeed, his stunning work on eschatology presupposes a Christian vision of time, one that
    is in some measure shared with Europeans. Cf. his *Concepts of God in Africa* (New York:
    Praeger Publishers, 1970); also *New Testament Eschatology in an African Background: A Study
    of the Encounter between New Testament Theology and African Traditional Concepts* (Oxford:
    Oxford University Press, 1971).
19 James Clifford, "On Ethnographic Allegory," in *Writing Culture: The Poetics and Politics of
    Ethnography*, eds James Clifford & George E. Marcus (Berkeley: University of California
    Press, 1986), pp. 98–121.
20 Walter Jackson, "Melville Herskovits and the Search for Afro-American Culture," in
    Malinowski, Rivers, Benedict, and Others: Essays on Culture and Personality, ed. G. W. Stocking
    Jr. (Wisconsin: University of Wisconsin Press, 1986), pp. 95–126; cf. John Hope Franklin,
    George Washington Williams: A Biography (Chicago: University of Chicago Press, 1985); also
    see Carter G. Woodson & C. H. Wesley, *The Negro in Our History* (Washington, D.C.: The
    Associated Publishers, Inc., [12th printing], 1972).
21 Herskovits, *The Myth of the Negro Past*, p. 227.
22 Herskovits, *The Myth of the Negro Past*, p. 207.
23 Herskovits, *The Myth of the Negro Past*, p. 214.
24 Herskovits, *The Myth of the Negro Past*, p. 214.
25 Herskovits, *The Myth of the Negro Past*, p. 221.
26 Newbell Puckett, *Folk Beliefs in the Southern Negro*, (Chapel Hill: University of North
    Carolina Press, 1926), p. 545, cited in Herskovits, *The Myth of the Negro Past*, p. 224.
27 At this point in his text, Herskovits cites for support of this position the work of Zora Neale
    Hurston who as he says writes with the "intimacy of inside knowledge," (*The Myth of the*

Negro Past, p. 252). Of course, this inside knowledge is not of Christian belief, but of blackness. Zora in Herskovits' thinking has inherent *racial* knowledge which is theological.
28 Walter Benn Michaels, "Race into Culture: A Critical Genealogy of Cultural Identity," in *Identities*, eds. K. A. Appiah & H. L. Gates, Jr. (Chicago: University of Chicago Press, 1995), pp. 32–62.
29 Talal Asad, "Toward a Genealogy of the Concept of Ritual," in *Genealogies of Religion*, p. 60.
30 W. Jackson, "Melville Herskovits and the Search for Afro-American Culture." Jackson also observes that, "Herskovits had noted Hurston's motor behavior while she was singing spirituals, and he suggested that these movements had been 'carried over as a behavior pattern handed down thru imitation and example from the original African slaves who were brought here.'" p. 107.
31 Baker, *Modernism*, p. 56.
32 Zora Neale Hurston, *The Sanctified Church: The Folklore Writings of Zora Neale Hurston* (Berkeley: Turtle Island, 1981). Of course, it is important to remember that Hurston did not put together the collection of this particular text. Also see her *Mules and Men* (New York: Harper & Row, 1990).
33 Hazel Carby, "The Politics of Fiction, Anthropology, and the Folk: Zora Neale Hurston," in *History & Memory in African-American Culture*, eds G. Fabre & R. O'Meally (New York: Oxford University Press, 1994), p. 40.
34 Thus one finds this necessary clearing away in the work of a wide variety of theologians, ethicists, and Afro-scholars of religion. Take for example, Peter Paris, *The Spirituality of African Peoples: The Search for a Common Moral Discourse* (Minneapolis: Fortress Press, 1995), pp. 1–61; E. Townes, *In a Blaze of Glory: Womanist Spirituality as Social Witness*, (Nashville: Abingdon Press, 1995), pp. 19–30. Dwight N. Hopkins, *Shoes that Fit our Feet: Sources for a Constructive Black Theology* (Maryknoll, New York: Orbis Books, 1993), pp. 16ff.
35 "The Other Question: Stereotype, Discrimination and the Discourse of Colonialism," in *The Location of Culture* (London: Routledge, 1994), p. 67.
36 Smith, *Conjuring Culture*, p. 3.
37 Smith, *Conjuring Culture*, p. 3.
38 Smith, *Conjuring Culture*, p. 56.
39 Smith, *Conjuring Culture*, p. 71. Cf. Smith, "Ethnography as Theology." As with Mitchell, the work of Paul Tillich stands in the background.
40 Smith, *Conjuring Culture*, pp. 70–76. Cf. Sacvan Bercovitch, *The American Jeremiad* (Wisconsin: University of Wisconsin Press, 1978); cf. Werner Sollors, *Beyond Ethnicity: Consent and Descent in American Culture* (New York: Oxford University Press, 1986).
41 Smith, *Conjuring Culture*, p. 127.
42 Cf. Smith on Sojourner Truth, *Conjuring Culture*, pp. 167–174. Also see Amanda Porterfield, "Shamanism: A Psychosocial Definition," *Journal of the American Academy of Religion* 55:4 (1987) pp. 721–739; and Mircea Eliade, *Shamanism: Archaic Techniques of Ecstasy* (Princeton: Princeton University Press, 1964).
43 Smith, *Conjuring Culture*, p. 187.
44 Mitchell, *Black Belief*, p. 32, cited earlier.
45 Albert J. Raboteau, *Slave Religion: The "Invisible Institution" in the Antebellum South* (Oxford: Oxford University Press, 1978), p. 287. Also cited in Smith, *Conjuring Culture*, p. 145. Emphasis added.
46 Raboteau, *Slave Religion*, pp. 286–87. Emphasis added.
47 Smith, *Conjuring Culture*, p. 145. Also see Charles Joyner, "'Believer I know': The Emergence of African-American Christianity," in *African American Christianity: Essays in History*, ed. Paul E. Johnson (Berkeley: University of California Press, 1994), pp. 35–36. Joyner seems to imply that those slaves who held to voodoo were the ones authentic to their African heritage as opposed to those blacks who abandoned this heritage by becoming Christian.
48 Smith, *Conjuring Culture*, p. 145.
49 Mechal Sobel, *Trabelin' On: The Slave Journey to an Afro-Baptist Faith* (Princeton: Princeton University Press, 1988), p. 123.
50 Sobel, *Trabelin' On*, p. 109.
51 (Minneapolis: Fortress Press, 1990.)
52 Hood, *Must God Remain Greek?*, p. 120.

53 Frederick Douglass, *Frederick Douglass: The Narrative and Selected Writings*, ed. M. Meyer (New York: Random House, 1984), pp. 248–260. Cf. Williams S. McFeely, *Frederick Douglass* (New York: W. W. Norton, 1991). Also see Bill E. Lawson, "Moral Discourse and Slavery," in Howard McGary and Bill E. Lawson, *Between Slavery and Freedom: Philosophy and American Slavery* (Bloomington: Indiana University Press, 1992), pp. 71–89.
54 Douglass, *On the Union, Religion, and the Constitution*, p. 250.
55 Douglass, *On the Union, Religion, and the Constitution*, pp. 253–254.
56 Douglass, *On the Union, Religion, and the Constitution*, p. 254.
57 Douglass, *On the Union, Religion, and the Constitution*, p. 255.
58 Douglass, *On the Union, Religion, and the Constitution*, pp. 258–259.

Index